ADVANCE PRAISE FOR

# UBIQUITOUS ASSESSMENT

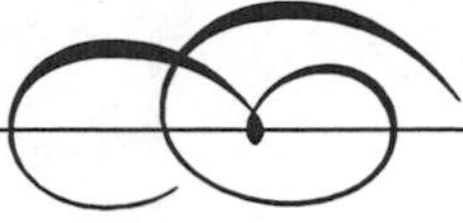

"Greg S. Goodman and Karen T. Carey create a needed context for assessment by their review of the field's historical and theoretical foundations. To this they add an ethical and political analysis that is both frank and compelling. With the stage effectively set, the authors go forward in laying out a detailed and practical case for 'ubiquitous assessment' in a family of human service professions including education and counseling. They are defining post-modern techniques at a time—and in a field—where such voices are most needed."

*Paul Shaker, Dean, Faculty of Education, Simon Fraser University, Canada*

"*Ubiquitous Assessment* leads the reader to reflect on the contrast between what educational and mental health professionals know about teaching, learning, and assessment, and the methods presently propagated by some policy makers. Goodman and Carey's discussion of our current testing obsession and its paradoxical and unethical consequences leads to a comprehensive coverage of evaluation strategies that will be instructive to psychologists, counselors, special educators, and other assessment providers. It is outstanding."

*Paul Beare, Dean, Kremen School of Education,*
*California State University, Fresno*

# UBIQUITOUS ASSESSMENT

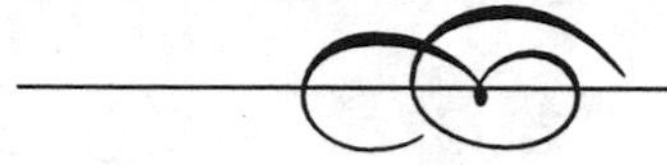

# Studies in the Postmodern Theory of Education

Joe L. Kincheloe and Shirley R. Steinberg
*General Editors*

Vol. 274

PETER LANG
New York • Washington, D.C./Baltimore • Bern
Frankfurt am Main • Berlin • Brussels • Vienna • Oxford

Greg S. Goodman & Karen T. Carey

# UBIQUITOUS ASSESSMENT

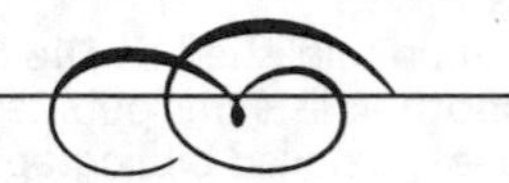

## Evaluation Techniques for the New Millennium

PETER LANG
New York • Washington, D.C./Baltimore • Bern
Frankfurt am Main • Berlin • Brussels • Vienna • Oxford

**Library of Congress Cataloging-in-Publication Data**

Goodman, Greg S.
Ubiquitous assessment: evaluation techniques for the new millennium /
Greg S. Goodman, Karen T. Carey.
p. cm. — (Counterpoints; v. 274)
Includes bibliographical references and index.
1. Educational tests and measurements. 2. School psychology. I. Carey, Karen T.
II. Title. III. Series: Counterpoints (New York, N.Y.); v. 274.
LB3051.G59 371.26—dc22 2004001653
ISBN 0-8204-7069-4
ISSN 1058-1634

Bibliographic information published by **Die Deutsche Bibliothek**.
**Die Deutsche Bibliothek** lists this publication in the "Deutsche
Nationalbibliografie"; detailed bibliographic data is available
on the Internet at http://dnb.ddb.de/.

Cover design by Lisa Barfield
Author photos by Andrea Goodman
Cover art by Gustavo Alberto Garcia Vaca / www.chamanvision.com

The paper in this book meets the guidelines for permanence and durability
of the Committee on Production Guidelines for Book Longevity
of the Council of Library Resources.

275 Seventh Avenue, 28th Floor, New York, NY 10001
www.peterlangusa.com



Printed in the United States of America

*Ubiquitous Assessment* is dedicated to Dr. Richard Goodman. A graduate of Harvard University, Dr. Goodman has worked as a professor of educational administration at the University of New Hampshire following a distinguished career as a school superintendent in Milford, N.H., and Wellesley, Mass. Currently a project director for the New England School Development Council, Dr. Goodman has authored several articles and books on the subject of superintendent and school board collaboration for high student achievement. Dr. Goodman's half century of professional service exemplifies the best in child advocacy for the promotion of high academic expectations within public education.

"Only connect."

*A Passage to India,* E.M. Forster

# Table of Contents

# Foreword

Assessment has been primary to the mission of modern psychology. Dating back to Galton in the late 1800s, much of the field's early reputation was based on the promise of formal and systematically constructed intelligence tests. This same pursuit continues to this day. The more recent applied fields of psychology—clinical, counseling, school, industrial/organizational psychology—are even more closely intertwined with assessment. Clinical psychology, the first of psychology's specialized applications, was first taken seriously during World War II when the armed forces recruited experimental psychologists to develop improved screening and selection techniques for military positions. Still today, the central task of many applied psychologists is psychological assessment.

The mainstay of these assessment attempts is norm-based testing. Typically, paper-and-pencil tests are developed to measure a trait or behavior. The new test is validated against similar older ones and/or particular behavior groups. At some point, norms are established. The assessment process presents on the surface as a clear, objective, and seemingly unambiguous science.

In *Ubiquitous Assessment*, however, Greg Goodman and Karen Carey convincingly demonstrate that over-reliance on norm-based testing is not only narrow but deceptively misleading. Norms, as any student knows, are simply averages—medians to be more precise. In the mind of the test evaluator, however, they too often signify normalcy. This is where the problems start.

To begin with, the test's criteria of normalcy take on legs of their own. No matter how many people take a given test, half of them will be above "normal" and half below; 25 percent will be in the top quartile and 25 percent in the lowest quartile. Additionally, the test tells us that a high scorer is "better than other people" but nothing about the significance of this difference for the real world. Goodman and Carey quote social critic Alfie Kohn: "It could be that everyone's actual scores are all pretty similar, in which case the distinctions between them are meaningless—rather like saying I'm the tallest person on my block, even though I'm only half an inch taller than the shortest person on my block."

On top of this is the sticky matter of culture. And when we enter the web of culture, answers come neither simply nor cleanly. The historian Lewis Mumford once observed that "each culture believes that every other space and time is an approximation to or perversion of the real space and time in which *it* lives." The truth of the matter is that there are no absolute rights and wrongs when it comes to cultural values. There are simply *different* values, each with their pluses and minuses. What's normal in one culture may be pathology in the next.

Almost by their very definition, cultural beliefs are so taken for granted—like the air that we breathe—that they are rarely discussed or even articulated. What is normal? Who is defining it? The answers to these questions have enormous consequences for norm-based testing yet are rarely spelled out or even considered. As a result, misuse of test scores are inevitable.

In this book, Goodman and Carey offer a bold new conceptualization of the process of psychological assessment. Assessment, they argue, has the potential to be something much more than a few standardized tests. It can and should become an integral component of the therapeutic process. In their concept of "ubiquitous assessment," evaluation isn't simply a precursor to psychotherapy; it is a central component of the ongoing conversation between the client and the therapist. Assessment is continuous and seamless.

The authors show when, where, and how ubiquitous assessment can be applied in a wide range of counseling and psychotherapeutic contexts. On the surface, the book appears to be a training manual for specialized professionals, in particular for school psychologists. It is that. But the reader will soon see that Goodman and Carey also have more profound issues in mind. *Ubiquitous Assessment* has us rethink everything from culture, sexism, and racism to how we conceive of normalcy itself.

*Ubiquitous Assessment* is a noble and much-needed addition to the counseling and psychotherapy literature. It is totalistic, client-centered, and interdisciplinary. Ultimately, it is a return to humanism at its best.

Robert Levine
Professor of Psychology, California State University, Fresno

# Acknowledgments

We would like to thank the following reviewers for their insightful and informed critiques: Paul Beare, H. Dan Smith, David Oakley, David Weber, Robert Murray, Ricci Skei, Amy Myers-Parks, W. Dwight Webb, Debbie Riverhawk Helmns, Paul Shaker, Pauline Sahakian, Susan Schlievert, Doug Waugh, Alejandro Juarez, Dave Swain, Nora Lynn, Janet Cooper, and Bob Levine, and all of the students in Counseling 203 during the fall of 2003.

No book comes to life without the vision and support of individuals capable of making such a production possible. In this case, Joe Kincheloe and Shirley Steinberg are the genius behind the scene. Their leadership in the field of Critical Pedagogy has inspired and promoted many works directed toward the furthering of social justice and the provision of radical democracy. We are proud that they have supported Ubiquitous Assessment's bold vision, and we are indebted to them for their teachings. Much of Joe and Shirley's scholarship is woven into the fabric of this text.

Barbara Morton's skill and knowledge of editing and word processing gives this book distinction. And, most importantly, this book would never have come to be without the loving patience of our spouses, Andy Goodman and Allan Cohan. Thank you for enduring our other passion: social justice.

# Chapter One

## Critically Situating Assessment

This book is written with the purpose of introducing or enhancing knowledge of assessment to potential and practicing educators and psychologists. More specifically, these educators and psychologists may be counselors, teachers, administrators, school psychologists, marriage and family therapists (MFTs), licensed clinical social workers (LCSWs), recreational therapists, or any other clinicians for whom assessment is an important function of the daily practice. As a part of your professional growth and continuing education within the subject of assessment, this book is written to teach a new paradigm of psychological and educational evaluation: Ubiquitous Assessment. Akin to idiographic assessment in its focus upon the individual and her/his uniqueness, Ubiquitous Assessment sees the evaluation process as both continual and seamless in its role in therapeutic and educational settings. In Ubiquitous Assessment, evaluation of the student or client is enmeshed within the learning or therapeutic process and the diagnostic considerations are a natural outgrowth of the learning or therapy connection. Our hope is to introduce this concept to the student or practitioner and to demonstrate that this methodology is most appropriate given the diversity, knowledge, and necessities of the new millennium.

### Early Purposes of Assessment

The Greeks are credited with being among the first Western civilizations to use assessment to improve understanding of human differences and to thereby maximize the utility of their citizens. Plato's work, *The Republic*, discusses three possible functions or uses of citizens within the perfectly organized state: artisans, auxiliaries, and rulers. These three distinct types were comprised of individuals who were allegedly composed by God with unique aptitudes and attributes. Depending upon each citizen's classification, these individuals could be matched with a future occupation and role within the community. Although this period of history is considered and identified specifically as ancient, the reductive thinking that places or attempts to place thousands of individuals within three "types" was, to a large degree, the foundation of modern typology. As the world evolved over the next two thousand years, the Greeks' early work in assessment continued to play a major part in psychometric philosophy. Another example of early contributions to psychology comes from Hippocrates (ca. 460–377 B.C.E.), a Greek physician. Hippocrates developed a theory that individuals were born with "humors" (phlegmatic, sanguine, choleric, and melancholic) and that this typing was instructive in assessing differences in personalities. The popular, modern assessment True Colors (Communication Companies International, 1989) can be linked to Hippocrates' four distinct personality types.

As psychology (philosophy at the time of the Greeks was an inclusive field comprising most of what we divide among the various sciences today) evolved during the next thousand years, the purposes of assessment remained essentially unchanged. Psychological evaluation was conducted to examine individuals for purposes of placement, study, and the identification of pathology. The purpose of assessments was to determine a citizen's potential fit or lack of fit within a particular society or group. As an example of an early consequence of assessment, during the Middle Ages, large numbers of persons were confined within dungeons for their "madness." Individuals considered "mad" or insane were "shanghaied" (a metaphor for being taken far away) on boats (*A Ship of Fools*) and removed from society (Foucault, 1965). This practice continued until "madhouses," precursors of the "modern" asylum, were created. Because the insane were believed to be "possessed" by devils, treatment consisted of driving out the demons or exorcising the source of the illness. This thinking led to witch-hunts and reinforced the fanatic behavior Americans conducted in their efforts to root out mentally suspect individuals through pseudojustice, such as the Salem witch trials (Braginsky et al., 1969).

Madness in the early years of Western civilization was subsumed in the term *melancholia*. According to Foucault (1965), "the notion of melancholia was fixed, in the sixteenth century, between a certain definition by symptoms and an explanatory principle concealed in the very term that designated it. Among the symptoms, we find all the delirious ideas an individual can form about himself: Some think themselves to be beasts, whose voices and actions they imitate. Some think that they are vessels of glass, and for this reason recoil from passers-by, lest they break; others fear death, which they yet cause most often to themselves" (pp. 117–18).

As a further example of modernist conceptualizations of psychology concerning early questions of madness, scientists and physicians were interested in understanding all of the inner workings of the mind. As a part of a continuing curiosity with the mind and its mystery, investigations of individual differences were conducted where brains were measured, weighed, and counted for variation in shapes and sizes. Craniometry was the early forerunner of modern intelligence testing (Gould, 1981). Through this process, an early form of factor analysis was developed. Charles (1995) defines factor analysis as "A process that identifies clusters of highly correlated variables, referred to as factors, and then correlating those factors with the criterion variable" (p. 321). The initial use of factor analysis was an attempt to link specific quantities such as brain weight with more vague constructs or qualities such as intelligence (Gould, 1981). "Disciplines" such as phrenology, the science of assessing cranial bumps and dents, became validated through functional (factorial) analysis's pseudoscientific connections (Gould, 1981). Another "mismeasure of man" was described by Flores and Obasi (2003), "The hypothesis that Africans had inferior brains and limited intellectual capacity was illustrated by measuring the differential amount of pepper corns held in the skulls of Africans and Europeans (Clark, 1975)" (p. 42). In a more current example of factor-analysis misplaced logic, Philippe Rushton, a racist Canadian psychologist, developed a "criteria for Civilization" checklist. In his research, he concluded that only "Caucasoids" met all twenty-one of the criteria. Another of Rushton's research projects involved asking men of differing racial groups to specify the distance their semen traveled during ejaculation. Rushton concluded, the farther the distance, the lower the person's intelligence (Kincheloe & Steinberg, 1996). The modern thinking of the Enlightenment's psychologists and physicians and the individuals continuing modernist logic with people today appears primitive in these postmodern times.

Exceptions of absurd proportion aside, small scales and individual studies were the major bastions of the psychologist's research efforts until the first part of the twentieth century. Industrialization and the development of the modern age required more specialized and widespread uses of psychometrics to speed the assessment process and effectively categorize large numbers of individuals for use within differing occupations (Gregory, 2004). The most often cited example in this period of psychometric expansion is Yerkes' development of the Army Alpha test (Sattler, 1988). This group intellectual ability assessment was based upon Otis's work on intelligence testing (Kelves, 1968). During World War I, thousands of men were screened (assessed) for placement in positions in the army ranging from fighting infantrymen to interpreters. Group assessment was born out of modern necessities.

## Twentieth-Century Developments Within Assessment

The term *assessment* was coined during the late 1940s by the United States' military Office of Strategic Services (Gregory, 2004). This use of the term *assessment* implied a process and purpose more substantive than is involved in simply testing. Over the past half century, assessment's definition has evolved and expanded to include the entirety of the "process of collecting data for the purpose of making decisions about individuals and groups" (Salvia & Ysseldyke, 2004, p. 4). Another definition of the purpose of assessment includes the improvement of student learning and, in the case of counseling, to enhance client/counselor understanding (National Forum on Assessment, 1993). As a functional definition befitting both teaching and counseling, the term *assessment* has implied a comprehensive collection of personal information that is gathered both informally (observing, interviewing, and reviewing previous assessments) and through the administration of more formalized techniques (standardized, norm-referenced psychological tests and measures).

Psychological and educational tests are generally of two types: individual and group. Individual assessments are the only type of psychological appraisal techniques that can be administered and interpreted with sufficient validity to be of any important use. Therefore, in clinical psychological evaluations (court ordered or forensic) and in other assessments such as those that are considered to be "high-stakes decisions" in education (graduation and retention), only individual assessments by trained clinicians have value worthy of their purpose. Further examples of these important client assessments include the diagnosis of depression within psychology or placement of students in a special education setting. Although individual psychological tests are included within the model of Ubiquitous Assessment for high-stakes decision making, much greater emphasis in educators' and therapists' daily practice is placed upon the information gleaned from nonstandardized and informal assessment techniques—for example, through clinical interview and observation gleaned from direct client or student contact. By focusing upon informal, nonstandardized procedures, Ubiquitous Assessment breaks ranks with traditional psychological testing textbooks that predominantly emphasize training in the administration of formal, standardized, and norm-referenced techniques (Anastasi, 1988; Gregory, 2004; Groth-Marnat, 2003; Salvia & Ysseldyke, 2004; Whiston, 2000).

Post-Freud and Jung, the modern Western, philosophic foundation of psychometrics has been characterized by the development of efficient tools (tests) to sort and regulate individuals for utilitarian purposes. Stemming from the military's need to sort and deploy hundreds of thousands of individuals, psychometrics was designed in an industrial age for mass productivity. An apt industrial psychology metaphor for psychometry is human engineering. The implication inherent in this metaphor is that we are using humans as a depersonalized entity or commodity for an industrial model nation. In industrial or other large-scale uses, providing the right individual for each slot in the factory or in an army and finding the information for placement quickly and efficiently was the singular goal of most large-scale assessment systems. This purpose is distinctly separated from individualistic and humanistic goals fundamental to teaching, counseling, and therapy within multicultural communities such as these United States (Swope & Miner, 2000).

The modernist thinking that envisioned group tests was supported by a belief that science and engineering, even human engineering, could fundamentally and completely support the new society. Ironically, modernist thinking predates the industrial era by several hundred years. Modernism's grip on mainstream Western thinking was such that it provided legitimacy for the industrialized factory, scientific technology, and advances on almost every level made by twentieth-century men and women. Most of America was enamored with the advances of technology, and the modernist conceptualizations of life were deified and used as justification for improvements in twentieth-century American life. For domestic life, the invention of the refrigerator and the development of methods of distribution of electricity to power modern appliances were tremendous boons. In psychometrics, this modernist thinking led to a proliferation of test development and to the public acceptance of large-scale implementation of group IQ (intelligence quotient), professional competency, and achievement testing. Unfortunately, because of reductive, causal thinking, people were situated as points to be compared on the continuum of linearity known as the bell curve. Now the individual's success or failure in society could be explained logically (Herrnstein & Murray, 1994) by literally seeing how one person compared with another. Science's dominance could explain everything.

## The Bell Curve

The bell curve is the principal tool in the domain of research methodology known as descriptive statistics. The essential function of the bell curve is to graphically represent a total population or group—for example, all eighth-grade boys and girls. The bell curve shows this population and their distribution or ranking in supposed relationship to all of the others in the group. The data analysis tools of parametric statistics work to define and characterize traits and to fit the distribution of individuals, animals, or things onto a graph known as the normal or bell-shaped curve (Charles, 1995). Using this graphic representation, research scientists can display results and construct visual images depicting so-called normal distributions.

Normal distributions are constructed through the use of what are called the measures of central tendency. Two major deficiencies of this process are at the heart of the current debate on assessment: (1) what is normal? and (2) what can we conclude by comparing individuals within this norm group? Norm-referenced testing seeks to describe and define "average." Using the statistical properties known as mean, median, and mode, the emphasis is upon the construction of a mathematical representation of the distribution of individuals and their position relative to a majority, or mean, definition of average. This result is commonly referred to as the bell-shaped curve.

The authors of this book take issue with several fundamental assumptions of norm-referenced testing. First, in a diverse, multicultural world, we do not have large groups of similar individuals with whom we can use statistical models to make fair comparisons. Even if we were to generate data from monocultural regions (known as local norms), we cannot generalize from that information to compare results with groups from outside of those areas. The second flaw of the process involves the end result of norm-referenced assessment: interpretation of the individual examinee's results. Alfie Kohn (1999), an articulate and informed critic of norm-referenced assessment, succinctly summarizes this second-most controversial aspect of norm-referenced assessment:

> Think for a moment about the implications of this fact. No matter how many students take the test, no matter how well or poorly they were taught, no matter how difficult the questions are, the pattern of results is guaranteed to be the same: exactly 10 percent of those who take the test will score in the top 10 percent, and half will always score below the median. That's not because our schools are failing; that's because of what "median" means. A good score on a norm-referenced test means "better than other people," but we don't even know how much better. It could be that everyone's actual scores are all pretty similar, in which case the distinctions between them are meaningless—rather like saying I'm the tallest person on my block even though I'm only half an inch taller than the shortest person on my block. (p. 77)

In a horrifying and twisted misapplication of the bell curve, racist scientists and sociologists have used this statistical tool to construct an argument that whites are superior to blacks. Misusing science to perpetuate oppression of blacks and others through fabrications of normal that are exclusive and support the domination of one group over another is racist and immoral. In their controversial and specious book *The Bell Curve* (Herrnstein and Murray, 1994), the authors make an argument that implies that blacks (and, by implication based upon IQ test results, Hispanics) are genetically inferior to whites. Herrnstein and Murray erroneously deduce that the discrepancy between blacks' IQs and the IQs of their "more successful" white counterparts may be a genetic marker of superiority. Because blacks and Hispanics score, on average, one standard deviation (15 IQ points) or approximately 25 percent lower than whites on intelligence and scholastic aptitude tests such as the Scholastic Aptitude Test (SAT), Herrnstein and Murray's writing leads readers to assume that this may reflect the advantage whites maintain. What is incomprehensible in this calculus is the fact that the majority of intelligence tests were normed on whites, and the tests are essentially an examination of Caucasian cultural knowledge (Sattler, 1988). According to psychometrics noted expert Jerome Sattler (1988), "Intelligence tests are culturally biased against ethnic groups" (p. 78). We must ask, if the test's norms were constructed by blacks and centered around African American culture such that whites scored lower than blacks, would Herrnstein and Murray have concluded that whites were genetically inferior to blacks?

To underscore the absurd notion that intelligence is culture-free and that only innate, genetic characteristics are measured, R. Williams (1974) created a black IQ test to demonstrate the importance of language. The test, the Black Intelligence Test of Cultural Homogeneity (B.I.T.C.H.), uses a combination of Ebonics and other cultural codes to make the test essentially incomprehensible to anyone outside black culture.

Commercial test manufacturers and psychometrists have tried to circumvent the thorny issues of culture by attempting to construct IQ tests that are culture-fair (Cattell, 1940) or language-free (Roid & Miller, 1997). Nonverbal and culture-free tests appear to be a good solution on the surface; however, many questions remain concerning the possibility of isolating the individual from culture and society (Kincheloe, Steinberg, & Gresson, 1996; McLaren, 1996; Orfield & Wald, 2000). Spring (1972) offers,

> The measurement of intelligence is at all times based on a conception of the good society and the good man [woman]. The criteria used to define and grade intelligence are directly related to these two sets of values. Often these values are hidden under the language of psychology. Intelligence is a term that invites constant reinterpretation either directly or indirectly. It is also a term that gains meaning and value only when related to a social context. Of course, many psychologists today claim to be scientific by not correlating their tests with social values but with previous tests. The rub here is that former tests mean the values of Binet, Terman, Thorndike, Goddard, and other social efficiency men. Unwittingly, today's test constructors and users are only perpetuating the beehive concept of society and intelligence. (p. 14)

In tests that compare individuals within a culture or society, it is impossible to be "culture-fair:" The culture is not fair (Kozol, 1991).

### Institutionalized Racism

Standardized, norm-referenced testing may be the most widely applied form of institutionalized racism we have ever witnessed. Institutionalized racism (Sleeter, Gutierrez, New, & Takata, 1996) is defined as practices of large organizations, such as schools, that have a negative or deleterious effect upon a particular culture or group. According to Sleeter et al. (1996), "Institutional racism comes about when a group of people have the power to enforce their prejudices by creating social institutions to buttress their privileges" (p. 186). Examples could include failure to provide adequate protection for gay and lesbian students, not responding to issues related to disproportionate dropout rates within the black and Latino populations, or failing or retaining grossly greater numbers of one racial group over another. The negative and racist effect of standardized testing is attacked by Orfield & Wald (2000): "Despite the political popularity of the testing 'solution,' many educators and civil rights advocates are suggesting that it has actually exacerbated the problems it set to alleviate. They claim that these [high-stakes testing] policies discriminate against minority students, undermine teachers, reduce opportunities for students to engage in creative and complex learning assignments, and deny high school diplomas because of students' failure to pass subjects they were never taught" (p. 74). Educational practices that increase stratification of schools and the students they include are not supportive of multiculturalism and diversity and may, in effect, exemplify institutional racism (Miner, 2000; Sleeter, Gutierrez, New, & Takata, 1996).

Recently, many notable educational and political leaders within America have stood up to refute test manufacturers' mistaken attempts at creating fairness and to oppose the racist implications of blacks' failure to achieve on a par with whites in this supposedly fair contest (Kincheloe, Steinberg, and Gresson, 1996; McNeil, 2000; Orfield & Wald, 2000; Wellstone, 2000). As one of the leading spokespersons for democracy and egalitarianism, Toni Morrison (1994) takes exception to Herrnstein and Murray's misuse of science and language to justify and perpetuate the oppression of blacks based upon bogus conceptualizations of normal. As cited by Joyce King (1996),

> In her acceptance speech upon receiving the Nobel Prize for Literature in Stockholm, Toni Morrison (1994) exposes the role that language plays in societal oppression. Morrison described oppressive language this way: She said, "it drinks the blood, laps vulnerabilities, tucks its fascist boots under

> crinolines of respectability and patriotism" (p. 17) and—I would add—"accepted standards" of scientific evidence. Morrison's critical appraisal of language and its mis/use is instructive and worth quoting further: "Oppressive language does more than represent violence; it is violence; does more than represent the limits of knowledge; it limits knowledge. Whether it is obscuring state language or the faux language of mindless media; whether it is the proud but calcified language of the academy or the commodity-driven language of science … or language designed for the estrangement of minorities, hiding its racist plunder in its literary cheek—it must be rejected, altered, and exposed." (p. 184)

We take seriously Morrison's charge to expose the racist misuse of the bell curve. In yet another bogus misuse of factor analysis, Herrnstein and Murray (1994) take racism to a new low by using science and modernist, linear logic to deduce that higher crime rates, higher poverty rates, and higher school dropout rates are, too, a function of lower intelligence (IQ). Throughout *The Bell Curve*, blacks are suggested to be biologically inferior in their intellect, and this deficit is the reason for their societal disconnection. The fact that this norm-referenced intelligence is more a reflection of white cultural capital (Bourdieu, 1993) than it is a measure of the spurious factor of IQ known as "g" is not discussed by Herrnstein and Murray (1994). Values of a culture have a worth and, as such, are sometimes associated with capital (money). Cultural capital, a term coined by the French sociologist Pierre Bourdieu (1993), includes elements from one's culture that convey status and power. Examples of cultural capital include manners, vocabulary, social activities, affiliations and associations (club membership), clothing and other attendant actions, items, knowledge, and the accoutrements of a particular group. Usually this group is representative of a specific or dominant culture within the sphere of influence.

Because of the fact that tests of intelligence are biased in favor of whites to such a large degree as one full standard deviation, IQ test use with blacks has been legally abolished in the state of California. In the *Larry P. v Riles* case, a California judge decided that the overidentification for special education placement of African American students was a violation of their due process rights because of the IQ test discrimination in favor of whites. Because of this discrepancy in test results between whites and blacks and the effective perpetuation of exclusionary educational practice (removal to self-contained special education classrooms for mentally retarded students!), it continues to be illegal to administer IQ instruments to African Americans within the state of California (Jones, 1988). The social justice issues inherent in the misuses of IQ testing are clear. Standardized tests have become a metaphor for the larger issue of racism embedded (institutionalized) in our schools and mental health agencies under the guise of assessment. Deafness to the discrepancy between white student scores and the IQ scores of minority students is a glaring example of institutionalized racism.

Reginald Jones (1988), professor of education and Afro-American studies at University of California, Berkeley, further articulated, "concern with bias in assessment cannot be limited to test instruments and procedures or to examiner characteristics alone; we must give attention to possible bias in all facets of the identification-assessment-placement system including bias in the referral and screening process, the influence of bias on parental involvement, the educational validity of procedures adopted, as well as to theories of teaching-learning which explain the accomplishments of defined subgroups of learners" (p. 27). In sum, the issues inherent in the process of IQ assessment are hegemonic: challenging IQ measurement bucks majority intellectual definitions.

As a result of postmodern multicultural and diversity contributions, criticism of IQ testing resonates throughout the academic community. Representing the California State University, San Diego, researcher and leading author in the field of assessment Jerome Sattler (1988) stated, "Intelligence tests limit our understanding of intelligence and sample only a limited number of conditions under which intelligent behavior is revealed. IQs are used to sort children into stereotyped categories" (p. 78). How IQ tests unfairly categorize students is evidenced through evaluation of the test itself. Deconstruction of intelligence tests discloses one of these assessments' primary components: general knowledge. General knowledge is widely regarded to include information that is typically overlearned and is consistent throughout a culture. Examples of this type of knowledge as taken from the Wechsler test are: "Who discovered America?" and "How far is it from New York to London?" (Wechsler, 1991). The information is subsumed under what would be considered important to know, and this knowledge is related directly to the culture one lives within. Being able to articulate the answers is a function of language. Obviously, Native Americans and individuals unaccustomed to foreign travel would recoil or, possibly, be awed by the test maker's answers to the examples given. We can only imagine the responses of our non-English examinees as they wrestle with the dual issues of culture and language. H. Carl Haywood (1988), professor of psychology and of neurology at Vanderbilt University, sums this up nicely: "Since many minority children cannot be assumed to have had the same opportunities to learn the content domains of static intelligence tests as have other children (i.e., the majority of children in the test's normative samples), it is inappropriate to use such static achievement-oriented tests to estimate the children's future learning potential" (p. 44). He went on to say, correctly, "the best predictor of learning is learning" (p. 44). Although this observation is tautological, the validity of the conclusion is rock solid. Reevaluation of the relationship between crystallized intelligence and culture has had the effect of moving the general "information" subtest on the new Wechsler Intelligence Test for Children, Fourth Edition (WISC-4) to the diminished role of supplemental subtest (Wechsler, 2003).

As the construct of intelligence is concerned, a reader of *The Bell Curve* is guided to conclude that biological science can explain this difference of collective understanding or knowledge. Readers of Herrnstein and Murray quickly deduce that the explanation of IQ difference is through its attribution to genetics, and that this is a straightforward and scientific fact. *The Bell Curve* furthers the racist work of Arthur Jensen (1969) and William Shockley (Gould, 1981) by insinuating that biological determinism fixes intelligence, and that blacks' (and Hispanics') lower scores are genetically predestined. Continuing to use norm-referenced assessment to perpetuate genetic and cultural deficit hypotheses is quintessentially racist (Sue & Sue, 1999).

## Contributions of Postmodernist Thinking

Many gifted and knowledgeable psychologists, educators, and academics have taken exception to the use of the bell curve as a measure capable of explaining differences between individuals or groups (Apple, 1996; Giroux, 1992; Gould, 1981; Kincheloe, Steinberg, & Gresson, 1996; Kohn, 2000, McLaren, 1996). In fact, placement upon the bell curve neither defines one's capability nor does it correlate with individual predictions—for example, the SAT's predictive validity for success in college is 0.50. This level of predictability from the SAT means that one half of the individuals scoring within the average range on the test will do well in college and one half will not: a rather expensive and quite time-involved coin toss! Yet worse than economic costs, racism is implicated in *The Bell Curve*'s conclusions, as well. For example, because blacks and Hispanics score, on average, one standard deviation lower than whites, the SAT is strongly suspect in its racially disproportionate skewing. The bell curve, as it is currently used in education and psychology, is fundamentally biased, and it yields consistently racist evaluations (Kincheloe, Steinberg, & Gresson, 1996).

Further deconstructing the flaws of bell curve as an instrument inappropriate for education and psychology, Patrick Slattery (1996) stated, "For some reason writers such as Herrnstein and Murray continue to believe that straight linearity is the natural state of the universe, despite the devastating impact of this modernist philosophy on the human psyche, the environment, and social structures" (p. 292). Slattery further stated, "The basis of this repudiation of Herrnstein and Murray's thesis is not rooted in modernist notions of scientific validity and reliability of research methods. With the appearance of a postmodern philosophy and the accompanying deconstruction of modern notions of linearity, an emerging science of complexity offers an alternative vision of the universe that makes obscene the reduction of racial, ethnic, and social issues to statistical certainties. The postmodern vision rejects traditional research meta-narratives such as those underlying *The Bell Curve*" (p. 292).

Slattery's comments reflect a new type of thinking that emerged in the West at the end of World War II. Known as postmodernists, the intellectuals who survived the Second World War resisted fascism and the sorts of imperialistic thinking that supported Nazi hubris and aggression (Foucault, Adorno, Gramsci, Derrida, etc.). The term *post* implies a moving away from the term it proceeds—for example, postcolonialism means beyond the obsolete concept of colonialism (Shohat & Stam, 1994). The modern thinking that contributed advanced war machines, biochemical weapons, and blitzkrieg was being questioned and eschewed for conceptualizations of a world that supported moving away from imperialism and fascism (Habermas, 1994) and challenged concepts supportive of the domination (hegemony) of one group over another (Gramsci, 1971). As this relates to assessment, postmodernists tend to see the bell curve and other linear representations of individuals as, at the least, exploiting individual possibility and maintaining hegemony by forcing competitive sorting and, at their worst, racist because of the negative effect upon blacks and Hispanics. Because blacks and Hispanics score up to one standard deviation lower than whites, racist psychologists and sociologists have used this as an argument for black and Hispanic inferiority and societal disjunction. Nothing could be more racist than this claim.

Henry Giroux (1992) has been one of postmodernism's leading spokespersons for educational change in support of underrepresented groups. With over twenty-five books to his credit, Giroux continues to fight for the liberation of people imprisoned by poverty and for the emancipation of all Americans through radical democracy (Street, 2003). Concerning postmodernism's contribution to these causes, Giroux (1992) wrote, "For educators interested in developing an antiracist pedagogy, postmodernism offers new epistemologies for thinking both the broader and specific contexts in which democratic authority is defined; it offers what Richard Bernstein (1988) calls a healthy 'suspiciousness of all boundary-fixing and the hidden ways in which we subordinate, exclude, and marginalize.' Postmodernism also offers educators a variety of discourses for interrogating modernism's reliance on totalizing theories based on a desire for certainty and absolutes" (p. 124).

Postmodernism provides a fundamental philosophic foundation for Ubiquitous Assessment. Moving away from modernism's rigid and linear conceptualizations of what is to be considered and represented as normal, Ubiquitous Assessment is aligned with the practices of those supportive of social justice and improving relationships between all people. Overall, postmodernism provides a cogent explanation for leaving linearity behind in the process of assessment and understanding within diverse, multicultural contexts.

> Postmodern thought subjects to analysis social and education forms previously shielded by the modernist ethos. It admits to the cultural conversation previously forbidden evidence derived from new questions asked by those previously excluded along lines of race, class, and gender. Postmodern thinkers challenge hierarchical structures of knowledge and power which promote "experts" above the "masses," as they seek new ways of knowing that transcend empirically verified facts and "reasonable," linear arguments deployed in the quest for certainty (Greene, 1988; Hebdige, 1979). When postmodernism is grounded on a critical system of meaning that is concerned with questioning knowledge for the purpose of understanding more critically oneself and one's relation to society, naming and then changing social situations that impede the development of egalitarian, democratic communities marked by a commitment to economic and social justice, and contextualizing historically how world views and self-concepts come to be constructed, it becomes a powerful tool for progressive social change. (Kincheloe & Steinberg, 1997, pp. 37–38)

Barry Kanpol (1997) eloquently refines postmodernism's definition of diversity even further: "Simply put, what the relations of race, class, and gender may be to any individual will always be different and changing and forever in flux" (p. 12). Each individual is a complex amalgam of multiple dimensions and contributions.

### The Effect of Multiculturalism upon "Normal"

In nearly all assessment texts, the authors situate psychological testing within a broad, historical context. The authors of *Ubiquitous Assessment* agree that the traditions and foundations of assessment are noteworthy; however, our views of history's relevance to today's multicultural and diverse student is in the disjuncture between past applications of assessment, the modernist thought processes that supported psychometrics, and today's postmodern and critical multicultural knowledge and requirements. Whereas the majority of the traditional, formalized assessments had been normed on typically white and middle-class individuals, the history and philosophic foundations of test development in America are essentially and exclusively a reflection of Caucasian cultural identity and European or Western experience. *Ubiquitous Assessment* utilizes postmodernism's criticism of norm-referenced testing to build relationships between all diverse groups through validation of their cultural identifications. In the words of Kincheloe and Steinberg (1997), "Critical multiculturalism employs the postmodern critique to help to construct a vision of a pedagogy of race, class, and gender justice" (p. 38). We interpret justice to mean fairness in the application of assessment to all groups. As assessments such as the SAT continue to unfairly discriminate against blacks and Hispanics, we reiterate our appeal to your sense of social justice concerning this critical issue.

What is considered "normal" or normative continues to be very much the center of assessment's current debate. The fact that our country and most of the Western world is characterized by extraordinary diversity and the psychometric truth that norm-referenced assessments tell us very little about the individual have become the principal reasons for the turning away from norm-referenced testing. Despite the obvious flaw of using a norm-referenced group test for individual assessment, since the emergence of the civil rights movement, test makers have tried to expand the norm groups in an attempt to develop psychometrically and technically adequate instruments. Norms are not capable of accurately describing or defining individuals or any meaningful differences between examinees except in their positions relative to one another on a linear scale such as the bell curve. A far better theoretical foundation for assessment of diverse populations is found in physic's chaos theory (Goodman, 2002). Chaos theory describes the way people and spaces uniquely exist as opposed to explanations of individual differences based upon simplistic linear equation and quantifiable definitions (Ford, 1996). As we shall see through the lens of chaos theory, efforts of linearity such as the mathematical recalculation of the norms to include different ethnic or culturally diverse groups provides only partial information in support of each subgroup.

Chaos theory has evolved from work in the discipline of physics to explain nonlinear phenomenon such as the universe or other, more earthly entities such as the fractal Maine coast. As Edward Hall (1989) observes, "Western man sees his system of logic as synonymous with the truth. For him it is the only road to reality" (p. 8). Chaos theory attempts to shatter the links with modernist perspectives such as Newtonian order and logical predictability. "Speaking specifically to uniqueness, chaos theory works well to explain the phenomenon of diversity that represents our multicultural, multidimensional, and multifaceted communities" (Goodman, 2002, pp. 15–16). Without extending the standard error of measurement to such lengths that the resulting scores would be meaningless and given of the tremendous diversity of our country, it is statistically impossible to make a norm-referenced assessment that fairly and reliably represents any individual undergoing assessment. Therefore, we do not support the use of norm-referenced group tests as they are currently administered, and we believe that these tests should have never been intended to be used to make valid or reliable "high-stakes" decisions about individuals. The only exception to a total prohibition on norm-referenced assessment may be by an individual's psychology, clinical psychology, or psychiatry examiner where these tests can be correctly interpreted or dismissed as invalid given disparities between the intended use of the test and the subject's proclivities. According to Slattery (1996), "Human beings, like weather patterns, are complex systems that defy predictability and linear certitude" (p. 297). Linear mathematical models of normal do not fit with Ubiquitous Assessment's fundamental assumptions of a person's uniqueness and individuality.

Of even more significance than the argument based upon chaos theory against the use of norm-referenced standardized tests is the collective cognitive contribution of the Marxist, post-Marxist, feminist, and postmodernist critical multicultural theorists and educators (Freire, 1998; Giroux & McLaren, 1994; Kincheloe & Steinberg, 1997; McLaren, 1997; Nieto, 1996). Drawing upon the work of the mentor Paulo Freire (1998), critical multiculturalists debunk the myths of linear comparisons and take up the fight for the oppressed and underrepresented. The debate over that which constitutes average or normal is central to the shift in assessment theory and technique. Consistent with most of the world's other nations, America is increasingly diverse and represents multiple languages, cultures, experiences, and knowledge.

By placing a premium on white majority knowledge and experiences and using that as the definition of normal or average, many members of our diverse community are situated outside the sanctum of respectability and placed in the position of "other" (Giroux, 1992). As we shall examine, the net effect of the use of norm-referenced, standardized testing maintains minorities in socially subordinated positions. In an earlier work, one of these authors (Goodman, 2002) stated, "Often these students have been traditionally silenced because of their status as an 'other.' Either because of socioeconomic disparity, gay or lesbian identity, color or cultural diversity, or difference in learning ability or modality, these youth end up identified as outsiders in mainstream culture. In schools where the cultural centers are clearly mapped, the position of the outsiders vis-à-vis the mainstream is clearly delineated. Often the goal has been separation or removal that effectively excludes the disaffected from participation in a comprehensive program" (p. 6). Whereas an "other" could conform to definition as a clear departure from mainstream or normative social positions prior to suffrage and civil rights (non-male and nonwhite), the characterization of a person as an "other" is clearly immoral and racist within our diverse urban and multicultural communities.

In our changing culture, the term *multicultural* has evolved in its definition. The early twentieth-century term for merging culture was the metaphor "melting pot." Nieto (1996) defines melting pot as "a model that maintains that differences need to be wiped out to form an amalgam that is uniquely American but without traces of original cultures" (p. 392). Old conceptualizations of America as a "melting pot" where all cultures became one essentially white culture, have, among multiculturalists, given way to new metaphors that maintain the identity of the individual. One of the new metaphors that maintains individuality within the group is that of a "salad." All of the individual ingredients retain their identity within a diverse mix. These new metaphors are very different conceptualizations of the role of diversity than the monoculturalist metaphor of melting into one uniform culture and assimilating whiteness to support the singular vision of a single dominant culture (Kincheloe & Steinberg, 1997).

When we refer to white, we do not mean whiteness as a skin color, but whiteness as an attitude or set of beliefs. Whiteness has been so dominant within American culture as the norm for all groups that its hegemonic position is invisibly imbedded and is maintained securely as the status quo (McLaren, 1997; Sue, Arredondo, and McDavis, 1992). Multiculturalists such as these authors argue, 150 years after the European migration to Ellis Island, that white cultural hegemony never was nor should it any longer remain a sustainable position. In a multidimensional, pluralistic society, the myths that supported the "melting pot" concept are defunct. Former definitions of normal, such as those supported by the bell curve, are not valid in a diverse society. These authors' pedagogical position is that diversity and individuality are of paramount importance, and we align with critical multiculturalists. Peter McLaren (1997), author of *Revolutionary Multiculturalism*, stated, "Whiteness constitutes and demarcates ideas, feelings, knowledge, social practices, cultural formations, and systems of intelligibility that are identified with or attributed to white people and that are invested in by white people as 'white.' Whiteness is also a refusal to acknowledge how white people are implicated in certain social relations of privilege and relations of domination and subordination. Whiteness, then, can be considered as a form of social amnesia associated with modes of subjectivity within particular social sites considered to be normative" (p. 267).

That white, and we shall add male and heterosexual, identities are enmeshed with conceptualizations of normal in psychology and education is no surprise. What is unfortunate is that we, as a culture, have not until recently been more vociferous in our writing to refute the use of these norms upon our multicultural and diverse citizens. Our diversity is our strength, not an exception needing "normalization" or adjustment. As Audre Lourde (1984) eloquently stated, "Difference must not merely be tolerated, but seen as a fund of necessary polarities between which our creativity can spark like a dialectic" (pp. 111–12). By emphasizing the individual and her/his unique qualities, Ubiquitous Assessment allows psychometric and educational evaluation without the use of comparisons to "normal."

*Ubiquitous Assessment* also breaks ranks with traditional psychological testing texts in that we see the role of assessment in educational and therapeutic/intervention contexts from a more Eastern or Oriental position. This perspective views individuals holistically and attempts to integrate and accept that all aspects of a person comprise her/his being. Being aware of all of the dynamics of oneself is critical to developing acceptance and becoming healthy. Although therapy and Eastern philosophy are closely linked, assessment's fundamental principles and practices have been driven more by Western and scientific reasoning (Watts, 1961). Traditional thinking about assessment has generally been to follow the evolution of science. In many ways, the Western views of assessment have mirrored modernist obsession with economic efficiencies and utilitarian conceptualizations that, in effect, dehumanize individuals. "The history of social, economic, and educational organization from the late nineteenth century to the present must be viewed in the context of this scientific objectification of human beings" (Kincheloe & Steinberg, 1997, p. 59). Even the fact that testing and instruction or assessment and therapy are separated and treated as distinctly differentiated is consistent with Western ideologies and follows the Western tendency to divide and categorize knowledge (Willinsky, 1998). According to Foucault (1970), "The sciences always carry with themselves the project, however remote it may be, of an exhaustive ordering of the world" (p. 74). This is not to overgeneralize and say that all Western thought is one way and that all Eastern thought another. We do not support reductive, either/or thinking. We seek expanded conceptualizations of the world that include diverse positions such as those found in Eastern thought.

## Assessment and Affirmative Action

The twenty-first century has commenced with reenactments of battles begun decades ago by politicians and politician-educators eager to chastise professional educators and to usurp the processes of schools (admissions, instruction, assessment, etc.) under guises of constructive critique (Shaker & Heilman, 2002). Dating back to 1961 when President Kennedy coined the term *affirmative action*, modern America has been embroiled in debate concerning the elimination of racism masked by unequal opportunities and a wrestling of admission policy possessed by the white majority (Hendrickson, 1996). As Hendrickson predicted in 1996, "Affirmative action as a national policy is not only the primary issue of the last half century but one whose importance will dominate public opinion well into the next century" (p. 351).

Although far from being conclusive or definitive, the current University of Michigan case, *Grutter v. Bollinger*, furthers the cause and reinforces the intent of affirmative action: to reduce racism and to expand the diversity of our nation's leadership (Lemann, 2003). Following the June 23, 2003, Supreme Court ruling in support of affirmative action, Holmes and Winter wrote, "Statistics tell the story. On every major indicator of academic success—the SAT, the ACT, and the National Assessment of Educational Progress (given to elementary and secondary students)—the gap between white and minority students has persisted for decades. Though it narrowed somewhat in the national assessment exams from the 1980s through the early 1990s, the divide has only widened since then" (2003).

The recent *Grutter* case decision in support of affirmative action reiterates earlier Supreme Court requirements for colleges and universities to discontinue the process of establishing quotas with bogus systems such as adding points to SAT scores of underperforming students in an attempt to even the competitive field. Although the court appears to view quantitative assessment (norm-referenced assessments such as the SAT) as unfair, the more significant aspect of the current ruling is its call for the implementation of qualitative evaluation (interviewing, writing samples, letters of recommendation, etc.) of candidates for admission. Justice Sandra Day O'Connor said, "attaining a diverse student body is at the heart of the law school's proper institutional mission." And, she added, "a 'critical mass' of underrepresented minorities is necessary to further its compelling interest in securing the educational benefits of a diverse student body" (Schmidt, 2003, pp. S1 and S4).

In the current debate on affirmative action, the only clear result is that the controversy is not resolved and that groups representing the right and the left continue their claim of victory (Schmidt, 2003). For the time being and probably well into the immediate future, building college and university communities reflective of the diversity their citizens represent will continue to be contentious. Competition for limited admissions opportunities within prestigious undergraduate and graduate schools will further exacerbate the racist assumptions that undergird our meritocracy. To support affirmative action in admissions, qualitative assessment can be an effective technique for building a diverse student body and a healthy nation. According to Noam Chomsky (1999), "Democracy functions insofar as individuals can participate meaningfully in the public arena, meanwhile running their own affairs. Functioning democracy presupposes relative equality in access to resources" (p. 131). Affirmative action is a good starting point for reexamination of the racist foundations of quantitative assessment and its ally, the bell curve.

Unfortunately, the deification of competition and the continuing desire to turn schools into businesses continues in K–12 education wrapped in the euphemistic "No Child Left Behind" (NCLB). Conceived by the G. W. Bush administration, NCLB would like to use quantitative, norm-referenced tests as a stick to improve the performance of the lowest-achieving students. The No Child Left Behind Act mandates the use of standardized testing to hold schools accountable for failure to improve academic achievement. "If any racial or demographic group fails to advance for two consecutive years, the school has to offer tutoring and give parents the option of transferring their kids to a higher-scoring school. The danger of high-stakes testing, of course, is that schools become test-taking factories in which the only thing taught or learned is how to take high-stakes tests" (Reich, 2003).

Improving education, especially for our lowest-performing students, is a goal every citizen supports (Bushman & Goodman, 2003). Unfortunately, that the lowest-performing students, their schools, and the professionals who serve them should be punished or humiliated because of their low scores on norm-referenced standardized tests is in line with the George W. Bush administration's "get tough," business-first rhetoric. As stated by Kohn (1999),

> The dominant position is reflected in an endless series of reports on American schooling released by the Business Coalition for Educational Reform, the Business Roundtable, the National Alliance for Business, the Committee for Economic Development, and other clusters of corporations. Rather like a party game in which the players create sentences by randomly selecting an adjective from one list and a noun from another, these virtually interchangeable documents seem to consist mostly of different combinations of terms like "tough," "competitive," "world class," "measurable," "accountability," "standards," "results," and "raising the bar." (p. 15)

That this degradation of education and the concomitant coercion used by politicians eager to develop inappropriate profit models is constructive or in the best interest of children and the people who instruct them is folly. Education is primarily about learning; business is essentially dedicated to profit.

How nonprofessionals and "advocacy academicians" continue to invade the world of education and be allowed to create such chaos is an insult to the academy and the scholarship of the legitimate research community (Shaker & Heilman, 2002). Lisa Delpit (2003), gifted spokesperson of education, contributes: "we in education often allow politicians to push us to act as if the most important goal of our work is to raise test scores. Never mind the development of the human beings in our charge—the integrity, the artistic expressiveness, the ingenuity, the persistence, or the kindness of those who will inherit the earth. The conversation in education has been reduced to a conversation about one number" (p. 14). Certainly, critique of any occupation can be considered fair; however, fear-driven cries for the complete revamping of the educational process by politicians and noneducators such as the current one, No Child Left Behind (NCLB), has no equal in other professions. Moreover, the negative implications of these politicized critiques leave the public with great doubts concerning the future of their children in the local schools.

Criticisms such as the devastating indictment of inner-city and poverty-impacted schools implied through standardized assessment delivered by NCLB are effective destroyers of confidence and trust for urban educators and teachers of our nation's poor, rural students (Lewin & Medina, 2003). Only white, middle-class communities are left with pride in their accomplishment of above average or, at a minimum, mean test results. These scores are not solely a function of great teaching even though there may, in fact, be exemplary teaching going on within these esteemed institutions. When the measure of success is the standardized test, this is very often another example of one more method of the maintenance of white cultural hegemony. It is not only antidemocratic: this is a perpetuation of racist and exclusionary educational practice. According to Alfie Kohn (2000), author of *The Case Against Standardized Testing* and an articulate critic of standardized testing, "Norm-referenced tests are not about assessing excellence; they are about sorting students or schools into winners and losers. The animating spirit is not, 'How well are we learning?' but 'Who's beating whom?'" (p. 15). Teachers and the process of learning is essential to student outcomes; however, the desired result of producing success for all students with "high level, interactive, and thoughtful instruction" (Delpit, 2003, p. 14) is not achieved through the administration of standardized tests.

Political appeals for the implementation of standards, as if standards were a new phenomenon, are attractive to those desirous of maintaining the social hierarchy (Macewan, 2000). Having the standards and the tests to measure student competency is aligned with the thinking that supports competency testing for business and industry. Although we want our pilots and surgeons to be at least minimally competent, this is a different matter from the one that schools confront. Comparing competency testing for physicians to high school graduation requirements is as absurd as the assumption that a standardized measure could effectively include the millions of diverse learners with any fair chance of being valid or reliable without extending the error of measurement to run from the 10th to the 90th percentiles. A high school diploma means relatively little in 2004; however, the absence of one speaks volumes (Goodman, 1999). Ninety-five percent of all inmates incarcerated in California do not hold a high school diploma (Ingersoll & LeBoeuf, 1997).

Although much has been written in the literature of assessment to deride the process, test manufacturers and the politicians elected by the test-publishing industry continue to effectively market their wares to local politicians and state agencies eager to feign concern for the poor and underrepresented (Macewan, 2000). This is hegemony at work. Effectively maintaining positions of power by defining the cultural capital at the center of the controversy perpetuates the myth that the information being tested is *the* knowledge. For Hirsh's (1991) claiming control of cultural capital (*Cultural Literacy*), this ploy of largely testing those things central to white, middle-class culture maintains the position that white is right and white knowledge is not only superior, it is not subjective: it is absolutely and unquestionably correct. Such a monocultural judgment in our culturally diverse world is intellectually deficient and morally untenable. In our total of over sixty years working as psychological examiners, we have felt a strong resistance against the use of standardized testing. In particular, the use of norm-referenced group tests should never be used to make the type of high-stakes decisions that students face today. According to Kohn (2000), "Robert Glaser coined the term 'norm-referenced test' (NRT) many years ago to refer to tests that 'provide little or no information about…what the individual can do. They tell that one student is more or less proficient than another, but do not tell how proficient either of them is with respect to the subject matter tasks involved" (p. 14). Further, Kohn stated (2000), "In contrast to a test that's 'criterion-referenced,' which means it compares each individual to a set standard, one that's norm-referenced compares each individual to everyone else, and the result is usually but not always reported as a percentile" (p. 14).

Norm-referenced assessments perpetuate the myths of the meritocracy. People at the top are rewarded with honors and recognition and the people at the bottom get what they deserve. In this system, the winners are justified, and in the language of assessment, the rewards are validation of their victory. Michael Parenti (1996) puts this bluntly and precisely:

> Throughout history there has only been one thing that the ruling interests have ever wanted—and that is everything: all the choice lands, forest, game, herds, harvests, mineral deposits, and precious metals of the earth; all the wealth, riches, and profitable returns; all the production facilities, gainful inventiveness, and technologies; all the control positions of the state and other major institutions; all public supports and subsidies, privileges, and immunities; all the protections of the law with none of its constraints; all the services, comforts, luxuries, and advantages of civil society with none of the taxes and costs. Every ruling class has wanted only this: all the rewards and none of the burdens. The operational code is: we have a lot; we can get more; we want it all. (p. 46)

Standardized test critic Alfie Kohn (1999) reinforces Parenti's point succinctly, "In case I am being too subtle here, let me state clearly that I think standardized testing is a very bad thing, and the more familiar you become with it, the more appalled you are likely to be" (pp. 73–74). Standardized testing reinforces competitive sorting and perpetuates cultural deficit conclusions of the nonthinking and racist critics of multicultural education (McLaren & Carlson, 1996; Nieto, 1996).

## The Social and Societal Costs of High-Stakes Testing

That there are problems within the nation that our public schools can and need to address is without doubt. Issues of poverty, unemployment, the world's highest incarceration rates, violence, and myriad health problems are all issues that a well-educated and successful society could overcome (Kozol, 1991). Moreover, we agree with Henry Giroux that blaming the school's community (teachers, students, and administration) and threatening school closure for poor performance on standardized tests is scapegoating and shifts the blame from the perpetrators to the victims. Giroux (1997) stated:

> The claim by conservatives that these problems can be solved by raising test scores, promoting choice, developing a national curriculum, and creating a uniform standard of national literacy is cruel and mean-spirited.

> But, of course, this is where the discourse of critical democracy becomes subversive; it makes visible the political and normative considerations that frame such reforms. It also offers a referent for analyzing how the language of excessive individualism and competitiveness serves to make social inequality invisible, promoting an indifference to human misery, exploitation, and suffering. Moreover, it suggests that the language of excellence and individualism when abstracted from considerations of equality and social justice serves to restrict rather than animate the possibilities of public life. Increasingly, conservatives also have used the language of individual rights; that is, the right of individuals to think and act as they please, to attack any discourse or program that questions the existence of social inequalities. (p. 243)

As counselors, psychologists, and therapists, our students and clients may continue to be victims of high-stakes testing; however, we can work within the system to help to promote change by challenging norm-referenced assessment and by working to improve the education of all. As the politicians eye the potential hazards and supposed gains of the current testing and accountability craze, we who work directly with students and their families know the cost of failing to graduate and being pushed out of comprehensive schools into alternative programs or the street. While citizens watch dropout rates continue to climb, we are seeing further proof of the failure of NCLB. As recently reported in the *New York Times* (Lewin & Medina, 2003), New York City schools are counseling students to leave comprehensive high schools in order to improve the school's overall test results and thereby avoid sanctions. One school reported an enrollment of 1,266 students in the 9th grade and 325 in grades 11 and 12 (Lewin & Medina, 2003). An attrition rate of 75 percent is absurd and an abomination. Whereas one of us previously reported dropout and attrition rates in inner-city schools of 50 percent (Goodman, 1999), it is unfathomable to imagine 75 percent. In Fresno, California, home to these writers, approximately 7,000 ninth graders in the Fresno Unified School District yield a senior graduating class of roughly 3,800. Response to the demands of Annual Yearly Progress are not promising for the approximately 3,200 students left behind. Certainly, this result of NCLB spells disaster for inner-city schools.

The current testing obsession continues to create many paradoxical and unethical consequences. As in the example of the New York schools pushing out thousands of students to improve overall school-site test results, Houston schools have been reported to be in trouble as well (Schemo, 2003). Houston schools have recently been discredited for grossly undercounting their dropout rate. Once touted by President Bush as examples of successfully addressing the needs of underperforming students, many of Houston's public school students are failing to achieve at appropriate grade levels. This problem of failing students by not helping them to achieve appropriate academic gains is not limited to the students. Faculty and administration are also trapped in this negative game of testing to detect failure. Furthermore, the pressure to perform increasingly improved results has led to allegations of Houston's providing false information concerning their school's dropout rates and college plans (Schemo, 2003; Schemo & Fessenden, 2003). Ironically, Houston's former superintendent, Rod Paige, is now America's top school officer. Increasing test scores by the removal of miscreants is a heinous and immoral method of faking school improvement (Goodman, 2002).

Atrocious consequences of the No Child Left Behind Act are by no means limited to Texas. As a part of Massachusetts's attempt to use tests to improve education, the state adopted a Communications and Literacy Skills Test in 1998. In Lawrence, Massachusetts, Superintendent of Schools Wilfredo T. Laboy placed two dozen teachers on unpaid leave for failing to pass a state-mandated basic English proficiency test (Associated Press, 2003, August 4). The improvement measure appears to be just one more masked attempt to punish English as a second language (ESL) professionals and the effect is racist. Ironically, Superintendent Laboy has, himself, failed the required test three times. Laboy, a native Spanish speaker, said in his defense, "What brought me down was the rules of grammar and punctuation. English being a second language for me, I didn't do well in writing. If you're not an English teacher, you don't look at the rules on a regular basis." (Note: President Bush, in his January 11, 2000, speech in Grand Rapids, Michigan, could have employed the same excuse as Laboy when he queried, "Is our children learning?" [Begala, 2000].) It appears to these writers that forcing Laboy to dismiss teachers based upon a single skills test or, sometime in the future, removing him for failure to pass the same test (a test that may be racist in its conclusions) are both ethically incorrect. In our logic, the administrators should, if anything, be held to a higher standard because they are the most visible and valued leaders of the school. However, in this case, the use of a biased assessment throws the entire argument into disjuncture. It appears that the only logical alternative is to discontinue the test or at least limit its use on individuals already working within school systems. In situations such as the one confronting Laboy, it is absurd to discredit and/or remove a person who has the responsibility to lead his community's schools toward improvement. Using a test that was not normed for use with primary Spanish-speaking individuals is a violation of best practice and is unethical. From these authors' perspective, it appears that the political motivations behind the Communications and Literacy Skills Test are, in effect, racist. These types of masked attempts at school improvement are often thinly veiled examples of the new, covert racism that exists in America. Laboy's intent of school improvement is laudable. Removing people from the school's process because of learning deficiency should be, at the least, a red flag.

The final argument for using nonstandardized and Ubiquitous Assessments to measure individual student achievement is related to the high school exit exams and the political controversy that surrounds these new tests. As reported in the *New York Times*, "One out of every five high school students in California will be denied diplomas next year if the state forges ahead with a plan to require seniors to pass an 'exit exam' before graduation, according to a state-commissioned study" (Winter, 2003, May 2). As disastrous as this prospect appears, this percentage of the general student body is small in comparison to the effect this exam could have on specific subgroups. Winter (2003, May 2) went on to state, "The outlook is worse for so-called disadvantaged students. Only 54 percent of low income students, 37 percent of nonnative English-speakers and 22 percent of students with learning disabilities in the class of 2004 have passed their math requirement so far" (p. A30). With a picture as bleak as this, California has reconsidered using this test and recalibrating the cutoff to graduate a larger percentage of students (Winter, 2003). California's high school exit exam has been postponed until 2006.

As NCLB enforcement approaches, each state is wrestling with how it will implement comprehensive, statewide testing programs. Currently, fewer than one-third of all states test students in reading and math every year (Karp, 2001). Sadly, the decision makers and policymakers are often legislators and other elected officials who are following a get-tough, conservative political agenda. These politicians are not only outside of education, they are unresponsive to educational research and deaf to the advice of the professional educators in the state departments of education and in the state's universities. The goal appears to be a top-down dismantling of pluralistic policy and educational equity (Karp, 2001). Attacking education with tests and high-stakes consequences appears to be Washington's guiding principle. The result is a "pushout" of students in states with yearly standardized assessments. In response to New York City schools' pushout of underperforming students, Linda Kastner (2003) asked, "Isn't there anyone working in the city (school) system who is a child advocate?"

In Florida, Governor Bush has supported a statewide retention plan to remediate students before passing to the next grade. Despite decades of research refuting retention's benefit (most students retained two times in elementary school will drop out in grade nine), Florida has adopted mandatory retention with no exceptions. The effect this year is that 23 percent or 43,000 third graders will be retained in Florida during the 2003–2004 school year (Winerip, 2003, May 21). Continuing policies such as Florida's may result in the wholesale abandonment of the public schools. As parents experience their children's pain, more and more parents will choose homeschooling or alternatives to the public school.

Assessment is at the center of controversy over how to best improve education. In defense of assessment's goals, we have found that in many instances current school reform efforts in California provided an incentive for schools to initiate improvements benefiting instruction and educational outcomes for students (Central Valley Educational Research Consortium [CVERC], 2000; CVERC, 2002; CVERC, 2004). Although these authors do not agree with the use of academic performance indices because of the parallel to the stock market index and, in general, the manufacturing of images evocative of a commodification of education (McLaren, 1999), we agree with humanistic and critical school reforms that improve instruction within the classroom. Assessment, individual and criterion-referenced or authentic, used to measure actual academic skills and progress can be a valuable tool with which students, parents, and educators can measure achievement.

Unfortunately, individuals with little educational expertise outside their own spurious memories of attending school are making the decisions about how today's educators should move forward. For example, policymakers in Washington have created an accountability system (NCLB) that acts in opposition to state accountability formulas (Asimov, 2003). The disconnection between state mandates and national standards leaves many local educators confused and angry. Ironically, many of the individuals involved in developing these unreasonable double-standard policies are intelligent and well-meaning people (Asimov, 2003). Shaker and Heilman (2002) identify these pseudoeducator/policymakers as "advocacy academicians."

> A new brand of academic reflection and research has found its way into popular media penned by "advocacy academicians"—scholars often operating outside their area of expertise yet wearing the garb of objective, expert scholarship. These advocacy academicians employ the institutional forms of fostering and evaluating research—peer review and corroboration and the imprimaturs of universities and philanthropic foundations, for example—but do so under the umbrella of ideology-based interest groups. The message is often, though not always, conservative, free market, and illiberal, and interlocked with the positions of religious, political, and corporate entities. Many of these groups seem to be less interested in reforming public schools than in discrediting

> public institutions, gaining party advantage, and opening new markets for profit. (Shaker & Heilman, 2002, p. 1)

Since the publication of *A Nation at Risk* (National Commission on Excellence, 1983), the U.S. educational system has been besieged by individuals and groups eager to use fear to drive reform initiatives within the public schools. The implementation of large-scale, high-stakes testing proposals are the latest reform effort of groups pressing for greater school accountability. However, their ignorance of school improvement and accountability's mainstay, standardized testing, is no more apparent than in cries for reform such as NCLB. In standardized assessment, only 49.9 percent of the students can be above the 50th percentile. Continuing to use a bell curve to competitively sort students, it is inevitable that 49.9 percent of the class will be below the 50th percentile. With ill-informed and mean-spirited double-talk supporting NCLB, these "advocacy academicians" (Shaker & Heilman, 2002), in their politically motivated maneuvers, stand to cause considerably more harm than good for our children. The negative consequences of NCLB include sanctions against underperforming schools, diminished self-esteem of low-achieving communities, and, potentially, closings of neighborhood schools (Lewin & Medina, 2003). Unintended negative consequences are increases in dropout rates, assigning derogatory appellations to underperforming schools (we know of a school called Garfield that was labeled Garbage-field because of their test results), and increased stress and burnout among staff and administration. "Standardized tests have historically been used to legitimize social inequality" (Miner, 2000, p. 17) rather than as an instrument for the promotion of social justice such as implied by the title No Child Left Behind (NCLB).

As graduate students in education and psychology or as professionals and citizens within the community you represent, you can contribute your input into the process at school, in a mental health clinic, or in the voting booth. These authors hope that your understanding of the deficiencies of the traditional, norm-referenced measurement will lead you to see the value in making multimeasured Ubiquitous Assessments whenever high-stakes decisions such as graduation, retention, school closings, special education placements, or administrative changes are being considered. "Graduation should depend on a review of a number of factors (grades, other test results, faculty recommendations) and not one test" (Goodman, 2003). Having high expectations for student achievement should be everyone's main objective. However, high standards and expectations are not to be equated with high-stakes tests (Cook, 2003). How you can actively participate as an advocate for high expectations through the collection of valuable assessment information that will benefit your clients or students will be the focus of the remainder of this text.

# Chapter Two

## Critically Situating Validity and Reliability

*Ubiquitous Assessment* does not eschew technical adequacy in the delivery of best practices as described in this volume. Every student and client we see deserves to be given our best, and we must make certain that what we do really makes a difference for each individual. Thus, the concepts of reliability and validity require special attention as they are cornerstones to ensuring we are providing best practice to those we serve. This chapter begins with an overview of the traditional definitions and methods for reliability and validity and concludes with our thoughts regarding the integration of these concepts within Ubiquitous Assessment.

### Traditional Definition of Reliability

Reliability is the degree to which our methods stand up to the test of time. In traditional norm-referenced assessment, reliability is the confidence we have in our test scores to be consistent from one testing session to the next. The stability, consistency, and predictability of our scores across time are important as we make decisions about our students or clients and the educational and psychosocial opportunities they are afforded.

Importantly, "the concept of reliability is the possible range of error, or error of measurement, of a single score" (Groth-Marnat, 2003, p. 12). All scores we obtain on any assessment measure consist of a true score and an error. A true score would be stable, consistent, and predictable in all cases. For example, if an individual were given an IQ test today, she/he would obtain the exact same score at a later time, this being the true score. This, however, is rarely the case primarily because our instruments are not precisely reliable. For example, while IQ tests and tests of achievement do tend to be somewhat more stable than tests of personality because of steady developmental changes, all tests reflect our own human variation (Groth-Marnat, 2003, pp. 12–13). Furthermore, we simply cannot ask all of the questions in any given domain on any one test. A true score would refer to the score a student would obtain if all questions in any given area were answered by a student. However, it would be impossible in most areas (including academic, psychological, intellectual, or behavioral) to give a student all items in one particular domain—for example, spelling. For reasons of efficiency, the instruments we use generally assess a sample of all the items that would be possible.

Furthermore, no assessment situation is ever ideal, because individuals vary in performance day to day. The student or client may be hungry, cold, or depressed. The examiner may also be stressed because of scheduling demands, fatigue, or physical discomforts. In addition, the setting may be in a busy office or school where phones are ringing and interruptions are a factor. Thus we will never obtain a "true" score on any student or client we assess because there will always be some type of error. The question that must be addressed is how much error there is as related to a particular score. While we may never know for certain how much error is contained in any assessment, we can estimate the error through the use of statistics involving a reliability coefficient and the standard error of measurement (see Salvia & Ysseldyke, 2004, for the procedures to obtain these statistics).

There are five primary types of reliability described in the literature. They include test-retest reliability, alternate forms reliability, alternate forms and test-retest reliability, internal consistency reliability, and inter-rater reliability. Each can be determined through the use of statistics. To assist your understanding of these important concepts, we present each type and its definition.

**Test-Retest Reliability**

Test-retest reliability is the extent to which the scores obtained by a particular student or client on one test are consistent with the scores the same student obtains on the same test at a later date. A correlation statistic is used to determine the association between the two administrations. For making decisions about individual students or clients, the correlation coefficient should be a positive .90 or higher for all types of reliability. Many of the tests used on a daily basis to diagnose individuals do not attain this standard. Thus, when we use tests with reliabilities below this standard, our decisions based on the scores obtained provide us with little information in terms of the stability of the scores, the consistency of the results, the predictability we can estimate, or the accuracy of our measures.

**Alternate Forms Reliability**

Alternate forms reliability is the use of two different versions of the same instrument, each administered at one point in time. The two forms must be equivalent in terms of construct measured, difficulty level, and scaling (Creswell, 2002). Oftentimes, items on the same test are divided into odd and even numbered tests and alternate forms reliability is established using correlation coefficients. In other situations, two tests appearing to measure the same construct are developed, the two tests are administered, and correlation is performed to determine if the two tests are indeed measuring the same construct. Again, reliability is determined using the correlation coefficient. The higher the positive correlation, the more likely it is the two tests are measuring the same construct.

### Alternate Forms and Test-Retest Reliability

A third method involves both of these concepts. Alternate forms and test-retest reliability is a combination of the two methods discussed above. Here, the test is administered twice but different forms are administered at testing session one and at testing session two. This type of reliability allows the comparison of the construct as well as the stability of the test. A positive correlation indicates that test one is reliable and that both tests measure the same construct.

### Internal Consistency

Internal consistency reliability involves one administration of the same instrument. Scores are considered reliable if the student or client answers the questions in a consistent manner throughout the test. In other words, the way a student or client responds at the beginning of a test is the same as the way the individual answers at the middle and end of the test. There are several methods for determining if a test has internal consistency. One method is the Kuder-Richardson split half test (KR20), used when categorical variables are used for response (i.e., yes/no; true/false) whereby the test is divided into equal parts, often using even and odd items, and correlating the results of each part. A second method is the Spearman-Brown formula, in which all items of the test are used and compared. A final method is the Coefficient Alpha. Coefficient Alpha is used to make comparisons when continuous variables are used as the response mode (i.e., Likert scale; strongly agree to strongly disagree).

### Inter-rater Reliability

Inter-rater reliability is often used when two or more individuals score the same tests or observe the same student or client. The point is to determine whether or not the two individuals are scoring the test or rating the student or client's behavior in the same way. Oftentimes, two individuals can come to very different conclusions in scoring test items or in observing an examinee in the classroom. Inter-rater reliability allows comparisons to be made between the scorings or ratings of one individual to another. Again, correlation is used and high, positive correlations indicate that the two individuals scored or rated the item or behavior in the same way.

All practitioners have an obligation to be aware of the reliability (and validity) of the tools they are using. As stated above, the higher the reliability coefficients, the more confidence we can have in our interpretations of the data and in the predications that we make related to the clients/students we are assessing.

## Validity

Validity is defined as the degree to which a construct measures what it purports to measure. Unfortunately, many test publishers base the meaningfulness of their tools on cash validity. Cash validity simply refers to whether or not the instrument makes the corporation money or not. If it does, it gets re-normed and republished. However, the Standards for Educational and Psychological Testing (American Educational Research Association et al., 1999) identify the specific components of tests that publishers should adhere to, although it is up to the individual practitioner to determine whether or not the instruments she/he uses actually do meet the standards. Some of the questions one should ask when evaluating an instrument for validity include: Does a test, concept, or other definable thing actually measure what we believe it does? If it does, can we use the results to make "good" decisions about what we should do? If a test measures attention problems, for example, does it really measure that construct or is it measuring some other construct, such as memory? And if the scale is measuring attention, can we use the results to begin to develop interventions for the student or client in question?

There are three major types of validity that are discussed in the literature: content validity, criterion-related validity including predictive and concurrent validity, and construct validity. However, validity should be viewed as a universal concept that incorporates all three types (Thorndike, 1997). In actuality, a measure will not be valid unless all three types are determined to be valid. A test is deemed to be valid if the scores are useful and if the scores result in positive outcomes for those individuals taking the test (Creswell, 2002).

### Content Validity

Content validity is the degree to which the content of a particular instrument, test, or construct is fair and representative of the domain in question. Does the test represent all aspects of the area being measured? Generally, content validity is based on common sense and logic. Related to tests, test publishers hire individuals whom they consider to be experts in an area to analyze the test to determine if the questions are representative of that domain. In the school setting, the content validity of a student who is verbally abusive and refusing to complete class work would include observations of the student's specific behaviors, such as cursing, yelling, screaming, or ignoring authority figures. This behavior set includes the settings where the behavior most often occurs (certain classrooms, only at school, at home, or in the community); whether or not the adult is asking the student to do something the student is able to do; whether the request is appropriate for the student's age, ability, gender, and/or ethnicity; whether the student is capable of understanding the request; and whether there are other factors or issues that might contribute to the student's behavior, including adult anger, student or adult depression, physical problems, language differences or difficulties, and/or religious beliefs (Carey, 2004).

### Criterion-Related Validity

Criterion-related validity is the association between the score on a test and a criterion of performance such as a student or client's behavior. Criterion-related validity can be separated into two parts: concurrent and predictive validity. Concurrent validity involves the association between what we observe or the scores on a test to some already established measure or criterion. For example, an individual's ability to make friends can be related to her/his verbal aggression or social withdrawal. Predictive validity requires that the scores from a particular test are used to predict future performance or the effectiveness of some program on a student or client's behavior over time. A common example is the use of the Scholastic Aptitude Test (SAT) to predict how well a student will do in college.

### Construct Validity

Construct validity seeks to evaluate the "significance, meaning, purpose and use" of scores on a test (Creswell, 2002, p. 184). Do the test items measure what we think they measure? Construct validity can be evaluated in either statistical or nonstatistical ways. According to Creswell (2002), statistical procedures can be used to: (1) "See if scores to items are related in a way that is expected" (for example, determining if an item on some test like a scale measuring attention deficit hyperactivity disorder [ADHD] is related to the overall, total score obtained); (2) "Test a theory and see if the scores, as expected, support the theory" (for example, determine whether a theory of ADHD is supported by results on some instrument that is designed to assess ADHD); and, (3) "Correlate the scores statistically with other variables or scales that should be similar or dissimilar" (for example, determine if scores on one test of ADHD relate to scores on some other scale measuring ADHD) (p. 184). Construct validity is the most common form of validity used within psychological tests measuring psychopathology such as depression, anxiety, bipolar disorder, and other forms of mental illness.

### Nonstatistical Procedures

Nonstatistical procedures can also be used and include: (1) "Examining the consequences of interpreting test scores in term of values" (Creswell, 2002, p. 184) (for example, when scores on a test of ADHD are high, does this indicate the student has "severe" ADHD, "mild" ADHD, or does not have ADHD?); (2) "Examining the relevance and use of test scores" (for example, can the scores be used to determine the need for medication and/or special school placements?); and, (3) "Examining the consequences of using test scores" (for example, are the scores on a test of ADHD useful for developing a cognitive/behavior intervention program?) (Creswell, 2002, p. 185).

A valid test should measure what it is meant to measure and should provide results that are useful in decision making. Test publishers should provide information related to both validity and reliability in the test or technical manuals. All practitioners have an obligation to review those manuals to be sure the tools they are using are valid and reliable for the individuals with whom they are working.

## Qualitative Concepts

The field of qualitative inquiry is relatively new and is, unfortunately, quite foreign to many individuals trained in the "scientific method." Qualitative analysis grew from the field of anthropology and today is used by researchers conducting ethnography (culture in context), case study, life history, historical analysis, and surveys. Such research has been conducted in the areas of education, psychology, feminism, symbolic interactionism, sociolinguistics, Marxism, and democratic evaluation. If one thinks about the anthropologist in the field who discovers a small chard of clay and attempts to determine what the piece was used for, by whom, and when, one can get an idea of what occurs in qualitative research. The field requires systematic inquiry that must occur in a natural setting, such as a classroom or a home, and not in a contrived situation such as an artificially contrived experiment (Marshall & Rossman, 1995). Much like the anthropologist's examinations, qualitative research requires the practitioner to immerse himself/herself in the everyday life of the individuals chosen for study in an attempt to understand the day-to-day lives of the participants, their values, and their beliefs. The researcher can be a participant observer or nonparticipant observer; however, she/he must be fully engaged to the extent possible with the participants either through daily interaction or at a minimum through nonparticipant observation. The method emphasizes flexibility as the study evolves over the length of time the researcher is in the natural setting. We believe qualitative research methodology is ideal for practitioners serving in schools and mental health settings. These techniques allow the practitioner to become fully engaged with the client/student and attempt to understand what it must be like to be that individual and live her/his life.

Data for qualitative studies are generally collected from three sources: interviews, observations, and documents. The researcher collects field notes from observations (conducted over a long period of time), conducts interviews to verify observational data and gain additional insights, and uses data from documents to again verify other information collected. The method, known as triangulation, requires the researcher to look for patterns, themes, and categories within the three sources to confirm or disconfirm her/his findings. The strengths of qualitative study were outlined by Marshall and Rossman (1995). Qualitative study is:

1. research that delves into complexities and processes;
2. on informal and unstructured linkages and processes in organizations;
3. research on real, as opposed to stated, organizational goals;
4. research that cannot be done experimentally for practical or ethical reasons;
5. research for which relevant variables have yet to be identified or research on little-known phenomena or innovative systems;
6. research that seeks to explore where and why policy and local knowledge and practice are at odds; and
7. research (p. 23).

Naturalistic or qualitative research has provided us with a different way to look at the issues of reliability and validity. Qualitative methods require the description and explanation of events accurately and as completely as possible so that such descriptions represent, as closely as possible, the individual or group being observed.

According to Lincoln and Guba (1986), "credibility" and "transferability" are "analogs to validity," and "dependability" is "an analog to reliability" (p. 76). "Confirmability" is analogous to the scientific method concept of objectivity (p. 76). They refer to these as addressing the "trustworthiness" we can place on our data (p. 77).

Credibility refers to the researcher's ability to demonstrate that the study was conducted in such a way that the participants and their behaviors, thoughts, and feelings are accurately described. Transferability is the equivalent of generalizability in traditional quantitative research. However, in qualitative research, the burden of transferability is on the readers of the work, and not on the original researcher (Lincoln & Guba, 1986). The best way to ensure credibility and transferability is through triangulation, which allows the research to "corroborate, elaborate, and illuminate the research in question" (Marshall & Rossman, 1995, p. 89). Dependability refers to the researcher's efforts at understanding and describing the changes that occur in the setting. The qualitative researcher understands that the world and the study participants are constantly changing and must be described as doing so. Confirmability is determined through the use of the data in order to authenticate the findings and develop implications from the findings.

Qualitative researchers attempt to ensure the technical adequacy of their data by controlling for their own biases and other mitigating circumstances that could affect the data. Some ways in which they do this are to work with a partner who can confirm through her/his own observations, interviews, and documentation of findings, and call biases to each other's attention; search repeatedly for negative instances of patterns in the data; evaluate and reevaluate the data for other possible explanations; and ask questions of the data to demonstrate themes along the way (Marshall & Rossman, 1995). Qualitative researchers also explain and explore the setting and methods in depth; overtly state their assumptions, values, and biases; gather as much data as possible to demonstrate relationships between the research setting and the "real" world; search for alternative explanations of the data; use efficient and accurate data collection procedures, and present the data for reanalysis.

## Other Types of Reliability and Validity

There are a number of other important types of reliability and validity that should be considered when preparing to conduct an assessment. These are generally not included in the traditional types discussed in the sections above, but are no less important for practitioner consideration.

"Decision reliability refers to the consistency of outcomes across such factors as alternative instruments or methods, raters, and assessment occasions" (Barnett & Carey, 1992, p. 30). The instruments we use for any assessment, whether they be observations, interviews, or actual test kits, should provide us with the ability to make consistent decisions across time and students. Thus, the reliability question refers directly to the outcomes of decisions. Unfortunately, in most cases, our assessment methods are likely to identify different children due to different assessment times, different raters completing scales, different assessment tools that measure the same construct, and error.

Decision validity refers to the suitability of using information from an assessment for making specific decisions (Messick, 1989). The question becomes whether or not the decisions developed from our assessments will lead to beneficial changes for the client, the parents, and/or others over a long period of time in the areas where the individual assessed has been found to experience some difficulties. Assessment should lead us to treatment and the decisions made related to treatment should have long-term positive outcomes.

Social validity refers to the judgments, beliefs, and values made by others about the acceptability of goals and plans for a specific treatment or intervention, the procedures used in the treatment or intervention, and the potential outcomes of such a treatment or intervention. In other words, do parents and other teachers and educators feel our focus on change is okay and our plan is good one? For example, does the student who is experiencing problems in school believe that additional tutoring will make a difference in her/his grades? Do the parents? Does the family of a student who has difficulty paying attention in class believe that the only way to assist the student is through medication? Social validity emphasizes the importance of taking into consideration the feelings and beliefs of the individual identified, the family, the culture, and the larger society.

There are two methods for attaining social validity. First, social validity involves social comparisons, so it may be necessary to compare the client/student to her/his peers. Second, the subjective attitudes, beliefs, and evaluations of parents, teachers, and community members regarding the client/student's behaviors must be considered, as they are directly effected by the behavior.

Ethnic validity was first proposed by Savage and Adair (1980) to ensure the fairness of assessment procedures for African American students in response to concerns about test bias as it relates to this population. They recommended that five domains of behavior be sampled, including affective, behavioral, cognitive, cultural, and social, through the immersion of the evaluator in the African American culture. This immersion over a long period of time would provide the evaluator with an in-depth understanding of the client/student's life experiences. However, they readily admitted that there were potential problems with the model, in that most people would simply not be able to spend extended periods of time immersing oneself in the culture.

Further, they felt that some individuals might experience difficulties when attempting to become a viable part of the African American culture.

Tyler, Brome, and Williams (1991) proposed another model of ethnic validity specific to psychotherapy. They suggested that the psychotherapy model was ethnocentric and based on white American male values. However, to meet the needs of all people, including those of different ethnic groups, they proposed a model based on three assumptions. The first assumption was that there are many different lifestyles and each one has both positive and negative aspects. The second assumption was that people are influenced by the characteristics and social contexts of the individuals with whom they interact as well as their own and others' ethnic/cultural backgrounds. The final assumption was that a person's identity is established at both individual and group levels. The foremost idea of this model was that the therapist needed to recognize, accept, and respect the similarities and differences in every individual's development and experiences. Thus, while a therapist might have different opinions, perceptions, ideas, and attitudes about the world in which she/he lives, each clinician is responsible for developing the ability to empathize and understand the views of every client with whom she/he works. Thus, the emphasis is placed on what is acceptable and meaningful to the individual within the client's cultural group.

The model proposed for educators was developed by Barnett and associates (1995). They expanded on the two models described above and incorporated the concept of social validity into their model. Barnett et al. (1995) defined ethnic validity as "the degree to which problem identification and problem solving are acceptable to the client in respect to the client's belief and value systems, as these are associated with the client's ethnic/cultural group" (p. 221). Thus, ethnic validity stresses values associated with one's particular gender, cultural, religious, or ethnic group and focuses on the student experiencing difficulties as a member of a group or groups with shared values and perspectives.

To ensure ethnic validity when working with students and families of differing backgrounds, a collaborative process using educators of the same gender, culture, religion, social status, race, and/or ethnic background as the student and family should be used to establish and "anchor" the cultural appropriateness of meeting with parents, identifying problems, and developing solutions. This allows parents and students to feel safe and understood and to get their point across.

## Reliability and Validity of Observations

In order to conduct meaningful observations, we must first make many decisions, initially including what, where, who, when, and how to observe. This requires planning and a thorough understanding of the reason we are observing. If we are not clear on what and why we are observing or we are observing at inappropriate times (such as in the classroom, when the problems occur outside), we are simply wasting our own time and that of others.

There are, however, many controversies about whether traditional categories of reliability and validity should be used when conducting observations or whether new frameworks such as those described as related to qualitative research are needed (Nelson & Hayes, 1986; Suen & Ary, 1989). Regardless of such controversies, however, the quality of observational measurement procedures must be evaluated for technical adequacy if our decisions based on such measures are to have any meaning for the individual student/client.

To ensure our observations are valid and reliable, the basic strategy is to make comparisons between observers who are watching the same behaviors. The quality of observations may reflect on the skills or training of the observers, the characteristics of the behavior(s) observed (such as bursts of cursing or aggression, specific problems confined to one or more episodes, or concealed behaviors), the clarity of the reason for observing or referral, the time of day the observation occurs, and the different settings in which in the observation is conducted. If after two observers (or more) conduct their observations and agreement between them is low in terms of what they observed, they should consider the possibility that one or more of the above is contributing to the disagreement.

There are several ways to determine agreement between observers to ensure reliability and validity. The first, total agreement, refers to a summary of agreements between the two observers concerning the total number of occurrences of the behavior within an established time interval. Total agreement does not measure the agreement on each specific instance of behavior, so there may be disagreement between the observers on specific occurrences of the behavior even if the total agreement percentages are high (Page & Iwata, 1986). To determine total agreement, the smallest estimate is divided by the larger estimate. For example, a teacher may report seven acts of cursing during the day while the teacher aide may report five. The total agreement would then be 71 percent (Barnett & Carey, 1992). Again, when we obtain this type of disagreement, we should look at the quality of our observations carefully to determine why such a difference occurs. Two observers may be seeing behaviors very differently and the behaviors identified for observation may not be all that important for the student/client in her/his day-to-day activities.

A second way to determine agreement between observers is through interval agreement. This involves examining the specific occurrences of the behavior under study within specified time intervals. The observers simply agree or disagree about whether or not the behavior was seen and we can use this method to investigate both occurrences and nonoccurrences of the behavior. We simply add the numbers of agreements and disagreements, and divide the total into the number of agreements (Hopkins & Hermann, 1976).

The agreement of estimates between observers is necessary in order to examine the effects of observers, the adequacy of the reason for referral, and the methods used for observation. The estimates of agreement also are important to use when we are observing at different times and in different settings.

Several problems can arise when we conduct observations that affect the reliability and validity of our observations. Observer drift can occur, which means that the observers unintentionally change the definition of the behavior being observed while conducting the observations. For example, the observers may be looking for evidence of aggression against others, but one may define a sneer as such evidence while the other does not. Expectation bias can also occur. Expectation bias occurs when the observers think or believe that they see improvement when no such improvement really exists. This can also occur when the observers believe they see problems that do not really exist. They may see problems as being much worse than they really are.

Finally, the location of observers needs to be considered. Observers who sit in the back of a classroom or in the dining room of a home may miss important events and interactions. Thus, the need to move throughout the classroom or home (if you can) in order to get "different takes" on the behavior under study should be considered.

The challenge in Ubiquitous Assessment is to select measures that are reliable and valid for the individual students/clients with whom we work to ensure that the decisions we make related to their lives are meaningful and accurate. Thus, validity is viewed as the appropriateness of the behavior(s) we have selected for treatment/intervention.

## Reliability and Validity of Interviews

The technical adequacy of interviews has received insufficient consideration and the reliability and validity of our interviews must be examined to ensure we have accurate and meaningful information if we are going to use this method to assist in developing treatments/interventions. Peterson (1968) warned that interviews should not necessarily be "regarded as the 'truth' about the individual and his environment, but as another form of data whose reliability, validity, and decisional utility must be subjected to the same kinds of scrutiny required for other modes of data collection" (p. 13). The greatest problem surrounding the use of interviews is the reliance on self-reported information. Furthermore, important information may be "out of awareness" (Bowers & Meichenbaum, 1984) of those providing the information during the interview. Parents and other people we interview may simply not have thought about a particular behavior or such a behavior may be seen as typical in the student/client's home or school but not appropriate in the larger community.

Parents, of course, need to be the most important persons in a client/student's life, and as such they may view their child as having no problems at all. They may blame others for the child's problems and view the behaviors that are causing the child difficulties as occurring because of unfair treatment of the child by others. Other parents are simply in denial of the severity of the problem behavior. Thus, their judgments may be biased and the information reported during interviews not accurate.

In order to address the issues of reliability and validity when conducting interviews, information from several sources must be obtained. Interviewing both parents (if possible), grandparents, babysitters, family friends, teachers, school administrators, medical doctors, psychologists, and counselors can assist in ensuring the accuracy and completeness of the information obtained.

An important problem that can affect the accuracy of interviews is bias on the part of the interviewer. Interviewers can bias the results by phrasing questions in a subjective way, leading those being interviewed by the questions asked, and disregarding important information provided by the individuals interviewed. The interviewer must carefully evaluate her/his style during interviews to ensure such problems affecting accuracy do not occur.

In order to verify our observations, we must follow them up with observations of the student/client in his/her actual environment. In our experience, practitioners often simply conduct interviews and never observe the student/client. By doing so, there is no way to determine whether what is being reported by others is accurate.

### Reliability and Validity for Designing Treatments/Interventions

The treatments or interventions we select must demonstrate reliability and validity. However, research studies have revealed the potential for significant discrepancies between professionals when selecting targets of our treatments and interventions. For example, Wilson and Evans (1983) sent descriptions of childhood disorders to a sample of members of the Association for Advancement of Behavior Therapy. The survey described children experiencing fearful and anxious behavior; conduct-disordered and disobedient behavior; and withdrawn, shy, introverted behavior. Each psychologist was asked (a) to judge whether treatment appeared necessary, (b) to indicate the child's major difficulty, (c) to identify treatment goals, and (d) to indicate and rank intervention targets. The psychologists agreed on the need to provide some treatment in each case; however, the question of what behaviors to treat was very low, resulting in 38.6 percent agreement (Barnett & Carey, 1992). This disagreement between psychologists of over 60 percent in determining what behaviors to treat alerts us to the fact that there is the potential for each one of us to select a different problem to focus on when working with the same student/client.

To control for this problem, we must make certain that we have fully explored the problem in question and conducted interviews and initial observations prior to determining our focus for treatment. Discussing the case with other professionals can also help ensure the accuracy of our decisions.

The results of selecting different behaviors for treatment come under the broad concept of validity. Unfortunately, there is no direct one-to-one correspondence between the accurate and complete description of a specific behavior and its treatment or intervention. Our selection of the behavior for treatment or intervention should be guided by the probability of changing a current problematic situation. We do so by referring back to the traditional concepts of validity.

Content validity for selecting our behavior for change refers to the adequate analysis of the behavior and requires (1) a specific determination of the behavior for change; (2) the settings where the behavior takes place; (3) an analysis of what is required in the setting, including the instructions and expectations for the setting/situation; (4) and the individual's own interests, attitudes, and beliefs that may affect her/his performance (Strosahl & Linehan, 1986). Criterion-related validity for selecting behaviors for treatment involves the examination of the relationship between the behavior as described by the parent or teacher and other measures of the problem, as well as the student/client's day-to-day functioning. Predictive validity refers to the effectiveness of our treatments over long periods of time. Construct validity for selecting behaviors for change requires the analysis of descriptions of the presenting behavior by referring to diagnostic classifications and other descriptions of similar behaviors.

These concepts of reliability and validity occur in general ways as related to the selection of the behavior for intervention/treatment. Mental health professionals in all fields need to address the technical adequacy of their reasons for referral or the behavior under consideration in order to develop treatment/intervention plans that will address the problem and have beneficial outcomes for the client/student.

### Reliability and Validity for *Ubiquitous Assessment*

As we noted in chapter 1, Ubiquitous Assessment refers to the focus upon the individual and her/his distinctiveness, viewing the assessment process not as a measure of the individual at one point in time but as ongoing and continuous. We believe reliability and validity for Ubiquitous Assessment should not only be based on the traditional methods above but also on those utilized by qualitative researchers in their quest to discover the uniqueness of students or clients and those individuals' values, beliefs, and behaviors.

Technical adequacy is a must in all of our endeavors, and we need to ensure that our methods and techniques are consistent over time. Factors of technical adequacy include evaluating what we think our methods are measuring, whether we are using traditional assessment tools, observations, and/or interviews in developing our treatment/intervention plans.

Therefore, if you do use traditional assessment measures such as IQ, personality, or achievement tests, be certain that they meet the rigor of the Standards for Educational and Psychological Testing (American Educational Research Association et al., 1999). Carefully examine the test or technical manual for information relative to reliability and validity to ensure the standard of coefficients above .90 for individual decision making. Clinicians need to use the methods outlined by qualitative researchers to ensure that data are consistent over time, that the patterns observed in the data are valid, and that the examiners immerse themselves with the individual student/client to the greatest extent possible in order to obtain certain understanding of her/his world. Counselors, therapists, and psychologists need to make use of interobserver interviews to confirm findings. When conducting interviews, be sure to talk with several different individuals with knowledge about the student/client's problems. Assessments will lead to the development of valid treatment and intervention plans if the clinician is certain to have fully explored the problem from all perspectives.

# Chapter Three

## Assessment in School Counseling

School counselors face tremendous challenges in their mission to provide quality counseling services to an increasingly diverse and multitalented educational constituency. Working with highly motivated and talented gifted students in one session and subsequently providing supervision for a large group of students and parents attending a cocurricular function later that day requires tremendous flexibility and well-honed assessment skills. One of the most challenging problems that counselors face is in accurately assessing their clients' needs. Whether the counselor is performing individual or group counseling, accurately assessing her/his client and correctly adjusting her/his role in the delivery in what has come to be referred to as "best practice" educational services is crucial to the professional school counselor's success.

The concept of best practice is borrowed from medicine and psychology and implies making the most well-informed, professional judgment given the necessities and requirements of the present time. Sometimes referred to simply as professionalism, best practice effectively translates into behaviors or responses that can stand as well-reasoned reflections of competency. Best practice implies thoroughness, reflection, and ethical behavior. Conversely, best practice means avoiding mistakes, from the most rudimentary such as not returning phone calls to committing the most egregious moral and ethical wrongdoings such as engaging in sexual improprieties.

For school counselors to perform optimally and in concurrence with best practice in the process of their daily functioning, assessment must be ubiquitous. By Ubiquitous Assessment, we mean that counselors must continually assess the needs of both the individuals whom they serve in an immediate sense and the groups of students for whom they are responsible throughout the course of the entire year. For some counselors, this means being available for crisis interventions, handling discipline issues as they arise, scheduling conferences with students referred for academic counseling, returning parent phone calls in a timely manner, and accepting administrative duties as assigned. Throughout the entire day, and often into the night, counselors must continuously assess the needs of the clients they serve.

Having worked as school counselors and psychologists for over sixty years, we are well aware of the multiple tasks set before school counselors. Of all the requirements of the profession, the most challenging task is that of accurately assessing the needs of those immediately before us. For us to accurately assess our client's mental status, we must be fully engaged or present in the gestalt sense. Irving Yalom, one of America's most famous and widely read psychotherapists, sees the role of the therapist as being seamless from the client. He conceptualizes the therapist and client as "together" in a process of growth and healing. According to Yalom (1989),

> Patienthood is ubiquitous; the assumption of the label is largely arbitrary and often dependent more on cultural, educational, and economic factors than on the severity of pathology. Since therapists, no less than patients, must confront these givens of existence, the professional posture of disinterested objectivity, so necessary to scientific method, is inappropriate. We psychotherapists simply cannot cluck with sympathy and exhort patients to struggle resolutely with their problems. Instead, we must speak of *us* and *our* problems, because our life, our existence, will always be riveted to death, love to loss, freedom to fear, growth to separation. We are, all or us, in this together. (p. 14)

Through forming real, meaningful connections with our counseling clients, we are able to understand the issues they face and to accurately assess the support they require.

Seeing the counseling relationship as a partnership between the client and the counselor, the introduction of formalized assessment procedures would not appear to enhance the rapport or maintain the appearance of equality. By implementing formalized procedures such as tests, the counselor situates herself/himself as separated from the client in her/his role as an examiner. Because of the awkwardness and inefficiency of using formal techniques, in almost all of the cases where we are performing our duties as counselors, we are using informal evaluation techniques. By informal assessment, we mean the use of nonstandardized methods such as interviewing, observing, and other information-gathering methods. The rare exception to the use of informal assessment methods occurs when counselors administer group achievement tests, the Armed Services Vocational Aptitude Battery (the ASVAB), college tests such as the Scholastic Aptitude Test, achievement batteries like the California Achievement Test (CAT), or other large-group test administrations such as the college entrance exam precursor, the PSAT.

### Assessment and School Counseling: Melding Theory and Practice

As students and practitioners continue their education, the development of a personal style of counseling evolves from first learning and selecting from traditional techniques. In this section we will examine the use of Ubiquitous

Assessment techniques within each of the major modalities of counseling theory: multimodal, Rogerian, rational-emotive, cognitive-behavioral, and Gestalt. Although most counselors choose a position that is a unique combination of differing approaches that suit their individual personality, we will discuss the interrelationship of Ubiquitous Assessment with respect to each of the major theories of counseling.

**Multimodal Therapy**

In the development of multimodal therapy, Arnold Lazarus conceptualized a unique system for assessing the individual client and integrating that assessment into the therapeutic process. Using a model that encompasses all major mental and physical health components, Lazarus provides the counselor with a method of integrating the assessment and the therapy in a ubiquitous style. Multimodal therapy is defined through the use of a simple acronym: BASIC-ID. The letters of BASIC-ID correspond with the following psychobehavioral factors: behavior, affect, sensation, images, cognition-interpersonal, and drugs (biological). In the process of the therapy, Lazarus evaluates each of the BASIC-ID components and identifies therapeutic needs based upon his assessment. Observing Lazarus in his film *The Assessment/Therapy Connection*, it is clear that the assessment and the therapy are interwoven. As the therapist and the client work together to discover or assess the "problem," trust and rapport are enhanced. From these foundations, therapy is a natural evolution. For Lazarus, the two components of counseling—assessment and therapy—appear seamless.

Gopaul-McNicol and Thomas-Presswood (1998) describe the process of the BASIC-ID:

> The multimodal assessment focuses on behaviors that get in the way of a person's happiness, and how a person behaves when he or she feels (affect) a certain way, as well as what the sensations (e.g., aches and pains) are and what bearings these sensations have on behavior and feelings. In addition, the goal is to examine one's perception of body and self-image, how one's cognitions affect emotions, and one's intellectual interests. The most important people in a person's life (interpersonal) and how they affect that person are also explored. Moreover, the focus is on a person's concerns about her or his state of health and drugs or medications used. (p. 144)

Of special appeal in multimodal therapy is the participation of the client in all aspects of the therapy. As the therapist assesses each of the components of the BASIC-ID, the client is included in the process. For example, the therapist might ask the client, "I get the feeling that you are a shy or sensitive person. Is this true?" The client is encouraged to help the therapist describe herself or himself to validate the therapist's assessment. Having a valid and open process of assessment, the development of greater self-knowledge becomes integrated in the therapy. Ubiquitous Assessment borrows this technique from multimodal therapy and incorporates this process in an eclectic manner.

**Rogerian Client-Centered Therapy**

In Carl Rogers's view, client-centered therapy is fundamentally a deep and personal relationship based upon a respect for the client's ability to resolve her/his own problems (Corey, 1977). In Rogers's (1961) words,

> Gradually I have come to the conclusion that one learning which applies to all of these experiences is that it is the quality of the personal relationship which matters most. With some of these individuals I am in touch only briefly, with others I have the opportunity of knowing them intimately, but in either case the quality of the personal encounter is probably, in the long run, the element which determines the extent to which this is an experience which releases or promotes development and growth. I believe the quality of my encounter is more important in the long run than is my scholarly knowledge, my professional training, my counseling orientation, [or] the techniques I use in the interview. In keeping with this line of thought, I suspect that for a guidance counselor also the relationship he [or she] forms with each student—brief or continuing—is more important than his [or her] knowledge of tests and measurements, the adequacy of his [or her] record keeping, the theories he [or she] holds, the accuracy with which he [or she] is able to predict academic success, or the school in which he [or she] received his [or her] training. (pp. 89–90)

Rogers's client-centered therapy is relationship based; however, it does not exist in the same manner as counseling's nonprofessional relative: friendship. Client-centered therapy is based upon fundamental elements. The first component of Rogers's therapy is congruence. The counselor must honestly be himself or herself. Also referred to as transparency, congruent counselors are genuine in their representation of themselves and their feelings. In this manner, counselors are able to present as real persons. This openness improves the quality of the relationship and invites the client to participate honestly and congruently, too.

The concepts of empathy and positive, unconditional regard complete the philosophic foundation for Rogerian or client-centered therapy. Empathy for Rogers meant fully feeling the experience of the other person. This author heard Rogers say that he wished that he could, metaphorically, take the eyes from the client and place them in his own eye sockets so that he could see, from the client's perspective, how it feels to be that person. This is not scientifically analytical or purely evaluative. Rogers' (1961) wanted to intimately perceive and comprehend the client's being. In conclusion, Rogers wanted to communicate unconditional positive regard. Rogers said, "I believe that when this nonevaluative prizing is present in the encounter between the counselor and his [or her] client, constructive change and development in the client is more likely to occur" (pp. 94–95).

Rogerian therapy is eclectically incorporated within Ubiquitous Assessment because of the focus upon process. Throughout the process of the counseling, the counselor is integrating the information the client or student is sharing. This unconditional acceptance of the client and the information that she/he shares allows the counselor to respond in a loving and honest way. Because of the strong emphasis on deeply connected relationships, client-centered therapy may be the best choice of therapeutic modalities for an emerging counselor. According to Corey (1977), "this approach is far safer than many models of therapy that put the therapist in the directive position of making interpretations, forming diagnoses, probing the unconscious, analyzing dreams, and working toward more radical personality changes. For a person with limited background in counseling psychology, personality dynamics, and psychopathology, the client-centered approach offers more realistic assurance that prospective clients will not be psychologically harmed" (p. 68). Certainly, client-centered techniques provide a basis upon which the client and the therapist can establish a meaningful and therapeutic relationship.

## Rational-Emotive Therapy

Rational-emotive therapy (R.E.T.) was created by Dr. Albert Ellis and is based upon the mind/feeling interaction. According to R.E.T. authors Ellis and Harper (1975), "human emotions do not magically exist in their own right, and do not mysteriously flow from unconscious needs and desires. Rather, they almost always directly stem from ideas, thoughts, attitudes, or beliefs, and can usually get radically changed by modifying our thinking process" (p. 11). Following the logic that feelings follow an antecedent (thoughts), R.E.T. therapists are most concerned with cognition and its relationship to feelings or affect and, subsequently, behaviors. By assessing the ideation of the client, the therapist is able to comprehend the inherent rationale controlling the behavior. According to Aaron Beck et al. (1979), "Ellis links the environmental or

Activating event (A) to the emotional Consequences (C) by the intervening Belief (B). Thus Rational-Emotive Psychotherapy aims at making the patient aware of his [or her] irrational beliefs and the inappropriate emotional consequences of these beliefs" (p. 10). The essential notion here is that individuals create their feelings to serve functions or to achieve goals. When these thoughts or ideas work effectively to continue your client's success and survival, these thoughts are rational. The problem exists when your client's thoughts are irrational and lead to conflicts and dissonance (Ellis & Harper, 1975).

Assessment in R.E.T. is conducted through a therapeutic conversation where insights about the intellectual (rational) and emotional (feelings) connection are explored. In this therapy, the assessment is conducted by the therapist, and the client benefits by understanding her or his role in maintaining or eliminating irrational thinking. This therapy may be eclectically linked to ubiquitous technique because it involves continual assessment of the individual's behavior, feelings, and ideation. Working to eliminate conflicts of daily living, R.E.T. therapy can be an effective tool for clients willing to accept the mind/feeling connection and who agree to work to change their irrational thoughts. For school counselors, this can be an effective and brief therapeutic tool for helping students struggling with irrational beliefs and their resultant ill feelings ("everyone hates me," "school sucks," "I'm ugly," etc.). Rational-emotive therapy has had considerable success among teachers and counselors. Because of its similarity to teacher/student relationships, its applicability within school counseling practice is easy to conceptualize. Teaching students to understand how their thoughts influence their feelings can be an effective method for helping students to take an active role in their personal growth.

### Cognitive-Behavioral Therapy

Expanding on the notions of Ellis's rational-emotive therapy's work in the area of developing and reinforcing coping strategies and skill training, cognitive-behavioral therapy guides the client through cognitive restructuring by taking a dynamic, behavior-oriented approach. According to Zarb (1992), "Cognitive-behavioral psychotherapies are active and goal-oriented, incorporating educational methods such as agenda setting, structure, clarification, feedback, reflection, practice and homework. The teaching component also involves therapist modeling of new ways of thinking and approaching problems. Continual evaluation of therapy in progress, along with evaluation of results, is also part of the therapy process" (p. 5). Cognitive-behavior therapy is particularly well suited for work with adolescents because of its dynamic, behavioral components.

Because of cognitive-behavioral therapy's feedback components, evaluation of therapeutic goals eclectically links with the techniques of Ubiquitous Assessment. This technique is especially effective with students who self-refer to the counselor. From the initial interview and through acceptance of the client and her or his presenting problem, the school counselor can begin to establish trust and rapport. Using the student's motivation for referral as the impetus for communication, the counselor can often receive good information from the student in the initial interview. During this interview, most of the emphasis is placed upon information gathering in all of the major areas of the student's life: family, peers, school, cognitions, affect, and other relevant information. Assessment can be enhanced through observations of the client and significant others, behavioral checklists and reports, and formal self-reports. Formal self-reports such as the Behavioral Assessment Scales for Children (American Guidance Service, 1999) can be helpful because of their comprehensive nature; however, they often lack sufficient validity and reliability to trust conclusions drawn from these instruments.

As a basis for brief therapy, cognitive-behavior therapy is a good choice for school counselors because of its direct, problem-solving model. For many adolescent and school-aged children, getting a clear and concise treatment through cognitive-behavioral therapy is enough to help them resolve simple, but thorny, peer, family, academic, and self-esteem related issues. This approach can also be implemented by peer counselors with a minimal amount of training (Zarb, 1992).

**Gestalt Therapy**

Fritz Perls' contribution to counseling theory, Gestalt therapy, provides an approach that can also be effective in school settings. Dealing primarily in the "here and now," Gestalt therapy attempts to get right at the issues and not take an analytic or deconstructive approach. According to Perls (1969), "I believe strongly in integration. I have unified quite a few of my opposing forces and there is still more to come. By now, I believe, it has come clear that Gestalt Therapy is not analytical but an integrative approach" (n.p.).

Gestalt therapy can be eclectically joined with a ubiquitous approach in that the therapy is integrated with the assessment. The insights from the current behaviors and feelings are integrated (Perls, 1969) with the therapist's work. Using structures such as completing "I" statements, the counselor can assist the student in the expression of her/his inner feelings. Working with students who are inhibited in her/his feelings, Gestalt therapy can help to release painful emotions. By encouraging students to live in the "here and now," you, the counselor, can help them experience the release of their emotions and encourage a healthy letting go of hurt and loss. The concept of "baggage" or unfinished business is central to the Gestalt therapist's work. Living in the "now," the client is carrying within her/him unfinished business or unexpressed feelings of abandonment, grief, anger, shame, guilt, and other feelings. These feelings affect the student's daily functioning and cause diasatisfaction and functioning difficulties. Later in this chapter, we provide a specific example of a student who struggled with his older brother's suicide. This boy's daily fights and disruptions were an expression of his repressed grief and a manifestation of his rage. According to Perls (1969), "you are related to whatever happens" (p. 30). The now (what is currently happening) is a manifestation of the totality of your experience. The question of what becomes much more important than why.

## The Counselor's Daily Practice

The most rudimentary informal assessments occur in the counseling office and involve basic academic reviews. Checking credits, grade point averages (GPA), attendance, behavior, and general performance is a consistent function of the counselor. For many students, these meetings are regularly scheduled as freshman, sophomore, junior, and senior conferences. Each of these conferences has as its purpose the opportunity to establish both long-term goals and short-term educational objectives, to review progress toward those accomplishments, and to plan to meet appropriate postgraduation hopes and expectations. Depending upon the philosophy of each school district, general counseling services can take on different forms. The best school districts require counselors to follow routine procedures for these conferences in an attempt to provide uniform and consistent services for all of their students. Written notes documenting the meeting with the student are kept in a counseling file. Examples of counseling protocols for grades ten through twelve from the Clovis Unified School District in Clovis, California, are included in the appendix.

In concert with regularly assigned conferencing, students need to visit their counselor for schedule adjustments, attendance issues, and other related academic concerns. In this process, the counselor needs to evaluate the student's connection to her or his studies and evaluate the individual's overall relationship to the school. Talking with a young woman or man who is deeply involved or engaged with academic and cocurricular activities at school is an entirely different experience from what the counselor sees and hears when talking with a prospective dropout (Jimerson, Campos, & Greif, 2003). Sometimes referred to as school engagement or school bonding, counselors are checking for student connection to school within three dimensions: cognitive, behavioral, and affective (Jimerson, Campos, & Greif, 2003). Jimerson, Campos, and Greif (2003) define these dimensions as follows: cognitive engagement includes the student's "perceptions and beliefs related to self, school, teachers, and other students" (p. 7); behavioral engagement includes "observable actions or performance, such as participation in extracurricular activities" (p. 7); and affective engagement or bonding includes the "students feelings about the school, teachers, and/or peers" (p. 7). Within the counseling interview, the counselor listens for student comments that can indicate levels of attachment, bonding, and engagement.

Each student has a unique history and identity. Listening to the story each student shares is essential in the process of establishing a relationship and being able to know where the student is "coming from." Knowing the story of each student is the key to being able to form a meaningful rapport or connection by understanding his or her challenges. Freud referred to this as connecting on a "soul" level (Bettelheim, 1983). Although school counselors are not psychotherapists, the best counseling professionals have a keen appreciation for the struggles we all experience and what is meant by "the human condition." We all share a connection to the continuum of hope and despair. By first assessing the student's position on the continuum of hope–despair and subsequently helping that student to affirm her/his hope for the future is an important role for the counselor.

In order to better know your students and to comprehend the difficulties they face, the use of a structured interview can be a most effective technique (Merrell, 1994). Taking thirty to sixty minutes, a counselor can learn much about a student's life by asking about her/his family background, living arrangements, parent's educational and vocational experiences, health history of family members, and other salient information. Very often counselors will quickly learn that the lives of their clients are distinctly different in school compared to their lives at home. Often saddled with responsibility to work, provide for a sibling with a major health problem, or having a parent with a chemical dependency issue, students' situations are far more complex than they appear to the eye as they stand posed with their friends about the school's campus or innocently seated within the classrooms. By focusing the interview on the student's personal experience and family, the counselor will gain valuable insights into the student's self-esteem, her/his culture, and other resources available to support school success. "Although changing family structures in the society make it difficult to assume a dominant family profile, all families are best understood as systems in which each individual affects all other members" (Taylor & Whittaker, 2003, p. 53).

Unfortunately, in too many cases, students' familial support is either very weak or nonexistent. Ranging from living in a group home to being homeless, students' needs to connect to an adult at school in a meaningful and deeply personal, loving way may be essential to the enhancement of their chances for future success (hooks, 2001). This connection is more closely identified as an act of love in the manner with which Brazilian educator Paulo Freire (1970) used the term. We are performing our duties in a loving way by deeply caring about the fate and future of our client. James Fraser (1997) said, "For Freire, this level of respect and love means that each individual must be the maker of her or his own liberation" (p. 177). For us as educators, this means that we are all ultimately responsible for ourselves. In a Rogerian (Rogers, 1961) sense, the counselor's role is to assist the student in this process of becoming her/his own person.

In addition to conversations or interviews with students or in situations where an interview will not be appropriate or reveal much information (such as with young children or nonverbal youth), observations can assist the counselor in gaining knowledge of the student's behavior, emotional state, and psychosocial status (Salvia & Ysseldyke, 1998). Observation includes collecting information concerning specific behaviors ranging from obvious examples such as sleeping in class to noticing more subtle body language like daydreaming. Students reveal much about their attitude toward school and their self-esteem through their behavior and body language. Especially during adolescence, styles of dress and accouterments such as tattoos and body piercing can communicate a plethora of messages ranging from sexual preference to gang affiliation. From the initial greeting of the student, the observation process is cueing both the client and the counselor to important messages about willingness to engage, trust and comfort levels, openness to new experiences, and possibly, fear or mistrust (Lukas, 1993). Observation is ubiquitous.

Observations can tell part of the student's story, however; only by knowing a student over a long period of time and by having all of the student's story will the counselor be sure to have a valid or true picture of the client's identity (Walker, 1983). Providing interesting activities for the client, such as art or craft activities, can be helpful tools in the assessment stage. Some students become verbal when they have something to do with their hands. One counselor with whom we are acquainted keeps a gigantic bag of peanuts in her office. She believes that the peanut shucking process helps her reticent students open up communication.

Dangers inherent in the use of observation include the influences of prejudice (prejudging) and stereotyping. It is important to guard against falling victim to reductive thinking and developing inappropriate impressions. Observation provides an important part of the assessment and needs to be validated by gaining further knowledge of the student's situation. The keys to minimizing observer error include using multiple observations or other measures of social comparison such as teacher report or rating (Salvia & Ysseldyke, 2004).

## Crisis Counseling and Interventions

One of the best examples of the use of informal assessment occurs when students appear at the counselor's door with affective concerns. Most often preceded by a crisis, students with immediate needs pose unique challenges to the counselor and frequently to the rest of the counseling office staff. Counselors need to be able to quickly and reliably assess the specific nature of the student referral and immediately provide an appropriate response. In the case of drop-in, voluntary referrals or for students sent by the classroom teacher, preparation on the part of the counselor places her/him at an advantage. Although it is impossible to allow an hour or two in a day's schedule to be available for immediate or crisis student counseling or disciplinary issues, failure to schedule for spontaneous student services means having to either miss the student in crisis or postpone meetings already scheduled. (Note: In many schools, counselors provide a dual role of personal counselor and disciplinarian. We believe that this is not appropriate for counselors and it is confusing to students. Asking someone to trust you and then in the next hour meting out a consequence for rule infractions is not consistent with best practice as a school counselor.)

To be prepared for any contingency is not only impractical, it is impossible. However, counselors do not want to miss an opportunity to try to help prevent a suicide, a dropout, or a fight. Therefore, in order to maximize the counselor's effectiveness, the use of triage skills is essential. Triage is a term adopted from the hospital's emergency room (E.R.) to describe the doctor's initial diagnosis or assessment of the patient. Triage is used by the counselor in much the same way as the E.R. physician; however, the goal of the quick assessment is to determine the degree of need that the client expresses and to provide appropriate therapy. As is the case with most professional competencies, developing triage skills takes considerable experience and knowledge. The best method of training or educating emerging counselors in these skills is through modeling. The head counselor can be the best resource for demonstrating the triage method and its implementation.

For some individuals, coming to the counselor's office to share a concern is as routine as any casual "hello" in the hallway. For other students, there are many cultural taboos causing resistance to the process. This is especially true for some males because of their cultural taboos against expression of certain emotions such as fear and sadness. This difficulty is further exacerbated in black and Hispanic males because of cultural taboos regarding mental health and the process of psychological disclosure. According to John Ogbu (1995), "Because they do not trust the schools (personnel), many minority parents and adults in the community are skeptical that the schools can provide their children with good educations" (p. 98). Unfortunately in this case, students frequently carry their parents' opinions with them into the counselor's office. This fact, often coupled with the student being faced with a counselor of different race, culture, and or gender, can create even more obstacles in the process of establishing and maintaining rapport (MacLeod, 1995).

Complicating matters still further, students are often unwilling to disclose intimate details of their situation in a few seconds while standing in the open doorway of the counselor's office. In the moments that the student stands before you, it is essential that you read the student's body language, listen for inflections, and quickly estimate the severity of the presenting problem. While simultaneously establishing a rapport worthy of trust (Pianta & Walsh, 1996), the counselor needs to make an immediate decision and to take an action that reflects the use of best practice. No one cluster of decisions can have so much potential ill effect or, conversely, provide as much help as when the client is at his or her most willing to share deeply personal problems or concerns with a caring professional. As we explore some of the more specific and technical assessments such as suicide intervention, the key issues surrounding the establishment of rapport will be obvious: trust and safety are the foundation for all successful personal counseling (Maslow, 1968).

## Referrals from Parents and Teachers

Very often, counselors receive referrals from parents and teachers to provide either assessment or intervention services for their students. Most frequently these referrals are precipitated by an event or an interaction that has given immediate attention to an issue seen as needing the counselor's attention. That is the perception of the person making the referral. At this point in the process, the student is usually unaware that referral is even a consideration.

When taking referrals from parents and teachers, counselors need to be concerned with several important factors related to the appropriateness of the referral. Being clear about the type of services the counselor provides and the extent of their availability is the first consideration that needs to be addressed. Many times a parent or teacher will discover a student in stress over an issue, and they will want a counselor to help the student process those feelings. A perfect example is the breakup of a relationship, and one of the partners arrives to class in a state of extreme grief. The teacher wants to send that student to the counselor immediately.

Another example of a typical referral involves the parental request for counseling for their student. Ranging from issues as minor as needing financial aid or an SAT application to requests for placement in an anger management group, parent requests need to be handled expeditiously, professionally, and successfully. By the time a parent has reached you on the phone, she/he has generally spoken with some other staff person: secretary, teacher, administrative assistant, or other person on staff. When they reach us, they would like to be rewarded or reinforced with appreciation for their concern for their student's well-being. This translates into a simple admonishment for counselors: Never say "No" to parent requests. Putting up roadblocks to parent or guardian calls for help is unprofessional and discourteous. Parents are asking for help, and it is our job to provide it. Responses such as "I don't run groups" are inappropriate. Even if the assistance involves referral to another agency, we provide phone numbers and personal assistance to smooth the process.

An additional consideration for counselors when referrals are made is how we introduce ourselves to students if we are calling them into our office at another's request. Because of the variability of referral possibilities, it is impossible to delineate all of the possible contingencies one could encounter. This is where the counselor's understanding of student's developmental levels and concomitant comprehension of a counselor's role come into play. For elementary students, simply introducing oneself and saying that we want to meet all of the school's students can be sufficient. For an at-risk youth, the introduction needs to be brief and clear: "You are not in trouble. Your father asked that I call you in and introduce myself to you. He thought that you might benefit from an opportunity to talk about your feelings in a confidential setting."

It is important to remember that the assessment process is a two-way affair. Students are assessing your communicative intent, your trustworthiness, and your capacity for comprehending their problem just as you, the counselor, are assessing the student. Remembering that this process is ubiquitous and two way is critical to your success in the case of referrals from parents and teachers. Having the ability to establish rapport with involuntary and perhaps completely resistant counselees is one of the biggest challenges counselors must confront. Having the dual liability of rejection by the student and a negative evaluation of the counselor's effectiveness by the referring person can be daunting, especially for a young professional needing to establish credibility in a new school. If you sense the need for support, consult with a supervisor or peer (Corey, 1977).

To overcome resistance on the part of students in the initial interview, we like to begin with giving the student simple choices and allowing her/him to develop a sense of control of the process. For example, asking a student to come in to the office is a different experience than being told to come in and sit down. Further, giving the student the choice about leaving the door open or closing the door can remove anxiety about being trapped. This is especially significant for male/female counseling relationships or for other students fearful of new situations. Being sensitive to these issues of choice can make or break the connection with the student. We find that by treating students with the same degree of respect that we expect, we are able to forge the rapport and trust necessary to overcome the resistances that can attend being referred by a parent or teacher.

One last aspect of the rapport process involves the office environment and its impact upon the student in the initial interview. It is important to include the effect of the office environment upon the student's assessment and acceptance of the counselor. Having an office that is well designed and open can be conducive to student communication. Comfortable chairs, appropriate space between the student and the counselor, confidential accommodations, and diverse art and artifacts all communicate the counselor's availability and sensitivity. The feeling of safety is communicated not only by the counselor's affect but by the space the counselor provides (Lukas, 1993). When inviting the student into the office, be sure to give her/him choices and the opportunity to freely enter and exit. Inviting someone into the office and asking if it is ok to close the door extends a healthy respect to the student and sense of safety concerning their participation in the process.

## Suicide Assessment and Intervention

Suicide is one of the leading causes of death among adolescents and young adults (Centers for Disease Control, 1992). For individuals between the ages of fifteen and twenty-four, suicide is the third leading cause of death. Although the great majority of suicides tend to occur among white males, suicide rates are increasing rapidly among black males. Regardless of the demographics, having a suicide by any student or staff member at your school can have catastrophic consequences for the entire community. Suicides are shocking, and the loss of a student for any reason causes grief within the community. Grieving the loss of a peer, many students will relate the pain to other losses they've experienced. In debriefing activities such as group counseling, many students will relate that the current loss reminds them of another, and often unresolved, loss of a pet, friend, or family member. Sometimes this multiple grieving or experiencing the sadness of the current loss will trigger more powerful emotions that had been repressed.

In some situations, the suicide of one student prompts the suicide of another. The phenomenon is so common among adolescents that it has been identified specifically as contagion. According to staffers at the Center for the Advancement of Health (Allen, 2001), "Suicide contagion is 'the process by which a prior suicide facilitates the occurrence of a subsequent suicide.' In addition to contagion through exposure to media reports of suicide, contagion can occur through exposure to suicide or suicidal behaviors within families or peer groups. Suicide contagion affects individuals already at risk for suicide and is linked to increases in suicidal behaviors especially in adolescents and young adults" (p. 8). Because of an adolescent's susceptibility to contagion, the copying of behavior, a completed suicide by one student can lead to copycat behaviors by individuals unable to cope with their loss. Suicidal behavior can include, but is not limited to, excessive or irresponsible alcohol and/or other drug use, reckless driving, fighting, violent behaviors, self-injurious behaviors (carving on self), and inappropriate and high-risk sexual behaviors.

Although the literature is replete with programs to prevent adolescent suicide (peer counseling, education in health classes, community gatekeeper programs, etc.), these programs do not replace the need for competent assessment by the counselor when the student is presenting with suicidal ideation. It is impossible to prevent all suicides with protective features or programs such as health education; however, good schools are ones with many opportunities to build resiliency within their students (U.S. Public Health Service, 1999). Whenever a student looks depressed or the counselor is suspicious of suicidal thinking, this direct question should be asked: "Have you ever or do you now think about committing suicide?" In evaluating student concerns, the most direct approach is best practice. Being vague or offering the student a possibility to deny the thought, such as "You're not thinking about hurting yourself, are you?" does not get to the issue. You must be clear and direct without appearing clinical or impersonal.

In assessing possible suicidal behaviors, there are several questions that are considered standard or conforming to rules of best practice. During this interview it is important to take accurate notes, because you may be called upon to answer questions of a specific nature regarding this conversation. Memory is not as reliable or as credible as a documented, written record. During the interview process, it is best if the questions are posed in an empathic and open-ended manner. "How did you come to feel this way?" or "Please tell me some more about those thoughts?" can help the client feel more comfortable expressing her/his feelings. Questions commonly asked and the themes that they generally cover are:

1. Have you been thinking about committing suicide?
2. What are some of your current thoughts about suicide?
3. Do you intend to kill yourself?
4. Do you have a specific plan and are there available means to implement this plan?
5. Have you attempted suicide in the past? What method did you employ?
6. Do you have a family history of suicide? Do you know anyone who has committed suicide?
7. Is there a history of violence in your family?
8. What are the most recent stressors in your life (divorce, loss of relationship, change in economic status)?
9. What is your current living arrangement?
10. Alcohol or other drug use?
11. Do you often feel depressed? (Frierson et al., 2002)

This clinical interview may lead to further questioning regarding the individual's affective state. Very often, individuals contemplating suicide are experiencing depression. Their suicidal thinking may be a logical extension of extensive or pervasive depression. In this case, additional assessment to investigate possible depression is most appropriate. Assessment for depression is covered later in this chapter.

At the conclusion of the suicide intervention interview, the counselor may wish to think of the client as low risk, moderate risk, or high risk. Regardless of the clinical impression, it is the counselor's responsibility to report the interview and conclusions drawn from the student's remarks to the parent if the student is under the age of eighteen. As in other cases of a client threatening to hurt herself, himself, or others, it is the counselor's responsibility to intervene on the student's behalf.

It is best practice to state the ethical responsibility and limits of confidentiality at the beginning of the interview; however, its requirement stands regardless of the timing. We try to always remember to explain the process of the counseling services to our clients at the beginning of each initial session, but in reality, it sometimes is overlooked. One possible cause for the counselor forgetting to inform the client of her/his "rights" is that the client's need to open up and express herself/himself immediately overwhelms the counselor or the counselor is slow to understand the severity of the student's need to talk. We know we are most vulnerable for committing this mistake after a long vacation or when we're feeling stressed for time.

The mistake of not informing the client of her or his rights concerning confidentiality can be avoided when the counselor is remembering to use Ubiquitous Assessment and is, thereby, fully prepared and present to listen as a professional. Being remiss in informing clients of their right to confidentiality and also of the limitations to confidentiality frequently leads to feelings of a breach of trust and, possibly, the destruction of a future counseling relationship. A solution to this problem is to have a written statement of client rights on the table before the client or posted on the wall in a conspicuous location. This document can serve as a reminder to the counselor and as an informational aid to the client. Certainly one of the essential components of best practice is the ability to shift gears from casual, friendly conversations outside and around the office and moving into the office to conduct professional counseling conversations. Although on the surface to a layperson or nonprofessional these interactions may appear indistinguishable, the quintessence of counseling is in the counselor's ability to be clinically correct while functioning in a manner free of any nuance of detachment. In Ubiquitous Assessment, there is no seam in the counselor's role change from inside the office to the outside. However, the counselor is aware that the assessments she/he conducts outside the office are distinct from the work conducted when the door is closed. Outside the office, the observations and interactions are professional but casual. Although confidentiality is not implied outside the counselor's office, all interactions with the counselor should be kept as private as the situation or environment will allow. A student's tears or anger cannot always be protected in a public setting. Inside the protection of the office, we are looking for deeper and more intimate interactions and confidentiality is clearly a part of the process. It is within the office that we are responsible for maintaining confidentiality and for informing our clients of its limitations as Children's Protective Services (CPS) mandated reporters.

Depending upon the conclusion of the interview, the counselor may decide to follow up with the student's assessment in one of several ways. If the student appears to be low risk, the counselor may be comfortable calling the parent and explaining the referral, assessment, and results of the conversation. This telephone call elicits a wide range of emotion from parents. Some are aware that their child's suicidal expressions are an ongoing issue; some are shocked to get this news. In Ubiquitous Assessment, this is pertinent information, too. What have the parents done with this information in the past? Are they aloof to their student's problem? Are they angry? Do they want to share in the process of helping their child resolve his or her suicidal feelings? However, no matter what level of risk one assigns to the client, no client should be released from the office if there is a strong suspicion that the person may actually hurt herself/himself. If you have any question concerning this issue, be sure to clarify the school's position with your administrator. This is not an area for risk taking of clinical experimentation. The stakes are too high for counselors no matter what level of training or degree of experience (Lukas, 1993).

In cases believed to be moderate or high risk, the decisions made by the counselor require the parent's input or the imposition of another professional's assessment. In some cases, the campus officer or a law enforcement representative is included because of possible violence or the need for restraint. In one intervention, a young woman was brought to the office because she reported the desire to commit suicide. In the interview, the student admitted that she had been sexually molested by her mother's boyfriend, and that she not only wanted to kill herself because of her shame, she wanted to murder the boyfriend for perpetrating the molestation. Ironically, the mother was reached by phone while on her way to court to testify in the case, and she refused to come to school to pick her daughter up for further assessment. The mother's refusal to come to school complicated the resolution. Fortunately, this case was concluded by compromise with the mother. She agreed to let the school nurse and this psychologist bring the daughter to the family's pediatrician. The pediatrician diagnosed the girl as needing hospitalization, and she was brought by ambulance to the psychiatric assessment center for observation and further assessment.

Clearly, the case of the suicidal/homicidal student required that the counselor work collegially; however, each situation of suicide intervention is individual and requires strong assessment skills. Above all, communication with parents and other qualified professionals is essential. This collaboration requirement is particularly true for beginning counselors. When the stakes of the counseling are high, collaboration can greatly reduce the possibility of counselor error. Because we are human, we want to be sure to enlist appropriate support to ensure the provision of best practice and to protect our client's well-being (Keyes & Magyar-Moe, 2003).

In the case of many suicides, someone knew that the person was in trouble, and that she or he was crying out for help. Too many examples exist of students writing suicidal poems, songs, or letters before attempting or succeeding to take their lives and their "cries for help" were unanswered. "The fact is that most people who take their own lives have given some sign of their intentions to at least one other person—and often to several other people—within the last few weeks or months" (Lukas, 1993, p. 114). Although not all suicides are foreseen or preventable, parents can become litigious when they learn that teachers or counselors knew of their student's suicidal plans and that their child's cries for help were ignored. Not the least of the cost of the repercussions of the loss of a student would be the guilt caused by knowing that following best practice could possibly have prevented a death. In suicide intervention, as in all of the work performed by the counselor, there is no room for carelessness or lack of attention to the needs of your clients. When in doubt, consult with a colleague (Corey, 1977).

If you are in the position of having to provide debriefing services for your school community, it is important to remember that many youth want to glorify the deceased. Because so many youth contemplate suicide, a completed suicide gives credence to the concept. Completed suicides give the imagined event a reality or validation (Centers for Disease Control, 1992). This is especially true when an icon of youth kills herself/himself. After the suicide of punk rock star Kurt Cobain, hundreds of adolescents were sporting T-shirts with his face emboldened on the front of the shirt. Wearing the shirt was akin to displaying a badge saying, "My idol did this. Guess how I feel?"

To reduce the very high chances of a suicide's contagion, the following recommendations from the surgeon general (U.S. Department of Health & Human Services, 1998) are appropriate: "Efforts must be made to avoid normalizing, glorifying, or dramatizing suicidal behavior, reporting how-to methods, or describing suicide as an understandable solution to a traumatic or stressful life event. Inappropriate approaches could potentially increase the risk for suicidal behavior in vulnerable individuals, particularly youth" (p. 10). In one school with which we are acquainted, a young girl's suicide was "commemorated" in a large, schoolwide memorial exercise in the gym. Later, a tree was planted outside the principal's office window, and a plaque was placed on the campus. Not surprisingly, a fellow classmate attempted suicide on the campus just weeks after the girl's death. The student's image was captured by a local reporter as he was being loaded onto the ambulance, and the picture was prominently displayed on the front page of the paper.

When we were called to the school to provide psychological support to staff and students, our first job was to inform the administration of the need for greater sensitivity in the protection of student information and restricting the press's public access to the school grounds. Obviously, the time for intervention is before the suicide takes place. Having a plan for emergencies can prevent the further injury caused by contagion.

### A Death in the Family

One of the most challenging and potentially devastating experiences students face is the loss of one of their parents or siblings. Over the course of sixty years of professional practice, we have both experienced the grief of our own losses as well as assisted others in recovery from their pain. Drawing from our training in grief/loss therapy (Kubler-Ross, 1981), we know that each experience is unique and that every person's process of recovery is governed by her or his needs and individual requirements. The work of recovery within the context of the work of the school counselor becomes more complicated by the dynamics of the student's loss and the chaos created by the removal of one of the members. Accepting the losses we encounter is often the final step in our recovery (Vorst, 1986). Working through the various resistances is the difficult work of the student.

The pain and rage associated with the loss of a family member is frequently converted into a symptom seemingly unrelated to the deceased. Frequently, school counselors will receive a referral concerning a child or adolescent and their manifest oppositional and defiant behavior. One example of such a case presented in an intermediate school where we worked. An adolescent, Joey, was repeatedly referred to the psychologist's office for fighting. The incidents were unusual because of the boy's small size and especially pugnacious nature. Coming from the administrator's office to the psychologist, it often took Joey an hour or more to calm down so that we could have any semblance of a conversation. Anger of Joey's magnitude was intimidating to all the adults in the school, and it was clear that the anger was not caused by what the teachers and administrators saw as the precipitating event. Joey was explosive, and he was waiting for any excuse to vent the tremendous anger inside himself.

Because Joey was not able to understand his own motivation and rage, we needed to contact his family to assess Joey's case. Through interviews with his mother, we could understand the magnitude of the family's situation. Joey's story was tragic. His older brother, star of the high school football team, honor student, and hero of the Carlson family, had recently committed suicide. Crushed by the breakup with his girlfriend, Joey's brother unraveled his own rage and frustration and used the family shotgun to end his pain. Shocked by the overwhelming force of this event, the family took differing approaches in dealing with their feelings of grief.

Mr. Carlson, who had been described as a "heavy drinker" before the incident, increased his alcohol consumption. Typical of individuals with posttraumatic stress disorder (PTSD), problems that existed before the suicide (trauma) were exacerbated by the traumatic event. Further, in the dad's attempt to deny his son's loss, he placed the boy's pickup truck on an elevated "shrine" in front of the house. With the son's name written on the side of the truck, it was a constant and bizarre reminder of the boy whose suicide could not be accepted. Denial, often represented in keeping the room the same, not giving away the clothes, or other possessions of the deceased, was manifested in the maintenance of the truck for all to see. For our student, Joey, this created more loss and separation: his father faded further away and was emotionally unavailable to support his grieving family.

Querying Joey about the fights, he would recall the instigation by another student with hyperbole. "He asked for it. He called me a [name]." Joey was trapped with rage over the loss of his brother and he couldn't comprehend the loss because the family patriarch was leading the denial. Joey was confused because something tragic happened and no one could talk about it. The family was isolated in an emotional lockdown and discussing or showing grief was taboo. The family refused to participate in therapy, and the anger continued to fester inside Joey. The notion of therapy seemed to feel like the family was betraying the deceased brother by letting go of their denial and anger. Years later, the truck still stands in front of the house, like Henry Stamper's amputated arm that he affixed to his boat's mast in *Sometimes a Great Notion* (Kesey, 1970): the ultimate symbol of defiance. The Stamper family, a logging family in the Northwest, held the motto: Never Give a Goddamn Inch. For the Carlson family, it seemed as if they would never move either.

Assessing a student's emotional response to a loss requires tremendous patience on the part of the counselor. Listening for any trace of acceptance that the event occurred and waiting for the student to be able to even discuss the problem may stretch the counselor beyond her/his bounds of a sense of professional responsibility. In these cases, referral to an outside therapist is best practice. In addition, as counselors, we need to understand that loss is difficult in even the most "normal" situations, such as the loss of a grandparent after a long illness where the family has prepared. Conversely, sudden losses and especially suicides can affect us very differently. For many individuals, it may take years to break the denial or overcome other resistance to dealing with the pain and loss. Assessing the meaning of each loss and helping the client accept it in her/his unique way is the sensitive responsibility of the counselor.

## Assessing Depression

In the counselor's work to assist students and families with their wide-ranging and diverse issues, the counselor will very likely encounter several of the more prevalent psychological conditions. As mentioned earlier, depression is one of the leading psychological problems within the world of adolescents and is known to be directly linked to suicide (Rebellon, Brown, & Keyes, 2000). According to the *Diagnostic and Statistical Manual of Mental Disorders,* "Up to 15 percent of individuals with severe Major Depressive Disorder die by suicide" (APA, 2000, p. 371). Conversely, students expressing suicidal ideation may very likely be experiencing depression, and at the minimum, require assessment to determine the etiology of their mood (U.S. Department of Health & Human Services, 1998). Unhappiness and general dissatisfaction with life's outcomes can be contributing factors and place individuals at high levels of risk for suicide (Keyes & Magyar-Moe, 2003).

Adolescent psychology, a field of study unto itself, contains a literature replete with diagnostic criteria for assessing adolescent depression. Although the medical diagnosis of depression is outside the scope of the counselor's training and practice, being able to identify depression so as to refer the parent and student to appropriate psychological or medical treatment is well within the counselor's responsibilities. In fact, the counselor may be key to breaking the denial that often attends depression. Being the person who identifies the school failure, excessive absences, or other dysfunctional behavior, the counselor has the ability to listen for signs of what is behind or responsible for the behavior at issue. The best counselors know that it is not the behavior itself, but the internal motivation or antecedents of the behavior that are the salient issues.

All stages of child development differ in the characterization of depressed mood. Young children can mask depression and present it in an angry form. Fighting, animal cruelty, and destructiveness can be forms of depression. In preadolescents and teenagers, depression more often presents attendant with the symptomatology we would expect: sadness, tears, sleeping too much or not enough, eating disorders, and so forth. According to the *Diagnostic and Statistical Manual of Mental Disorders Fourth Edition–Text Revision (DSM 4-TR)*, a major depressive episode is characterized by:

A. Five (or more) of the following symptoms have been present during the same 2-week period and represent a change from previous functioning; at least one of the symptoms is either (1) depressed mood or (2) loss of interest or pleasure. Note: Do not include symptoms that are clearly due to a general medical condition, or mood-incongruent delusions or hallucinations.

1. Depressed mood most of the day, nearly every day, as indicated by either subjective report (e.g., feels sad or empty) or observation made by others (e.g., appears tearful). Note: In children and adolescents, can be irritable mood.
2. Markedly diminished interest or pleasure in all, or almost all, activities most of the day, nearly every day (as indicated by either subjective account or observation made by others).
3. Significant weight loss when not dieting or weight gain (e.g., a change of more than 5% of body weight in a month), or a decrease or increase in appetite nearly every day. Note: In children, consider failure to make expected weight gains.
4. Insomnia or hypersomnia nearly every day.
5. Psychomotor agitation or retardation nearly every day (observable by others, not merely subjective feelings of restlessness or being slowed down).
6. Fatigue or loss of energy nearly every day.
7. Feelings of worthlessness or excessive or inappropriate guilt (which may be delusional) nearly every day (not merely self-reproach or guilt about being sick).
8. Diminished ability to think or concentrate, or indecisiveness, nearly every day (either by subjective account or as observed by others).
9. Recurrent thoughts of death (not just a fear of dying), recurrent suicidal ideation without a specific plan, or a suicide attempt or a specific plan for committing suicide.
10. The symptoms do not meet criterion for a Mixed Episode.
11. The symptoms cause clinically significant distress or impairment in social, occupational, or other important areas of functioning.

12. The symptoms are not due to the direct physiological effects of a substance (e.g., a drug of abuse, a medication) or a medical condition (e.g., hypothyroidism).
13. The symptoms are not better accounted for by Bereavement, i.e., after the loss of a loved one, the symptoms persist for longer than two months or are characterized by marked functional impairment, morbid preoccupation with worthlessness, suicidal ideation, psychotic symptoms, or psychomotor retardation. (American Psychiatric Association [APA], 2000, p. 356)

As stated earlier, it is outside the scope of practice for school counselors to clinically diagnose depression or other psychological disorders. However, it is in the best interest of counselors to be aware of the symptomatology of mental disorders and to know to refer these students and their families to appropriate sources for clinical consideration. In some school systems, the services of the school psychologist are available to assist parents and their students. The school psychologist is trained in psychological assessment and is capable of diagnosing depression in school-aged individuals. In addition to the option of internal sources for referral, having a list of clinicians and telephone numbers for contacting metropolitan, regional, or county mental health offices can be helpful for parents desiring additional help or information. By providing parents with several phone numbers, counselors allow parents to choose the option that best suits their family's needs.

## Assessing for Special Education and Gifted and Talented Education

The counselor's role in the identification and placement of students for special education and gifted and talented education (GATE) varies slightly depending upon the service delivery system set by each school district. However, the general guidelines for consideration of a placement in either of these specific programs are mandated by federal regulation. As a part of the process of identification and placement, the counselor's role is an important one.

In both special education and GATE programs, overidentification and underidentification are significant issues, and they relate to inappropriate use of standardized testing (Taylor & Whittaker, 2003). Typically, white, middle- and upper-middle-class parents have viewed GATE as a high-status achievement of their children and a reflection of their superior genetic and intellectual ability. Conversely, African Americans and other minority groups have often been overrepresented in special education classes and other pullout programs such as alternative education.

Although we will cover assessment issues for these programs in greater depth in the school assessment chapter, it is worthy of mention in the school counselor's chapter. The counselor's presence at Student Study Team (SST) meetings and other special education meetings is essential. At meetings where placement considerations are being discussed, the counselor is the team member best suited to report on the student's overall academic standing. Providing a current transcript and holding records of attendance and behavior, the counselor can provide an accurate report of factors related to the student's success or current difficulties. As changes in the Individuals with Disabilities Education Act (IDEA) become implemented, the counselor's role in providing immediate assessment information will be key in the provision of appropriate and immediate interventions (Lloyd-Jones, 2003).

## Assessing Attention Deficit Hyperactivity Disorder

Attention deficit disorder and its partner, attention deficit/hyperactivity disorder, have received greater and more widespread recognition since the initial appellation as hyperkinesis (hyperactivity disorder) in the early 1960s. According to the *DSM 4-TR* (American Psychiatric Association [APA], 2000), the incidence of attention deficit disorder (ADD) and attention deficit/hyperactivity disorder (AD/HD) is from 3 percent to 7 percent of the population. Although not all ADD and AD/HD students are rendered dysfunctional because of this disorder, many students are negatively affected within classroom settings. Those students who have not been identified as having the disorder are especially vulnerable for school failure. Untreated or unattended by classroom modifications, students with ADD or AD/HD are at risk for school failure.

With the advent of Section 504 of the Americans with Disabilities Act, schools are required to develop individual programs (as opposed to individual educational plans or IEPs) to meet the needs of students identified as having a disability that substantially limits their access to fundamental human activities such as learning (House, 2004). Although the 504 team may be comprised of many individuals, the counselor has a primary role in the process. The counselor's assessment of the student's progress is key in determining the impact of the disability and its relevance for 504 consideration.

Although not responsible for clinically identifying AD/HD, the counselor should be aware of the diagnostic criterion for AD/HD. If the counselor knows what to assess for screening AD/HD, she/he can make an appropriate referral to either the school psychologist or the family physician. If the student has already been clinically identified, the counselor can concur with the assessment and proceed with the 504 Plan if appropriate.

According to the *DSM 4-TR* (APA, 2000), the diagnostic criteria for AD/HD is as follows:

A. Either (1) or (2):

1. Six (or more) of the following symptoms of inattention have persisted for at least six months to a degree that is maladaptive and inconsistent with developmental level:
   - (a) often fails to give close attention to details or makes careless mistakes in schoolwork, work, or other activities
   - (b) often has difficulty sustaining attention in tasks or play activities
   - (c) often does not seem to listen when spoken to directly
   - (d) often does not follow through on instructions and fails to finish schoolwork, chores, or duties in the workplace (not due to oppositional behavior or failure to understand instructions)
   - (e) often has difficulty organizing tasks and activities
   - (f) often avoids, dislikes, or is reluctant to engage in tasks that require sustained mental effort (such as schoolwork or homework)
   - (g) often loses things necessary for tasks or activities (e.g., toys, school assignments, pencils, books, or tools)
   - (h) is often distracted by extraneous stimuli
   - (i) is often forgetful in daily activities
2. Six (or more) of the following symptoms of hyperactivity-impulsivity have persisted for at least six months to a degree that is maladaptive and inconsistent with developmental level:

   *Hyperactivity*
   - (a) often fidgets with hands or squirms in seat
   - (b) often leaves seat in classroom or in other situations in which remaining seated is expected
   - (c) often runs about or climbs excessively in situations in which it is inappropriate (in adolescents or adults, may be limited to subjective feelings of restlessness)
   - (d) often has difficulty playing or engaging in leisure activities quietly

(e) is often 'on the go; or often acts as if 'driven by a motor"

(f) often talks excessively

*Impulsivity*

(a) often blurts out answers before questions have been completed

(b) often has difficulty awaiting turn

(c) often interrupts or intrudes on others (e.g., butts into conversations or games)

B. Some hyperactive-impulsive or inattentive symptoms that caused impairment were present before age 7 years.

C. Some impairment from the symptoms is present in two or more settings (e.g., at school (or work) and at home).

D. There must be clear evidence of clinically significant impairment in social, academic, or occupational functioning.

E. The symptoms do not occur exclusively during the course of a Pervasive Developmental Disorder, Schizophrenia, or other Psychotic Disorder and are not better accounted for by another mental disorder (e.g., Mood Disorder, Anxiety Disorder, Dissociative Disorder, or a Personality Disorder. (p. 93)

Being able to identify the diagnostic criterion for AD/HD can help the counselor with the development of appropriate 504 or other intervention plans and activities. Positive identification for 504 eligibility can be accomplished by simply having a current diagnosis of AD/HD from a doctor or psychologist and proof that the student meets the 504 requirement of a "significant impairment in learning." Because of the prevalence of AD/HD in America today, prior knowledge of the condition and possible treatment options for managing schoolwork, including the implementation of 504 plans, are part of what is considered best practice for school counselors (Alper, Schloss, & Schloss, 1995).

Although treatment for AD/HD varies widely, the most common strategy involves the use of a stimulant called methylphenidate (Johnson, 2001). More commonly identified by trade names such as Ritalin, Concerta, or Metadate, these prescription medications are available through an individual's physician or psychiatrist. Other possible medications for AD/HD include Adderall, Dexedrine, Dextrostat, Cylert, or various antidepressants. Whatever medication is chosen, it is prudent to conduct clinical follow-up procedures to determine the efficacy of the medication. Bert Whetstone (2000) recommends a parent, teacher, and child rating scale for this purpose. The scale solicits information about behavioral and physical changes after the introduction of the medication. The surveys can be evaluated by the psychologist or physician to determine the effect of the therapy (medication). These surveys can play an important role in convincing parents who are unsure of the use of psychotropic medication with their child.

In addition to medicinal therapy, counseling, psychotherapy, cognitive-behavioral therapy, and support groups can be effective treatments for individuals with AD/HD. Dealing with the feelings associated with AD/HD can be one of the most difficult aspects of the condition. Although there is no cure for AD/HD, some individuals are able to be very successful, fully functioning adults. Many AD/HD individuals have tremendous energy, and when they find the appropriate outlet and opportunity for self-expression, they are extremely productive. In response to much of the negative criticism AD/HD has generated, therapist and outdoor educator Jason Holder (1999) has renamed the condition AD/HA, attention deficit/hyperactivity advantage. Holder's point is well taken: AD/HD does not have to be presented to the child or the family as a malady. Many AD/HD individuals lead productive and successful lives.

Because of the many misconceptions of ADD and AD/HD, the counselor may want to take an active role in reframing the teacher's and family's perspectives on how to proceed postdiagnosis. Although therapists can be effective with parents and children, the counselor needs to support the teacher in her/his adjustment with an AD/HD student. Having literature with classroom modifications available for the teacher can be helpful in identifying alternative strategies for instruction and behavior management. Above all, the counselor needs to support the affective state of the teacher and reinforce efforts made to accommodate the student's unique needs.

## Assessment of Child Abuse and Neglect

One of the most stressful situations counselors confront is the assessment of a child's sexual and/or physical abuse or neglect. As a mandated reporter of child abuse (physical and sexual) and neglect, it is incumbent upon the counselor to understand the characteristics and identifiers these children present and to promote their protection. Although there is variation in the legal requirements for mandated reporters from state to state, the essence of child protection is clear. Abuse of a child is defined as committing an inappropriate sexual or physical act upon the child. Neglect is failure to provide a necessary parental function such as feeding or providing proper medical care to the child.

As a mandated reporter, it is not necessary that you can prove that the parent or guardian is actually neglecting or abusing the child. The law is clear that the counselor must report if there is reasonable suspicion or knowledge that there are grounds for making the call to Children's Protective Services. Sometimes the allegations of abuse or neglect are very clear. Student statements that the abuse occurred, coupled with visible marks to corroborate the allegations, leave no doubt that the investigation by Children's Protective Services needs to occur.

There are three basic areas of assessment that can be employed in the evaluation of suspected abuse. In addition to the (1) physical symptoms such as those mentioned above, a child may exhibit (2) behavioral symptoms that relate to abuse and neglect. Children who are chronically absent from school may be involved in an abusive relationship or be experiencing neglect. Behavioral symptoms can also include stealing food, self-reporting of hunger, excessive fatigue, poor health and hygiene, or other appearance of neglect. The final marker of an abused or neglected child is found in the (3) attributes of the caretaker themselves. Parental disinterest in the child's well-being or detachment concerning responsibility are strong symbols of potential neglect or abuse. Other possible indicators of problems for the child could be parental substance abuse, parental mental health issues, criminal activity, or obvious social or personal problems.

Making the decision to contact the Children's Protective Services is best made in conjunction with your supervisor or another experienced staff member. The costs of not calling and being negligent are at odds with the harm that could be caused by creating an investigation of innocent and loving caregivers. In order to ensure that the referral is valid, Lukas (1993, p. 148) suggested the following "imminent risk assessment:"

1. The recentness and nature of the abuse.
2. The age of the child and, therefore, the degree of dependency on an adult for protection.
3. The ease of access the alleged perpetrator has to the child.
4. The need of the child for immediate medical care or evaluation.
5. The capacity and reliability of the person who is responsible for protecting the child.
6. Any known previous history of abuse or neglect of this or some other child in the family.

When the counselor has determined that a call should be made, procedures are followed to ensure the protection of the child. In reporting, several universal procedures apply. Caseworkers receiving the call require that the mandated reporter identify herself/himself and her/his location. This information is followed by the disclosure of all pertinent and relevant information such as the names of all of the known family members, their address, phone number, and other demographics. The alleged incident needs to be reported as accurately and with as much detail as possible. Finally, the name of the person to whom you report needs to be included in your notes for possible future reference.

Reporting alleged child abuse or neglect seems on the surface to be clear-cut or obvious. However, this is not always the case. In one situation with which we were involved, a counselor and a principal were informed by a student that a teacher was exhibiting excessive physical contact with his students. Not wanting to hear that this was a potential abuse situation, the principal did not investigate or initiate an investigation of possible sexual abuse. After the police were notified by the student's parents, the investigation disclosed that the principal did have prior knowledge of the allegations, and from the records, it was clear that she made no effort to call Children's Protective Services. This failure to report resulted in the principal's removal and loss of her administrative credential. Denial of the teacher's abusive relationships had negative consequences for students, parents, administrators, and the community.

## Assessing the Ecology of the School

The final area requiring the Ubiquitous Assessment skills of the counselor involves the evaluation of the overall school climate and culture. The important role of Ubiquitous Assessment is no more evident than when seen in the context of evaluating the school as a whole. As an integral member of the school's management team, the counselor has the opportunity to use the information that she/he has to interact with the faculty and administrative team to effect changes in school climate or ecology.

As the counselor participates in supervision of breaks, cocurricular activities, and general business throughout the campus, she/he cannot help but notice the differing degrees of affective and interpersonal harmony or disharmony that is manifested within the total community. Assessing attributes and attitudes along continuums such as friendliness–hostility, acceptance–racism, pride–disrespect, and warmth–aloofness, the counselor should be picking up vibes or feelings from the students and staff that identify the school's general affective state of campus affairs. Awareness of the school's ecology is an essential counselor function.

Through assessment of the daily operations of the school, the counselor can work effectively with other administrators to develop strategies to create a positive learning environment (Orpinas, Horne, & Staniszewski, 2003). Gauging the tensions and frustrations of the students by being with and observing their behavior in their breaks and lunch periods, counselors can keep their senses alert to issues causing conflict. Identification of gangs, groups, and other individuals and their needs is a relevant role for the counselor. The entire learning process comes to a stop when students are expelled or otherwise removed for perpetrating violent acts or other major educational code violations. The net effect of lost learning opportunities can also be true for the victims.

Since Columbine's tragedy, school safety has become a more obvious and critical concern than ever before (Goodman, 2002). Sparking a contagion of school shootings, Columbine has become a metaphor for school violence. America is one of the most violent Western cultures. American youths are ten times more likely to die from a violent attack than their Canadian neighbors (Hinds, 2000). The counselor's role is assessing the school's ecology becomes an important component in providing a safe learning environment because of the counselor's ability to identify feelings, read body language, and communicate with students in nonthreatening ways. Since Columbine, many school districts have added counselors to mitigate the risk factors that can make students act out in violent ways. Providing counseling for students suffering from divorce, loss of a close family member, or wounded by some other personal tragedy, schools can exemplify the values of love and compassion and avoid potential tragedies (Goodman, 2002).

Traditional school ecological assessments have followed psychology's tendency to evaluate individuals and to then draw conclusions about the whole from the average or mean response (Rasmussen et al., 2003). We contend that Ubiquitous Assessment methodology makes it possible to look at the whole school and to draw valid conclusions based upon the counselor's observations and conclusions. Although this method is more complex than using individual instruments, the process and result have a greater impact upon the total learning environment. "As school personnel [counselors] work collaboratively to understand students' environments and to address students' needs, more complex assessment instruments will continue to be used by professionals" (Rasmussen et al., 2003, p. 454). We suggest that each school form a cabinet or selection of administrative leadership and use this forum to discuss the issues as they present themselves. This process of assessment involves continuous and ubiquitous observation. Its reward, the development of safe and effective schools, requires critical conversations and the implementation of effective programs that address student concerns (Goodman, 2002).

The school's environment is a visible statement of the values of the community. The condition of the grounds, buildings, and other related facilities speaks loudly about the school's climate. The presence of graffiti and tagging implies not only gang activity but it says that the administration is not acting to remove the gang's claim of turf or territory. On an even higher plane, the environment of the school can be conceived as sacred space within the community. This is the highest tribute to the efforts of all those who work and learn there. Our attention to the environment of the school is a metaphor for our commitment to the world in which we live. David Jardine (2000) calls this educational consideration *ecopedagogy*. He stated,

> Ecopedagogical reflection thus involves drawing together our concern, as educators, for the presence of new life in our midst (Smith, 1988) (and for bringing forth this new life into the world, our world—educare) and "our most pleasing responsibility," caring for the earth. Such reflection simply asks: In what ways do questions of pedagogy interweave with questions of the continued existence of an earth in the embrace of which pedagogy is possible? Ecology and pedagogy interweave to the extent that separating them or separating our responsibilities for them can be accomplished only at a tragic cost. "No matter the distinctions we draw, the connections, the dependencies, remain. To damage the earth is to damage our children" (Berry, 1986 p. 57). (p. 21)

How the counselor can influence the school's environment is related to her/his commitment to the issues surrounding the environment. From the reflection of values reflected through the appearance of the counselor's office to larger, extended efforts for school improvement, the counselor can influence several students or many. One of these authors works with a class of peer mediators who conduct a schoolwide recycling program. This program not only teaches the values and practical benefits of recycling but the students also model environmentally sensitive behavior for other students to see. The school's environment benefits on many levels by participating in a campuswide recycling program. The counselor is rewarded, too, by taking an active role in the betterment of the entire school.

Although we will speak specifically to the use of Ubiquitous Assessment within the classroom in a later chapter, the teacher observation process is worth noting in this section on the counselor's role because of the counselor's influence on administration in this endeavor. How administrators want their school to look and feel is reinforced and supported by the teacher in the classroom. Given, of course, that the administrator is highly qualified and competent, those individuals would be able to recognize that supportive teachers provide meaningful instruction and are caring and compassionate professionals. The net effect of a competent professional educator's work in the classroom is reflected by student involvement and her/his active participation in the learning process (Kohn, 1998).

Obviously, there is much room for difference within a teaching staff. However, one constant needs to be governed by the administration and adhered to by the staff: core values. Whether they be centered around students' connectedness to school, compassion for all, academic competency, or a combination of these three values, there needs to be leadership and agreement within the school community that the values are worthy. Analyzing the participation of staff is purely qualitative; however, it is obvious how successful the school is by a simple walk-through. Walking into the classroom, anyone can see that there is a wide array of possible configurations ranging from tight control to organized chaos. Our preference is to see diverse learning modalities used to engage students in discovery and to sense that their motivation for participation is palpably high. Schools that represent respect for the environment and all of the participants within it feel safe and secure. As a counselor, this is where you want to work.

## Assessing the Need for Referral and Further Evaluation

For every professional, there are limits to her/his knowledge, experience, and scope of practice. Scope of practice refers to the ethical boundaries related to appropriate use of assessment procedures or, simply, practicing within one's limits (Whiston, 2000). As noted in the American Counseling Association's *Code of Ethics and Standards of Practice* (1995), "Counselors are responsible for the appropriate application, scoring, interpretation and use of assessment instruments, whether they score and interpret such tests themselves or use computerized or other services" (p. 36). Furthermore, counselors need to protect the client's rights to privacy, follow laws related to disclosure of assessment information, and avoid labeling or stigmatizing clients based upon test results. Overall, best practice dictates that use of assessment information will only provide benefit to the client.

Counselors provide a valuable function in their schools by serving as supports to their students in the selection and scheduling of classes, provision of counseling for crisis or other affective support, and planning for future education or training after high school. Best practice in Ubiquitous Assessment is defined by knowing the limitation of services that we can provide based upon our training, knowledge, and the scope of the counselor's practice (ACA, 1995).

One of the most effective services that a counselor can provide is that of referral. In the case of students needing more assistance, assessment, or counseling than the counselor can or should provide, referral to the school psychologist or an outside therapist or agency is appropriate. Knowing the limitations of either time and/or training, referral is an appropriate option when students need therapy or extended, specialized counseling for a specific issue. Examples of situations warranting referral are eating disorders, clinical conditions such as depression, and other significant psychosocial concerns. When situations indicate referral, it is best practice to provide the student and her/his family with the specific information necessary to make contact, such as phone numbers, addresses, and the names of individuals. Many large communities have organized the essential information concerning their agencies and publish a resource guide for referrals. In rare instances, interagency cooperation is organized to include mental health, probation, or other assistance on the school site and within easy access of the parent and their child.

As counselors confront issues as diverse as homelessness, runaways, pregnancy, abuse, and poverty, a guide to the resources of the community provides necessary support and information to the student and her/his family. In assessing the student's needs, we also evaluate our ability to provide sufficient service to help the individual overcome or resolve her/his current problem. In the case of academic difficulties, counselors may need to refer the individual to Student Study Teams (SST) for further assessment (Salvia & Ysseldyke, 1998). According to Salvia and Ysseldyke (1998), "Referral usually is a formal process involving the completion of a referral form and a request for a team of professionals to decide whether a student's academic, behavioral, or physical development warrants the provision of special education services" (p. 12).

In Ubiquitous Assessment, the counselor needs to assess her/his skills and remember that she/he is one part of a system of caregivers or mental health providers within the school or community. As a part of a team of service providers, counselors play a dual role as helper and referral source. A counselor needs the support of her/his team—the nurse, the site administrator, other counselors, the school psychologist, and other community members—in order to provide the best practice and highest level of service to the students. Working as a member of a team, counselors can be an effective part of the assessment process.

Being a part of a team can be a mitigating factor for the reduction of mistakes. Emerging counselors need the support of colleagues to reinforce the learning necessary for success at the school site and within the larger community. Coming from graduate training to the school, there is much left to learn. Being open to the fact that although school is complete, the real education is, as they say at graduation, commencing. Although you may feel confident because of your good training, it is important to temper that feeling with a balancing dash of self-doubt.

Within each of us are the seeds of success. The growth of our learning and the development of our skills is a function of our openness to new experience. Our colleagues can be our best resource for the development of professional competence. In the best of all worlds, you will have the opportunity to receive excellent support and supervision. If it is lacking, we strongly advise that you seek it wherever it is appropriate—for example, the local university, professional support groups, or in individual therapy. As an emerging professional, you need to assess yourself. Do so with the love and compassion you have for your students. Counseling is not so much a right and wrong methodology but a process—an evolution of experience. Your own authenticity and the integrity of the relationship will bode well for the client and the counselor. As you continue to develop your professionalism, stay open to the growth opportunities as they occur along the way.

# Chapter Four

# Assessment in Classrooms

For the work of the school psychologist or the school counselor within educational settings, the assessment of a student's classroom may be the most important part of any evaluation conducted. All of us who work with children as clients should be working closely with the school and classroom teacher(s), as most children who are having difficulties that would result in the assessment by a school psychologist, school counselor, or other mental health professional will involve problems functioning within the school setting.

Teachers generally refer children to us because they are having difficulty with them in the classroom, not in a one-to-one testing setting or in the counselor's office. However, we often fail to take the time to observe the client in the classroom, interview the teacher, or assess the learning environment. These are important functions that should not be overlooked. Because of the importance of this process, a review of the traditionally used measures in school settings will be reviewed first to familiarize you with such procedures and the problems encountered in using them. The second part of the chapter will explore methods used in Ubiquitous Assessment.

### Standardized Group Tests

Generally, students are assessed on their academic skills through the use of standardized tests. These tests allow students to be assessed as a group, so that entire schools can be assessed on the same day(s). Today, the emphasis on accountability has increased the use of standardized tests in school districts across the country, although this movement is not new. In Massachusetts during the middle 1800s, the state superintendent of instruction, in order to hold schools accountable, required the assessment of students' skills through written examinations (Linn & Gronlund, 2000). A number of other districts followed suit. Following World War I, the use of multiple-choice tests became conventional, and such tests were used to assess students in all academic areas. The trend continued and following World War II the testing movement for school districts became widespread. In 1983, *A Nation at Risk: The Imperative for Educational Reform* was published by the National Commission on Excellence in Education. The document spelled out several recommendations for the use of tests to enhance students' educational achievement, including: (1) certification of the student's credentials; (2) identification of the need for remedial intervention; and (3) provisions for the opportunity to complete advanced work (p. 28).

Attempting to motivate the educational community with fear by the reporting of systemic inadequacies, *A Nation at Risk* (National Commission on Excellence, 1983) spawned a tidal wave of interest in accountability. Although some of this motivation created the development of additional large-scale assessments, such as the California Achievement Test, there were other initiatives that actually attempted to benefit students on an individual level. This desire to provide improved outcomes for individual students led to the more recent developments of performance-based assessments. Performance-based assessments allow us to "observe students while they are performing or we examine the products they create and evaluate the level of proficiency demonstrated" (Stiggins, 2001, p. 184). The student is required to actually perform some activity rather than simply answering or knowing an answer (Linn & Gronlund, 2000). Other types of assessment have grown from this movement as well, including outcomes-based assessment, authentic assessment, and alternative assessment. Outcomes-based assessments refer to the "products" schools produce in terms of the knowledge and experiences students take with them (Ysseldyke & Thurlow, 1993, p. 3). Authentic assessment identifies the "knowledge, thinking, problem-solving skills, social skills and attitudes exhibited by those in the community, on the job, or in advanced courses as part of their normal work" (Tombari & Borich, 1999, p. 4). Those skills that are necessary outside of the school setting and needed in the real world are stressed. Alternative assessment is defined as anything other than the traditional model of multiple choice and other standardized tests.

Recently the federal government passed the No Child Left Behind (NCLB) Act (2002). This law requires each state to develop "world-class" standards for children in the third through eighth grades. Each state is required to then develop assessment measures that are aligned with the state's curriculum to meet specific standards. NCLB further mandates that educators assess all students in grades three to eight annually. Because these assessments will be conducted on a large scale, the traditional multiple-choice format has been selected as the most cost-efficient way to meet the letter of the law. Unfortunately, our knowledge about good assessment practices has been ignored.

Should schools and/or districts not meet their annual goals set forth by the state as outlined in NCLB, monies will be withheld from those sites, and remediations put in place for teachers at those schools (No Child Left Behind, 2002). Today, every school district includes some form of traditional standardized assessment of students, and many also now require students to pass high school exit exams in order to graduate.

These tests, however, are fraught with problems. As mentioned above, states are now required to develop specific standards and have them in place and, in order to ensure the standards are met, they have gone as far as to identify the curriculum to be used at every grade level. Unfortunately, only in rare instances do the assessment tools selected by the states to be used at the end of year match the curriculum used by classroom teachers. This results in a lack of content validity as there is no match between what is taught and what is tested. The only way students can actually do well on such tests is if the teacher prepares her/his classes for the test or if the students possess the cultural capital to do well on these types of tests because of their family background, opportunity, and experience. Only if the tests and the curriculum are aligned can the teacher be sure that the students will be tested on what they have been taught.

Another problem with standardized group tests is that such tests do not allow for any kind of changes in instruction or informed decision making by the teacher. They are one-shot summative evaluations that result in a student being stigmatized and her/his teacher being made to suffer whatever consequences the powers-that-be deem necessary. Such assessments tell us little about how the student learns, what she/he needs to learn, and the best way to teach the student the skills she/he will need for the future. In order to understand the problem fully, a brief review of some of the most common group standardized tests follows below.

## Specific Standardized Group Tests

The most common standardized group tests currently in use are the California Achievement Tests (CAT), the Iowa Tests of Basic Skills (ITBS), the Metropolitan Achievement Tests (MAT), and the Stanford Achievement Tests (SAT). There are major, significant problems with all of these tests.

The California Achievement Test, Form 6 (CAT6), also known as the Terra-Nova Second Edition (CTB/McGraw-Hill, 2002), includes subtests in reading/language arts, mathematics, science, social studies, word analysis, vocabulary, language mechanics, spelling, and mathematics computation. There are thirteen levels of the test, one for each grade kindergarten through twelve. The test was normed on over 264,000 students during fall and spring standardizations and includes students identified as eligible for special education. The problem with the CAT6 is that there is minimal evidence of any type of validity and no evidence of test-retest or alternate form reliability. A further criticism of this assessment tool is that it does not align with California's state standards for instruction even though it bears California's name (Bell, 2002; CVERC, 2002). For many reasons, the use of this test in schools to assess the overall achievement of students must be viewed with extreme caution.

The Iowa Tests of Basic Skills (ITBS) (Hoover, Dunbar, & Frisbie, 2001) consists of ten levels for students in grades kindergarten through eight and was normed in 2000. Subtests include vocabulary, word analysis, reading comprehension, listening, language, mathematics, social studies, science, and sources of information for students in grades kindergarten through three; and vocabulary, reading comprehension, spelling, capitalization, punctuation, usage and expression, math concepts and estimation, math problem solving and data interpretation, math computation, social studies, science, maps and diagrams, and reference questions for students from grades three through eight. Additional tests, the Tests of Achievement and Proficiency (TAP) (Scannell, 1996) and the Iowa Tests of Educational Development (ITED) (Forsyth, Ansley, Feldt, & Alnot, 2001), are available for students in grades nine through twelve. Subtests for these include vocabulary, reading comprehension, written expression, math concepts and problem solving, math computation, social studies, science, information processing for the TAP, and vocabulary, reading comprehension, spelling, language (revising written materials), analysis of social studies materials, analysis of science materials, and sources of information on the ITED. The TAP was constructed in 1992 and is primarily a norm-referenced test, while the ITED was standardized in 2000 and is a norm-referenced and curriculum-referenced test. The ITBS and ITED were normed on approximately 180,000 students. The construct and criterion validity of these tests is lacking and there is no test-retest reliability reported. Again, the use of these tests must be questioned when technical adequacy is so poor.

The Metropolitan Achievement Tests, Eighth Edition (MAT8) (Harcourt Educational Measurement, 2002) consists of thirteen levels from kindergarten through twelfth grades. Subtests include sounds and print, reading vocabulary, reading comprehension, open-ended reading, mathematics, mathematics concepts and problem solving, mathematics computation, open-ended mathematics, language, spelling, open-ended writing, science, and social studies. The test was normed on a total of 140,000 students during fall and spring standardizations in the 1999–2000 academic year. Again, as on the other tests discussed above, content and construct validity are lacking. Unfortunately, reliabilities reported for internal consistency and test-retest are too low to be used to make individual decisions about students.

The Stanford Achievement Test-Ninth Edition (Harcourt Brace Educational Measurement, 1996) consists of thirteen levels and includes five to thirteen subtests at each level. Subtests include sounds and letters, word study skills, word reading, sentence reading, reading vocabulary, reading comprehension, mathematics, mathematics problem solving, mathematics procedures, language, spelling, study skills, listening to words and stories, listening, environment, science, and social science. The test was normed on approximately 250,000 students. Validity is addressed in the manual, and the authors did go to some lengths to ensure the test had strong content and construct validity by having the items reviewed by subject matter experts, people of differing cultures and ethnicities, and teachers involved in the standardization. Reliability is reported for internal consistency and alternate form. However, conclusions concerning individuals based upon results of this assessment need to be viewed with caution.

Of the four tests reviewed, only one (the Stanford Achievement Test-Ninth Edition) appears to have adequate technical adequacy for screening students on academic achievement. However, all of these tests will be used by state departments to meet the No Child Left Behind requirements of yearly testing. Without technical adequacy, they tell us virtually nothing. Of gravest concern are the high-stakes consequences of such tests upon students and their families, teachers, and schools. Stigmatizing students and penalizing schools based on technically inadequate tests is unethical and unprofessional.

## Teacher-Made Tests

The most common form of academic assessment in the schools is the teacher-made test. For the most part, teacher-made tests assess students on what they have covered in the class. If we truly want to know how a student can perform, these assessments should be experiential and use the material taught to her/him in the classroom. Unfortunately, many teacher-made tests are not relevant to learning outcomes and often have only to do with the teacher being able to issue the student some grade or another. True/false and multiple-choice tests still tend to be the methods of choice for classroom tests. Often only one test is given on a particular area of content, and the results of that test "make or break" the student. Such assessments do not allow modification of instruction and no information related to a student's daily or weekly progress in a content area is obtained. Most importantly, teacher-made tests have not been used with any other group of individuals so comparisons cannot be made and thus, many teacher-made tests are not valid or reliable.

Teacher-made tests can be improved by ensuring (a) the test matches the content difficulty, (b) the test provides an adequate representation of the material covered, and (c) each question measures one or more learning objectives (Braus, Wood, & LeFranc, 1993). In addition, teacher-made tests should examine each student's ability to think critically, using some type of performance-based or experiential assessment. Often, tests given in the classroom tell how a student performed (i.e., by the grade obtained) but information relative to how the student obtained his or her answers is lacking. Taking the time to analyze a student's responses requires extra time on the part of a teacher.

## Individual Norm-Referenced Achievement Tests

School psychologists; school counselors; social workers; and marriage, family, and child therapists are often interested in assessing students' academic achievement to determine if potential problems faced by the student in everyday life could stem from academic deficiencies. Because of the inherent problems with standardized group tests and teacher-made tests, individually administered achievement tests are often given by mental health professionals. These tests tend to be normed on a national sample and assess the areas of reading, writing, spelling, and mathematics in a one-to-one setting as opposed to the group tests discussed above. Common, individually administered norm-referenced tests include the Kaufman Test of Educational Achievement-Normative Update, the Wechsler Individual Achievement Test-Second Edition, and the Peabody Individual Achievement Test-Revised-Normative Update.

The Kaufman Test of Educational Achievement-Normative Update (KTEA-NU) (Kaufman & Kaufman, 1998) is an individually administered, norm-referenced test for students in grades one through twelve. Subtests include reading decoding, reading comprehension, mathematics application, mathematics computation, and spelling. Standard scores are based on a mean of 100 and standard deviation of 15, and percentile rank, stanine, normal curve equivalent, and age and grade equivalent scores can be obtained. The normative update published in 1998 was normed on 600 students. The original test was published in 1985 and normed on 1,409 students in a spring sample and 1,067 students in a fall sample. All technical adequacy information is reported only for the original test even though the updated version shows students' mean performances have increased. Thus, the test should be used with extreme caution as there is no current evidence provided for reliability or validity.

The Wechsler Individual Achievement Test-Second Edition (WIAT-II) (Psychological Corporation, 2001) is also an individually administered norm-referenced test designed for students from prekindergarten to twelfth grades. Subtests include word reading, reading comprehension, pseudoword reading, numerical operations, math reasoning, spelling, written expression, listening comprehension, and oral expression. The test is based on a mean of 100 and a standard deviation of 15 with additional scores that can be obtained including percentile ranks, age and grade equivalents, stanines, normal curve equivalents, quartiles, and deciles. The test was normed on 3,600 students from grades kindergarten through twelve for a grade-based sample, 2,950 students from four to nineteen years of age for an age-based sample; 2,171 students were included in both groups. The test has adequate validity and reliability with test-retest reliability exceeding .80 and inter-rater reliability ranging from .71 to .99, depending on subtest. However, for individual decision making, reliabilities should be above .90. Thus, the WIAT-II, while meeting some technical adequacy requirements, does not meet the technical adequacy requirements for individual subtests, and many assessors ignore this fact when they interpret the subtests for individual students.

The Peabody Individual Achievement Test-Revised-Normative Update (PIAT-RU) (Markwardt, 1998) is an individually administered norm-referenced test for students in grades kindergarten through twelve. Subtests include mathematics, reading recognition, reading comprehension, spelling, general information, and written expression. Scores are based on a mean of 100 and a standard deviation of 15 with additional scores of age and grade equivalents, percentile ranks normal curve equivalents and stanines that can be obtained. The norm group consisted of approximately 600 students and unfortunately, the same problem with the KTEA holds true for the PIAT. No new data are reported for reliability and validity, and the user is referred to the previous edition.

### Individual Norm-Referenced Behavior Rating Scales

The tools used most often to assess problem behaviors are rating scales. Common scales include the Child Behavior Checklist (CBCL), the Behavior Rating Profile-Second Edition (BRP-2), and the Behavior Assessment System for Children (BASC). The problem with these tools is that while there are self-report scales for students to complete, the primary information comes from others such as parents and teachers, which "provide an index of someone's perception of a student's behavior" (Salvia & Ysseldyke, 2004). As can be seen from a brief glimpse of these commonly used rating scales, they are lacking in technical rigor. Unfortunately, there are similar problems with tests designed to assess behavior problems.

The Child Behavior Checklist (CBCL) (Achenbach, 1991), designed for students from ages four to eighteen, is an individually administered rating scale completed by the student's parent or guardian. There are two sections on the scale: competence and problems. Competence items include extracurricular activities, social interactions, and school functioning. This section includes twenty items on the three scales and are scored on a four-point scale (don't know, less than average, average, and more than average). Problem items are categorized into internalizing (withdrawn, somatic complaints, and anxious/depressed) and externalizing (delinquent behavior and aggressive behavior), with a total of 118 items. The parent scores these items using a three-point scale (not true, somewhat or sometimes true, and very true or often true). Scores obtained are T scores and percentile ranks. The scale was normed on 2,368 children who had not received mental health or special education services within one year of the standardization process. Reliability measures included inter-interview reliability across three interviewers with scores above .90; test-retest reliability on three samples with scores ranging from .56 to .87 for the competence section and .48 to .89 for the problem section. It should be noted that these correlations were obtained for only a small subset of the total sample. Validity coefficients were obtained for criterion-related validity above .80. Content validity was established through a thorough literature review and an analysis of the items by experts. Construct validity was established through a study of referred children and nonreferred children, resulting in the CBCL demonstrating the ability to discriminate among such children. Of the tools available to assess behavior problems, the CBCL appears to be the most technically adequate; however, when it comes to making decisions about individual children, the user must remember that the results are based on informants' perceptions of the student, not the actual behavior of the student.

The Behavior Rating Profile-Second Edition (BRP-2) (Brown & Hammill, 1990) was designed for students from six years six months to eighteen years six months. There are three student rating scales, a teacher rating scale, and a parent rating scale. The student rating scales consist of twenty items each related to home, school, and peers and are scored true or false. The teacher and parent rating scales have thirty items each. Each item is scored on a four-point scale from 1 (very much like the student) to 4 (not at all like the student). Scores obtained on the BRP-2 include standard scores and percentile ranks. The total norm group for the student scales included 2,682 students without social-emotional problems; 1,948 parents for the parent scale; and 1,452 teachers for the teacher scale. Information related to reliability and validity were published in the manual and appear adequate with the exception of inter-rater reliability (no information is reported). It is important to realize that the test was developed as a screening device and is not adequate for making decisions about individuals. Unfortunately, this tool is used quite often without that caveat.

Another common tool used to assess student behavior problems is the Behavior Assessment System for Children (BASC) (Reynolds & Kamphaus, 1992). The test was designed for children from four to eighteen years of age and includes of a teacher rating scale, a parent rating scale, and a self-report of personality. The teacher rating scale is composed of three forms—one for ages four to five (109 items), one for ages six to eleven (148 items), and one for ages twelve to eighteen (138 items). The items are scored on a four-point scale from N = Never, S = Sometimes, O = Often, and A = Almost Always. Scores obtained include T scores and percentile ranks. Norm groups for the teacher scale consisted of 2,401; for the parent scale 3,483, and for the self-report 9,861. Students diagnosed as having social-emotional problems were included in the norm group and included 693 for the teacher scale, 401 for the parent scale, and 411 for the student self-report. Overall the reliabilities and validities for the BASC appear good; however, the BASC did not adequately discriminate between students identified as having social-emotional problems and those students not identified. This could be a function of the small sample sizes utilized in these studies; however, for individual decision making, findings must be seriously questioned.

## Ubiquitous Classroom Assessment

The review of common standardized group assessments, teacher-made tests, and individually administered assessment tools demonstrates over and over again the problems evidenced with such tools. The question then arises, "How can we assess students in the classroom?" Using Ubiquitous Assessment, a number of far more useful methods can be implemented to give us the information we need to truly make a difference for students in our schools. Although these techniques take time, when one considers the wasted time and energy that goes into traditional assessment efforts without any payoff for the student in terms of alternative instructional strategies or programs, these techniques actually provide information that can help us make informed intervention and therapeutic decisions for our most at-risk students.

For those who are school personnel, particularly school psychologists, the federal law serves an important function in delineating our responsibilities. Part B of the Individuals with Disabilities Act (IDEA, Public Law 101–476), Section 300.533, specifically states that:

> As a part of an initial evaluation (if appropriate) and as part of any reevaluation under Part B of the Act, a group that includes individuals described in §300.344, and other qualified professionals; as appropriate, shall:
>
> (1) Review existing evaluation data on the child, including:
> (i) Evaluations and information provided by the parents of the child;
> (ii) Current classroom-based assessments and observations; and
> (iii) Observations by teachers and related service provides . . .

In many cases, school psychologists and others do not complete classroom observations when indeed they should. Educational and mental health professionals often say they do not have the time in their busy days to do so, yet classroom observations actually result in much more relevant and useful information for developing change strategies concerning the student than do any other kinds of assessments. Classrooms should be viewed as ecosystems that provide support for student learning. Hobbs wrote, "The group is important to the child. When a group is functioning well, it is extremely difficult for an individual child to behave in a disturbed way" (1966, p. 1112). Well-functioning classrooms have teachers who utilize an age-appropriate curriculum and who teach adaptive behavior skills that can help to prevent behavior problems (Dunlap & Kern, 1996; Nordquist & Twardosz, 1990). Teachers in well-functioning classrooms assess students as they engage curriculum in a natural environment. In this sensitive setting, any change for individual students may affect other children's and teachers' behaviors. Thus, assessors need ways to evaluate what is happening in the classroom setting, and the most effective technique is the use of structured observations in the student's classroom. The best method for evaluation to develop interventions is to observe in classrooms and obtain usable data by planning, conducting, and using classroom observations. The standardized tests reviewed above offer us nothing in terms of how we will help struggling students succeed. Using structured observations based on carefully developed problem solving, the assessor can select specific behaviors to observe and create appropriate interventions.

## Consultation with Teachers and Parents

The first step in assessing a student's functioning often involves engaging in consultation with the teacher, parent, or other caregiver. Consultation is a systematic way to guide problem solving. Our main task as mental health professionals frequently involves identifying the problem and then developing interventions or therapeutic approaches to rectify the situation. The stages of ecobehavioral consultation are problem identification, problem analysis, plan development, plan implementation, and evaluation. Consultation provides assistance to caregivers rather than direct services to students (Gutkin & Curtis, 1990). Individuals coming together to consult must have a mutual respect, trust, and openness for and to one another. As the consultant is viewed as the individual with expertise in problem solving and intervention design, consultees—including parents, school personnel, and other professionals—are viewed as experts in their knowledge of the child. Thus, two or more individuals, with their own specific areas of expertise, come together to attempt to solve a student-related problem (Barnett, Bell, & Carey, 1999).

Consultation or problem-solving interviews are conducted using effective communication skills, both verbal and nonverbal, and include genuineness, listening, empathy, clarification, and summarization (Gutkin & Curtis, 1990). There are twelve basic steps to the first stage of the problem-solving process—problem identification (Carey, 1989; Vedder-Dubocq, 1990).

1. Explain the problem-solving interview and its purpose. First, the tone is set and guidelines are established for the interview by giving an overview of what is to be accomplished.
2. Define the problem behavior. Question and probe as needed to determine the consultee's view of the problem. For example, what the student is doing and not doing, and whether others see this as a problem.
3. Prioritize multiple problems. If multiple problems are identified, help the consultee prioritize the behaviors. For example, ask the consultee, "What bothers you the most? Which of these is most pressing to you?"
4. Define severity of problem. Try to link estimates of the severity of the behavior with specific example and trends of actual occurrences.
5. Define "generality of the problem." Through probing and questioning, try to determine the length of time the behavior has been a problem and the situations where it is observed (Peterson, 1968).
6. Explore determinants of the problem behavior. This point of the interview is based on functional analysis of behavior.
   a. Ask the consultee to "Think about the times the problem is worse. What is going on then?"
   b. Ask the consultee: "What about times when the problem gets better? What is happening then?"
   c. Determine the consultee's perception of the origin of the problem. "What do you think is causing [the problem]?"

d. Antecedents, personal, and social influences. Ask "Think back to the last time the [the problem occurred]. What was going on then? Where were you? Were there others around? Who? What were you thinking?"

e. Consequences. Ask "What usually happens after [the problem] occurs? Does this happen consistently?"

For social consequences: "What did others do?"

For personal consequences: "What were you thinking about then?" (adapted from Peterson, 1968, p. 122)

7. Determine modification attempts. Ask, "What things have you tried to stop the problem behavior? How long have you tried that? How well did it work?" (adapted from Alessi & Kaye, 1983, appendix B).
8. Identify expectancies for improved behavior. Determine desired levels of performance or changes in roles and behaviors. Ask, "In this situation, what would you like [e.g., the student] to do instead of the problem behavior? If [the student] were to improve, what would you notice first? What is the behavior you would like to see?" (Alessi & Kaye, 1983, appendix B).
9. Summarize consultee's concerns. Give a rationale for the summary and then summarize the consultee's concerns and confirm the definition of the problem behavior.
10. Explore the consultee's commitment and motivation to work on the problem. Ask, "How would solving this problem make your day easier? Were this problem to go away, how would this change your day? If this problem were to get worse, how would this affect you? What do you think the chances of solving this problem are?" (adapted from Alessi & Kaye, 1983, appendix B).
11. Have the consultee summarize problems, goals, and plans. Ask, "In order to make sure I understand your concerns and goals, I would like you to summarize them for me."
12. Discuss and mutually arrive at plans for next steps. Next steps may involve further consultation to review uncertainties about information revealed, plans for observation, and/or referrals to others.

The problem-solving interview is the starting point for determining the problem behavior as viewed from the standpoint of the consultee. Once a definition of the problem behavior is obtained, the consultant can move forward with the next step: observation.

## Observation Basics

When conducting classroom observations, the assessor must make decisions about what to evaluate in the natural environment of the school. The best practice is to attempt sampling of behaviors across several classes and different days. For many students, especially adolescents, time of day is also an important aspect to explore. Some behaviors only occur at certain times of the day—for example, right before lunch. This information can only be obtained through an individualized problem-solving strategy making sure we observe at specific times. Intersession sampling addresses the assessor's decision related to when to observe. Selecting time checks as observation units requires that the (1) sessions must be equivalent in opportunities for the occurrence or nonoccurrence of behavior; and (2) conditions must be the same for all observation periods (Cooper, Heron, & Heward, 1987). From the consultation session, the consultant can get an idea of the usual time periods for activities, making it possible to have comparable sessions. Finally, it is important to select an adequate observation length. Behaviors with low frequency may require longer time periods; behaviors with longer frequencies may require shorter time periods. Sample behaviors from the observations must be representative and accurate.

## Methods for Observing and Recording Behavior

Observation includes "recording the stream of behavior, dividing it into units, and analyzing the units" (Wright, 1967, p. 10). The observation should be a "detailed, sequential, narrative account of behavior and its immediate environmental context as seen by skilled observers" (Wright, 1967, p. 32). Our observations need to be guided by our specific questions related to the environment, instruction, behaviors, skills, and tasks (Wolery, 1989). There are several useful ways to observe behavior in the classroom. Oftentimes assessors conduct so-called observations by simply writing down everything they see (or think they see) and developing impressions about a student's behavior. Conducting observations in this manner is haphazard and subject to bias and incomplete information (Linn & Gronlund, 2000). In order to get an accurate picture of a student's behavior in the classroom, whether it be academic or social-emotional, we must collect objective data on the problem behavior identified during our consultation.

### Real-Time Observations

The natural environment allows for ongoing observations to be conducted as the behavior actually occurs. Barnett and Carey (1992) recommended that preliminary observations be done using real-time observations to select those behavioral and environmental features that are important to note and may add to our understanding of the behavior identified during consultation.

Real-time observations focus on the child's situation (including actions of peers and teachers toward the child) as well as specific child behavior. The procedure shown in figure 1 requires the observer to record the exact times of the initiation and termination of behavior. Activity changes are recorded by time notations, and arrows are used for the observer to note the appropriateness (↑) or inappropriateness (↓) of the child's behavior. Each line of the observation protocol should include only one unit of behavior and each behavior should be mutually exclusive (one activity is recorded) and exhaustive (all time is accounted for) (Sackett, 1978; Suen & Ary, 1989). Time notations can be made at prespecified intervals such as one minute (Wright, 1967), two minutes (Bijou et al., 1969), or a variation (Barnett & Carey, 1992).

Data derived from real-time observations include:

1. Frequency or Event recording. Frequency equals the number of times behavior occurs in an observation session. Frequency can be useful for describing aggressive behaviors, time on task, or transition times.
2. Rate of Occurrence. Rate of occurrence is the frequency of behavior divided by the length of the observation session. Using the rate of occurrence allows for comparisons of frequency across sessions of different lengths, providing us with measures of reliability and validity. This is useful when our time is limited but we need to make comparisons across different days, again to ensure reliability.
3. Bout duration. Bout (one occurrence of behavior) duration is the length of time the behavior occurs. Bout duration can be useful for recording states of behavior (tantrums), on-task behavior (paying attention during instruction), or activity engagement (such as art instruction).
4. Prevalence. Prevalence is the proportion of time a bout is found within an observation session. Bout durations are totaled and divided by the session length (expressed in the same time units) and the result is multiplied by 100. Using prevalence allows us to compare states of behavior, such as paying attention in class, across observation sessions of different lengths.
5. Interresponse time (IRT). IRT is the time between bouts and is calculated by recording the time period from the end of a behavior to the beginning of the next behavior. The mean IRT is calculated by dividing the sum of all IRT durations by the number of nonoccurrences of behavior. IRT is useful for

setting observation intervals, particularly when only limited time is available for several observations.

**Figure 1. An Example of Real-Time Recording**

Setting: Special Day Class for Emotional Disturbed Students

Time: 8:15–8:35 Child: D

↑ 8:15 D enters classroom and throws book bag on table. Walks to get chair from stack for his desk. Takes chair back to his desk.

↓8:16 D sits down and then runs to the classroom door, shouting for S. Teacher intervenes and attempts to get D back to his seat.

↓ 8:17 D agrees to go back to his seat and as soon as he is seated he runs to the door again and starts shouting for S. Teacher intervenes and asks D to come with him to the office space in the classroom.

↑ 8:19 D and Teacher go to the office space in the classroom and the Teacher asks, "What is going on D?" D states that he "saw S earlier but that S said he wasn't coming to class today."

↑ 8:21 Teacher says for "D not to worry about S., that he would find out what is going on, but that D needs to get back to his desk and get to work." D agrees and leaves the office area.

↑ 8:22 D returns to his desk, opens his backpack and removes a notebook and a pencil. Other students in the class are working on writing in journals. D takes out his journal and begins completing the assignment.

↓ 8:24 S enters the room and D jumps up to greet him. D states "I thought you weren't coming today." "I thought I would have a good day but now you're here. How am I supposed to get any work done with you here?"

↓ 8:25 D begins to scream at S, telling him he hates him and that he is ruining everything for D. D hits S.

↓ 8:26 Teacher and aide tell D to not hit S but D continues.

↑ 8:27 Teacher and aide tell D again to calm down and D begins to move away from S toward the Teacher. Teacher tells D three times to stay calm, which D does.

↑ 8:29 D moves closer to the Teacher and when he is about three feet away says to the teacher, "I am really sorry, I don't know what happened." Teacher tells D he must apologize to S.

↑ 8:30 D tells S that he is sorry and hopes they can still be friends. S says he is sorry too about telling D he wouldn't be in class. Teacher encourages them to shake hands and they do.

↑ 8:32 Teacher directs D back to his desk to continue working on his journal. D follows the Teacher's directions, returns to his seat and begins working.

↑ 8:34 D continues working quietly.

Frequency: D engaged in inappropriate behavior five times and appropriate behavior nine times.

Two episodes of shouting

Two episodes of hitting.

Rate of Occurrence: 2 divided by 14 = .14 or 14 percent of the time D engaged in yelling behavior.

Bout duration: For hitting—lasted for 2 minutes

Prevalence: Four bouts of behavior divided by 14 = .2857 x 100 = 28.5714

Interresponse time = .7143

## Antecedent-Behavior-Consequence Analysis

Also known as A-B-C analysis, Antecedent-Behavior-Consequence Analysis is a basic strategy for the functional analysis of behavior (Bijou, Peterson, & Ault, 1968). Functional analysis of behavior refers to what function a behavior serves for a student. Antecedents are events that precede a behavior and may increase or decrease the behavior. Consequences can be either reinforcing, punishing, or neutral depending on which type is administered. In general, the setting is first described and then observations are recorded on a three-column form (see figure 2). Similar to real-time observations, a time column is also included.

**Figure 2. Antecedent-Behavior-Consequence Analysis**

| Date______________________ | Behavior of Concern: | ______________________<br>______________________<br>______________________<br>______________________ |
|---|---|---|
| Time: | | |
| What was going on before? | What was the behavior? | What happened after? |

## Frequency or Event Recording

Frequency recording involves simply tallying the number of times a behavior occurs in an observation session. Thus, only certain predefined behaviors or events are recorded. To use this technique successfully, only discrete behaviors of brief and stable durations, such as activity changes, calling out, or aggressive acts can be recorded using this method. There are many ways to record frequencies and events, including simply making tally marks on a piece of paper or using counters of some kind. One teacher known to us uses "pop beads" to collect frequency data by moving the beads from one pocket to another throughout the observation session.

Duration recording is the recording of the elapsed time for each occurrence of a behavior, and the total duration of the behavior. This method is used when the concern is the length of time a student engages in a specific behavior. For example, when a student is off task during instruction, duration recording is the method to use to record how long the student remains unengaged. In addition, the latency of the response can be recorded. Latency is the amount of time before beginning a behavior, such as the length of time it takes a student to comply with directions (Barnett & Carey, 1992).

**Time Sampling Techniques**

Time sampling enables the observer to record observations of several children or of multiple behaviors. Two types are used: momentary time sampling and interval sampling.

*Momentary Time Sampling.* Momentary time sampling is used with continuous behaviors when duration is of interest and behaviors have no clear beginnings or endings (Hartmann, 1984). It is also used when behaviors have high rates of occurrence. For example, this method is useful when a student is sitting in her/his seat but is on and off task continuously. In momentary time sampling, an observation session is divided into smaller intervals and the occurrence or nonoccurrence of a behavior is recorded at the specific moment during observation. For example, at a specified interval, such as fifteen or thirty seconds, the observer records whether the student is paying attention to the teacher.

*Interval Recording.* Interval recording is used to note both events and states of behavior. The observation session is divided into smaller time intervals, such as ten to fifteen seconds, and the observer records the occurrence or nonoccurrence of the behavior within each interval instead of at one precise moment. Two methods can be used: partial-interval sampling and whole-interval sampling. Partial-interval sampling involves the recording of the presence of the behavior during any part of the interval. Using the example above of the student on and off task during instruction, the observer would note whether or not the student remained on task at any time during succeeding ten- to fifteen-second intervals. Whole-interval sampling involves the recording of the presence of the behavior throughout the whole interval. Thus, again, using the example above, the student would need to remain on task for the whole ten- to fifteen-second interval.

### Other Methods

Many other methods exist for observing and recording behaviors. These include (1) Discrete skill sequences, which is similar to task analysis, whereby every component required to complete an activity is first recorded and then the student is observed to determine where she/he has difficulty. (2) Category sampling, which is used for behaviors that can be categorized, such as on-task behavior. All evidence of on-task behavior is recorded even if it takes different forms. (3) Permanent products, which include work and homework completion. All assessors should take the time to review actual student work products as they can tell us much about teacher expectations and how the student performs relative to her/his peers. (4) Trials to criterion, which involve how many times a "response opportunity" is presented before the student performs the task to a specified criterion (Cooper, Heron, & Heward, 1987, p. 74). In other words how long does it take a student to meet some teacher expectation, given the opportunity to do so. (5) Levels of assistance, which include recording the amount of support a student needs to complete a task or participate with peers. Some students need additional support from teachers and/or peers, and knowing how much support is necessary can provide us with information in terms of how to ensure the student gets such support. Finally, (6) Probes, which include structuring tasks in such a way that data can be collected. Oftentimes it is not possible to actually observe the behavior in the real world and we need to set up situations for the behavior to occur in order that we can observe it.

### Observing More Than One Child

Micronorms refer to the norms accepted in a classroom. As each teacher is different, it can sometimes be useful to know what is expected for a student assigned to a particular classroom. Appropriate comparison students (three to four) must be selected and, generally, observations are conducted using momentary time sampling, where each student is observed for one interval, before moving on to the next. Each student is observed engaged in a task for preset time period (e.g., ten seconds). Such data can help us see whether or not the student identified is actually behaving in ways significantly different from her/his peers.

**Self-Observation**

Self-observation is used when we are interested in the emotions and thoughts of a student; although it can also be used with overt behaviors, when we want the student to be cognizant of her/his behaviors. In order for self-observation to be effective, the student must be able to discriminate the occurrence from the nonoccurrence of a behavior. The results of self-observations must be recorded by the student. Based on the data recorded, the student needs to evaluate himself/herself. Generally the student needs to be trained in order to self-observe.

Students, however, are often not accurate at self-observation although several strategies can be used to improve accuracy. These include combining self-observation with other strategies used by adults to monitor the student's behavior, and agreement checks can be conducted to improve performance through the surveillance of an adult. It is important to recognize that complete accuracy is not necessary for the student to derive benefit from self-observation (Kanfer & Gaelick, 1986).

**Functional Assessment of Academic Behavior (FAAB)**

The Functional Assessment of Academic Behavior (FAAB) (Ysseldyke & Christenson, 2002) is a published measure that is used for gathering information on the instructional needs of students in the classroom examining the student-environmental match. The tool includes twelve instructional-environmental components: instructional match, instructional expectations, classroom environment, instructional presentation, cognitive emphasis, motivational strategies, relevant practice, informed feedback, academic engaged time, adaptive instruction, progress evaluation, and student understanding; five home-support-for-learning components, including home expectations and attributions, discipline orientation, home-affective environment, parent participation, and structure for learning; and six home-school-support-for-learning components, including shared standards and expectations, consistent structure, cross-setting opportunity to learn, mutual support, positive trusting relationship, and modeling. The FAAB is composed of observational and interview forms (including a student interview form, parent interview form, and teacher interview form) that allow the observer/interviewer to identify the instructional needs of students. Using the data collected from the interviews and observations, the practitioner completes the instructional-environment checklist using qualitative judgments throughout to determine the existence/nonexistence of each factor. In addition, the FAAB manual includes interventions that can be implemented both in the classroom and the home setting.

Observations are by far one of the best methods available to determine the extent of a behavior problem and to assess the classroom environment. They provide us with useful information for making relevant intervention and therapeutic decisions. As the classroom is where many behaviors are first reported, observations in the natural classroom environment can assist us in seeing where and what the problem is. There are numerous computer and Palm-type programs available today for recording behavior, making the pencil-and-paper method obsolete. In addition, these programs can tally the results quickly and reliably. Some of these include !Observe by Sopris West, and Ecobehavioral Assessment System (EBASS) by Juniper Gardens (Greenwood, Carta, Kamps, & Delquadri, 1995).

## Curriculum-Based Assessment

As was discussed above, many of the tools used to assess students in the classroom are neither reliable nor valid. However, one of the most useful tools for developing intervention and therapeutic plans is assessing the student in her/his actual curriculum. Whether the curriculum is academic, behavioral, emotional, or social, assessing the student on what he or she has actually learned provides us with information we can use to change the instruction and see the student make real gains. While the specifics of curriculum-based measurement are beyond the scope of this volume (for further information, see Shinn [1989] and Tindall & Marston [1990]), a brief overview is provided here.

Curriculum-based assessment allows for continuous, ongoing observations of the student's performance in the classroom setting. By analyzing the student's level of skill development we can determine the appropriate level of instruction for that particular student in a specified area (Barnett & Carey, 1992). According to Barnett, Bell, and Carey (1999), "the information gained from curriculum-based assessment includes: (1) current level of performance or functioning; (2) rate of learning new skills; (3) strategies necessary to learn new skills; (4) length of time the new skill is retained; (5) generalization of previously taught skills to a new task; (6) observed behaviors that deter learning; (7) environmental conditions needed to learn new skills (individual, group, peer instruction); (8) motivational techniques used to acquire skills; and (9) skills acquisition in relationship to peers" (p. 66).

Curriculum-based assessment has been relegated in the past to students in elementary school. However, this assessment tool can be used with any curriculum that is based on developmentally sequenced tasks and ongoing assessment (weekly or more often). For example, at the high school level where computer literacy classes are now required, the curriculum for these classes is based on an appropriate developmental progression. A student's knowledge of computer literacy can be assessed in such classes by conducting brief probes of her/his knowledge. One example would be asking students to find a particular file on the computer (a task that should take no longer than one minute). By gathering information on this task, the teacher would know whether the student is able to turn on the computer, find the correct program, use the mouse or keyboard in the appropriate way, go to the correct tool bar icon, and locate the file. Should the student break down at any step along the way, the teacher would know exactly when to begin instruction for that student in order to ensure the student continues to make progress. By engaging in such activities once, twice, or three times a week, students are less likely to fall behind their peers.

As another example, the area of social skills can be explored. Students who have difficulty making friends often do not know how to go about engaging with others. Practicing the steps for meeting someone new, modeling the steps with another person, and then practicing the steps can lead to the actual meeting of real-live friends for many students. Observations are required of the student in the real world to determine where, when, or if the student is unable to engage in the steps outlined.

Curriculum-based assessment is aligned with Ubiquitous Assessment. In many school districts, such assessments are relegated to the use of local norms developed to determine eligibility for special education. However, that is not what we are referring to here. Curriculum-based assessment should be viewed as a part of the seamless process from assessment to intervention/treatment. By continually assessing a student's areas of weakness and changing instruction, we can be assured that we are doing everything possible for the student to make academic, behavioral, and social gains.

## Summary

This chapter has provided those interested in classroom assessment with the basic, necessary tools to begin to engage in Ubiquitous Assessment. Understanding the complexities of the classroom and the methods for assessing what happens in the educational setting can provide the school practitioner with the means by which to ensure change and growth for all students.

Observations in the classroom are essential, required by law, and are the best methods for investigating what the student is facing every day. Remembering that the student is a whole person and not just made up of discrete academic problems or behavioral difficulties allows us to see the student beyond his or her internal issues and examine the environment and other people with whom the student interacts. We have seen many situations where the student would excel academically and behaviorally if she/he was simply removed from a particular teacher's classroom. Oftentimes, however, principals and other administrators are reluctant to change students' teachers because of some underlying belief that all teachers can teach all students. That is simply not the case. Personality issues abound for all of us in our daily interactions and sometimes a simple intervention for all involved is a change from one room to another.

Furthermore, every teacher has her/his own way of presenting material, structuring the classroom, and using academic time. Some students benefit from a classroom with lots of activity, group work, and noise; others simply do not. Knowing the students with whom we work through our interactions with them, observations of them in the natural environment, interviewing important persons in their lives, and assessing them regularly in the instructional material to which they have been exposed can provide us with the intimate knowledge of the student we need to make decisions in their best interests. This is Ubiquitous Assessment.

# Chapter Five

## Assessment in Marriage and Family Counseling

Since the first validation of the norm group for the national licensure examination for the Marriage, Family, and Child Counseling certification (MFCC) in 1975, there has been a revision and improvement in almost every aspect of the profession. Even the original name—Marriage, Family, and Child Counselor or MFCC—has changed to reflect the shift in focus from counseling to therapy: Marriage and Family Therapist (MFT). What has remained consistent for the past thirty years has been the theoretical foundation of systematic approach within the practice of the MFT. Fundamental to the foundation of the practice of the clinician is the belief that the individual exists within the context of familial interactions and that each family represents a unique amalgam of the individuals comprising the family system. The process of assessment and therapy is ubiquitous in that the patterns of interaction among participants are circular. All behavior is a consequence of an earlier action, and the current behavior is an antecedent of things to come. Although the symptom or problem that brings the family to therapy appears to be fixed as the product of one individual's behavior or one aspect of the family, such as the parent's cohesion, the systems approach sees the "identified patient" as only one element of the family's dynamic (Lukas, 1993).

Assessment in marriage and family counseling is differentiated from individual therapy in its requirements that the clinician evaluate the dynamics and interpersonal relations of all of the family members. "In family therapy the whole family is considered the client and your focus will be on the interactions between and among family members" (Lukas, 1993, p. 45). How this process differs from individual approaches is twofold. In family therapy, (1) the individual is viewed as a part of a family system, and (2) the assessment is conducted in a holistic manner. This holistic assessment seeks information about interaction routines between the family members, embedded patterns of behavior, and personality differences. This process is distinctly differentiated from traditional individual psychiatric intake evaluations with methods such as taking a mental status examination (Zimmerman, 1994). In family therapy, counselors examine a system and, more specifically, the interactions within the family for communicative intent (Bateson, 1958). Communicative intent refers to the meaning of the interaction. For example, desire to accomplish an avoidance of conflict may manifest in one of the family members spending inordinate amounts of time at work. Being a workaholic or exhibiting other behavioral manifestations of feelings among the family members can clue the clinician to assess why family members act the way that they do (Minuchin, 1974).

Marriage and family counseling requirements are well matched with Ubiquitous Assessment techniques. Because of the multifarious and multiaxial dimensions of family behavior and interaction, a plethora of familial dynamics, often referred to as the system (Kerr & Bowen, 1988), needs to be evaluated. By assessing family members' feelings of attachment, detachment, sexual behaviors, substance use/abuse, shared participation, common values, use of language, and numerous other distinct aspects of family life, the clinician can come to understand the function each behavior serves. The purpose of this chapter is to introduce different conceptualizations of interpersonal and intrapersonal family dynamics. These concepts or explanations of family interactions will aid the clinician in Ubiquitous Assessment of the dynamics of the system to point the therapy appropriately.

Basic to the practice of the MFT are two major schools of thought. The first, Bowen's systems theory, "is based on the assumptions that the human is a product of evolution and that human behavior is significantly regulated by the same natural processes that regulate the behavior of all living things" (Kerr & Bowen, 1988, p. 3). Bowen's system theory is an attempt to bring understanding to the client of the dynamics of the family. In essence, the client is learning about the emotional system or unit: the family. This conceptualization of the family is modernist and relates to Bowen's interpretation of the laws of nature. Because this system theory is heavy in the application of training, it can be effective with culturally diverse families (Gopaul-McNicol & Thomas-Presswood, 1998).

The second major theory undergirding family therapy work comes from Minuchin (1974). Minuchin's work revolutionized family therapy. Essentially, the therapist does three things in the process known as the structural approach: challenge the symptom, the family structure, and the family reality (Gopaul-McNicol & Thomas-Presswood, 1998). This approach is good for restructuring families that are too enmeshed (family members are too close or are indistinguishable as in the case of a mother and daughter "twinning") or that are lacking in cohesion (relationships are characterized by absence or detachment). For the purposes of understanding and applying Ubiquitous Assessment's role in family therapy, we combine the two approaches and use elements from both schools of thought.

The key to successful practice as an MFT is to develop a broad base of knowledge and experience. Having a deep understanding of the taxonomy of families and the processes of growth and decay within the sets of issues that comprise family experience, the therapist can successfully provide for the needs of most families seeking therapeutic interventions. Through the experience of the 3,500-hour internship required for licensure, the MFT has extensive opportunity to develop excellent interview and observation skills. This internship also provides ample time to acquaint oneself with the knowledge necessary to evaluate or assess the meaning of the information gleaned through interview, observation, and participation with the family in the therapeutic process. The importance of experiential learning within the field of marriage and family therapy is strongly underscored by the requirement for such a lengthy internship.

## The Role of Culture in Family Therapy

One of the most interesting domains of counselor expertise includes the MFT's understanding of cultural norms and how they translate into family behaviors. Families in therapy can benefit tremendously from the counselor's cultural awareness. Knowing special sensitivities and characteristics of cultural groups can assist the counselor in understanding actual or potential problems. As we have articulated in an earlier work, *Critical Multicultural Conversations* (2004), cultural understanding is not formulaic or "cookbook." "Diverse cultural groups in the United States differ as much within groups as they do between groups" (Taylor & Whittaker, 2003, p. 57). Because of this incredible complexity, cultural understanding is a multifarious and evolving process built upon the clinician's knowledge of differing cultures. This understanding can only come from the clinician asking questions to investigate the role of culture within each individual family. This process allows the family to experience the clinician's interest, knowledge, and participation in the family's unique amalgam of cultural identification. For example, within the Hmong culture, the traditional role of the father is represented as the family's supreme authority (Vangay, 2004). Within the traditional culture, all respect is given to the father, and his position of authority is virtually unquestioned. In the agrarian community of Southeast Asia, this model was efficient for getting work accomplished and maintaining cultural congruence. The father was the boss, and the family worked together to grow and harvest their own sustenance. In this culture, boys are valued more highly than girls because of their ability to work and to carry on the family progeny (Vangay, 2004). Asking a Hmong family to describe the role of the father, the clinician can use her/his prior knowledge of Hmong families and incorporate and evaluate the information the family is sharing concerning their likeness to or difference from the traditional family.

Coming to America after the Vietnam War, Hmong families experienced culture shock. Although many Hmong families continued farming traditions, the children of the traditional family began to acculturate within the new community. Watching television and attending school, Hmong children saw a very different lifestyle than the one to which their parents wanted them to adhere. Following the custom of having large families to provide labor for the farms, Hmong parents continue to need children to adopt parent roles when the children are old enough to perform them. Cooking, cleaning, and caring for siblings are difficult in a distinctly different cultural world where many typical young adolescents play after-school sports, have hours of homework, surf the web, and cruise the malls.

Drawing on old-world methods of discipline such as corporal punishment, Hmong parents are confused by the American cultural taboos against hitting and the irony of finding themselves to blame for acting in ways consistent with their culture. Hmong parents find themselves confronting a new culture with its foreign parenting customs and completely different relationships with their offspring. Girls who would formerly command a dowry and begin families of their own around the age of thirteen are now wanting to graduate from high school and move away for college (Vangay, 2004). Boys who were the backbone of the family farm now want cars and money for their vehicle's attendant "boom box," custom wheels, and conversion kits.

Children's and adolescents' attempts to break away from the traditional culture have often been met with violence and frustration. After counseling by Child Protective Services (CPS) for physical abuse, parents are left in a state of confusion concerning their role and authority. Follow-up from CPS interventions commonly includes referral for family counseling. In order to provide meaningful and effective interventions for Hmong families, marriage and family counselors need to be aware of the complex issues of culture (Vangay, 2004).

All cultural groups add influence to the individual family unit. Seeing the cultural influences as shared belief systems, attitudes toward self and others, ways of behaving, and other identifications, the therapist can better understand and be culturally responsive to the clients. In many instances, successful therapy with families representing different cultures will mean giving up some of the therapist's identifications and joining the family in order to experience their dilemma. Whether the family is in synchronicity with original culture or whether the family refutes the identifications synonymous with the original culture, this information is important to the family counselor. As we examine each family and continue to assess its functioning, the contribution of culture can be seen as an important component of the family system. In fact, within some families, the role of culture can be so strong that the family is very strongly influenced by the extended family of not only relatives but the larger ethnic community as well.

## The Functional Family

Families arrive in the office of the marriage and family counselor for many reasons. Either through referral from an individual therapist, referral from another professional such as the family physician, or self-referral, families are coming to therapy to seek solution to one or several identified issues. Most commonly, the family will express that the presenting problem is the result of behaviors manifested by the identified patient. Sometimes referred to as a dysfunctional family, families with serious issues can benefit from the intervention of a trained clinician. A more positive characterization of the family may be to identify the functional components that each family presents. After identifying what works in the family, the therapist can turn to the dysfunctional behaviors and assess these behaviors for their communicative intent. Communicative intent refers to the meaning of the behavior. For example, smoking a cigar may have the communicative intent "leave me alone."

Deconstructing behavior to unveil the communicative intent is the challenge for the family therapist. The system is revealed by the therapist determining each family's unique dynamics and developing meaningful conclusions from the clinical evaluation. In family therapy, this is best achieved as the clinician joins the family for an experiential therapeutic process and effectively becomes one of the family members during the hour of therapy (Minuchin, 1974). In functional families, the characteristic of closeness is readily evident. Sometimes identified as cohesion (Minuchin, 1974), the amount of closeness and distance each family member exhibits is a reflection of feelings family members share or shun (Olson, Portner, & Lavee, 1985). The behavior of the family members can either support or detract from the member's cohesiveness.

As mentioned earlier in this text, each behavior is a manifestation of thought and feeling and the behavior is perceived to be a means to achieving some goal. In another example, a child's gross misconduct can have the effect of bringing both of her or his divorced parents together to try to help support the child. This child's misbehavior is sometimes metaphorically referred to as "the bridge" because it reunifies the separated adults. By deconstructing the behavior and integrating the information gleaned throughout the assessment process, the therapist can situate this knowledge within the therapy. This information can help the parents to see that the misbehavior is reinforced by their attention. A more therapeutic practice for the family may be to provide the attention for positive behavior and deny the reinforcement for misbehavior. Being aware that the behavior is a code for expressing feelings, the therapist can help the parents create effective changes.

Because each family is unique, norm-referenced assessment instruments are often inadequate, invalid, and unreliable when used with families representing cultures excluded from or marginally included within the norm population. Furthermore,

> many practitioners are not trained to assess children (or adults) from culturally and linguistically diverse backgrounds. Often they do not understand how cultural incompatibilities bring about practices that suppress the performance of an individual from a culturally and linguistically diverse population. The lack of testing procedures that guide administration of psychological tests and interpretation of results adds to the inability to properly assess this population. The instruments often chosen to assess culturally and linguistically diverse children (and adults) tend to be inadequate and unable to yield results that reflect the true potential of this population. The standardization norms of these tests frequently do not represent the group of the individual being assessed when he or she is from a non-Western-European culturally influenced background. Hence, decisions about education and treatment are often grounded in inaccurate data. (Gopaul-McNicol & Thomas-Presswood, 1998, p. 47)

For these reasons, most clinicians do not use standardized testing as a part of their assessments with families (Boughner et al., 1994). The preferred evaluation methods include combinations of clinical interviewing, observation of behavior in therapy, observation in the home or other appropriate settings, and other nonstandardized assessment procedures. The overall goal of these assessments is to examine the quality of the family dynamics to determine sources of distress or dysfunction and to uncover protective and positive attributes from which to conduct therapeutic interventions. In addition, the assessment needs to be a gestalt or immediate evaluation. The family needs to stay situated in the here and now, and using techniques that require scoring and interpretation at a later date does not facilitate the process.

Because of the nature of family function, about the only constant within the family is change. According to Minuchin (1974), "The premises of change are different in family therapy. Change is seen as occurring through the process of the therapist's affiliation with the family and his restructuring of the family in a carefully planned way, so as to transform dysfunctional transactional patterns" (p. 91). As therapy proceeds, individuals change and the relationships between all of the family members evolve, too. Although some constancy remains, the effects of family dynamics cannot be overlooked. The family's evolution is natural and, if anything, problems today can reflect old coping mechanisms and ineffective adjustment activities. For example, when a child is young, indulging behavior on the part of the parent to adjust the child's mood can be very effective. Putting the child in the car and driving to the ice cream stand can have a restorative effect on a bored four-year-old and her/his onerous mood. However, turning the keys and a credit card over to a bored adolescent can result in an entirely different set of consequences. Both are parental acts to appease, yet the result and appropriateness are opposite.

The reality of family life is that it is composed of dynamics and the journey is not an approximation of reality: it *is* real life. As one of our friends is fond of saying, "This is not a dress rehearsal." Inherent in real life is the complex combination of wins and losses known as the human experience. Being and experiencing our humanness is an imperfect process. Life is loaded with many differing challenges. What makes each family unique is the way in which we cope with the challenges and issues we confront. Family therapy is a tool for us to use when we are at a loss for our own answers or when we are in denial that the problem even exists.

It is important to remember that families approach therapy with considerable experience and many good, "tried-and-true" family coping skills. The clinician's first instinct should be to look for the positive attributes within the family. Beginning with an inventory of "what works" is an appropriate starting point. This method is related to work in positive psychology (Lopez, Snyder, & Rasmussen, 2003). Looking at the health of the family encourages the members that their experience is not solely pathological. The family does have positive attributes, and within themselves they have the resources to find unique ways to solve their problems and improve the quality of their lives (Power, 2003). Assessing and discovering the family's sense of humor, hope, and vision can improve a sense of optimism about their ability to control their own destiny and future outcomes (Carver & Scheier, 1999). Although families present themselves to solve the problem for which they sought therapy, they will ally themselves and include the therapist within the family more readily if they feel that the family strengths and attributes are appreciated.

Just what comprises a high-quality existence is relative. This is a perfect topic for the inclusion of all of the members because it indulges fantasy and encourages imaginative play. As family members tell what would improve the quality of their life, they are invited to "join" in the discussion: a key component of family therapy (Lukas, 1993). By sharing her/his wishes for improved quality of life, all of the family members are participating and that is essential for the therapist's success. Nonparticipants are sending a message, too, but it is different one. Therapists need to welcome the challenges their clients give them, and view the resistant client (usually the adolescent who was dragged into the office) as a vital part of the family system.

## Ubiquitous Assessment of Family Dynamics

All behaviors can be interpreted to have a communicative intent. Coming to another family member for consolation or love, avoiding one another through physical detachment, or hiding behind the newspaper while sitting at the breakfast table—all that we do can be seen as a form of communication. Although Freud would attribute these behaviors to subconscious motivations, family therapists see the dynamic operations of the family from a systems perspective. That is, there exists a series of antecedents (initial acts) that create consequences or subsequent behaviors. The consequences, in turn, become antecedents and thus the system is maintained. Some family therapists refer to this dynamic as a merry-go-round. It appears that there is movement among the participants; however, the end result is a trigonometric, repeating sine function. Behaviors and motivations are continually revisited. Another term for these routines is "baggage." We carry these psychological issues with us wherever we go. In families, this experience presents differently than it does with individuals. Family baggage can include family secrets such as sexual abuses or fears of rejections such as being disowned or cut out of a will or trust fund.

Although we assess the family members individually, we are most concerned with the interactional patterns and system of family dynamics. It is impossible to ignore individuals within the family, but it is essential to remember that the goal is to avoid becoming focused on any one of the members, such as the identified patient, and to keep trying to see the family as a whole. In some ways this process can be represented by the parable of the three blind men. Three blind men are walking across a savannah when they encounter an elephant. The first man reaches out and touches the elephant's trunk. What a large snake, he thinks. The second man feels a giant leg and imagines a tree with a soft bark. The third man rests beside the elephant's stomach and thinks he is against a huge wall. In family therapy, we need to remember that we seek to understand the sum of the parts (Remen, 2000). Although we cannot ignore the role the individuals play in the family dynamics, the assessment is of the entire family as a system of interconnectedness.

Seeing repeated patterns of behavior and recognizing their function within the family is the work of the marriage and family counselor. Many times the therapist will see and hear similar scenarios. The patterns of behavior consistent with alcoholic families, families experiencing recovery from the loss of a parent or child, codependency within single-parent families, and other classic family problems can be easily identified by a skilled clinician (Jesse, 1989). Ubiquitous Assessment examines the entirety of the interaction patterns and analyzes all of the components to comprehend the family's dynamics. Evaluation techniques include interviewing, observing, and collecting information that allows insight into the daily functioning of the family. As the therapy continues, the information available to the therapist increases. In this way the assessment and therapy continue to intertwine.

## Birth Order and Children's Roles in Family Dynamics

Family therapists can gain insight into family dynamics by understanding the unique role children perform depending upon their birth order. This section will explain some of the current theory of birth order and the nuclear family's adoption of birth-order characteristics. For the clinician, seeing how each family handles the chores of their roles will provide insight into the dynamics of the family. In traditional and nontraditional families, roles are adopted, and members identify themselves around the positions they hold. Assessment of roles adds to the understanding of the family's cohesion and functionality.

The firstborn has a unique and special place within the family. Being the leader, the firstborn is imbued with the responsibility to carry out the family mission and to represent the identity to the world of the family (Hoopes & Harper, 1987). The pride and hope of the family is deeply invested in this child, and she/he is the object of considerable attention. This function of the firstborn creates a type of narcissism. Even if the role is only imagined, the firstborn perceives that the eyes of others are upon her/him, and she/he is the symbol of the family itself. In adolescents this phenomenon is called "imaginary audience." The assumption is that everyone is watching you, even if the act is as simple as walking across a school campus.

Being the firstborn can support success or it can lead to an opposite outcome. The leader has the opportunity to take control of younger siblings, to set examples for others to follow, and to comprehend more about the world because of her/his advanced age. The leader may also find the job to be too daunting and take an opposite tack. Jack Nicholson exemplifies this position in his role in the movie *Five Easy Pieces.* In this film, Nicholson is the son of a famous concert pianist. Nicholson returns home from his job as a honky-tonk piano player in Las Vegas after his father had experienced a stroke and was left with no speech or mobility. In one of the movie's most tender scenes, Nicholson wheels his father out onto a field and confesses that he couldn't ever live up to the standards of the family. That was why he gave up the family tradition of classical music and took an alternative path.

How the firstborn handles the awesome responsibility of being the leader can vary greatly. The responsibility of the firstborn can often lead to productive and goal-oriented behaviors. The firstborn wants to model success, and accomplishments are one of the best examples of one's achievements. Unfortunately, the firstborn can also become trapped in self-worth that is dependent upon good work. For these individuals, just being loved for who you are is not congruent with their achieving motivations. This can lead to the development of feelings of failure when attempted achievements go awry. According to Hoopes and Harper (1987), "First children tend to forget past accomplishments and focus on what they must do in the present. Because their self-esteem is linked to continuous productivity, and because they worry that their efforts are insufficient, first children are concerned if they are not involved in a task" (p. 44). The pressure is on, no matter what the outcome is.

Second children hold an enigmatic position within the family. Assuming that there will be a third child coming along to assume the "baby" role, the second child is in a sort of no-man's land. Not the baby and not the leader, the middle or second child can be a source of conflict for the family. Challenging the leadership of the firstborn, the second child can develop some disconcerting and oppositional behaviors. Not being able to successfully dethrone the firstborn, the second child may either continue the fight or take refuge in withdrawal (Hoopes & Harper, 1987).

The word most often used to describe second-born children is confused. Confusion is evident in the second-born child's fluctuation from one type of coping strategy to another in an attempt to define herself/himself. Seeking an explicit position, the second born may attempt several approximations at a behavior before completing the task. For example, dressing may take multiple robings and disrobings before the desired attire is selected. The second child is simultaneously looking to the leader for direction and trying to develop her/his unique way of being. As the second child continues to seek the answer to the question, "Where do I belong?," second-born children need special support and nurturing to relieve them of the threat of being rejected and to build a healthy self-esteem.

The third-born, or the baby, is in the enviable position of entering an established family. The advantages of having multiple opportunities for getting one's needs met is clear. Myths about the baby are often realized by family members indulgences. In families that function smoothly, the baby is well cared for and experiences ample amounts of attention. This creates a strong sense of self-esteem and protection. The negative result of this security can be a lack of acceptance of responsibility. Protection of the youngest can extend a form of denial or psychosocial amnesia. Adding denial to the natural immaturity and attendant irresponsibility can lead to some unpleasant behaviors. Often the baby can be the identified patient when the family comes to therapy because of the baby's lack of understanding of the consequences for her/his behavior.

In a counseling session with the youngest child of a divorced family with four boys, the teacher was commenting to the family that her efforts at correcting the youngest child were unrewarded. She felt that no matter what she did the boy would not change his behavior and her authority was undermined. When the boy was confronted by his parents concerning his lack of respect for the teacher's authority, the boy responded, "Well, so what? No one cares what Mrs. Miller thinks, anyway." The baby is very often unable to hear the criticism. Having been in a protected position since birth, they often refuse to accept responsibility for their behavior. They are the ultimate product of their environment, and they feel fully justified in their position. Why not? They have had all their family's support: certainly the whole family can't be wrong. According to Hoopes and Harper (1987), "One of the most frustrating characteristics of fourth children is their refusal to accept responsibility for their behaviors" (p. 78). It will be a relief to them to know that their role as the identified patient is not solely their fault. We are all part of a system and function in relationship to the family as a whole.

## The Dysfunctional Family

If anything is universally enmeshed within the American culture, it is the drug known as alcohol. Alcohol's presence is almost everywhere. Advertised across the street from our elementary schools on the local grocery store window, promoted on banners at sporting events, consumed in church as the metaphoric blood of Christ, sipped in celebration, and served as a balm at wakes: alcohol flows through almost every vein of American culture. Its use is so prevalent that its misuse is often undetected. Known as functional alcoholics, Americans' drinking and working habits mask the more stereotypical image of the bum on the street and the down-and-out drunk. In fact, many of our heroes, presidents, and family members were or are those euphemistically titled "heavy drinkers." Lyndon B. Johnson was reputed to consume a liter of 101 proof Wild Turkey every day of his presidency. Churchill was famous for his daily fifth of gin. President George W. Bush has admitted that he was a "heavy drinker" until he turned forty: a heavy drinker with two arrests and convictions for driving under the influence of alcohol (van Wagtendonk, 2000). Alcohol abounds.

So how do we sort out the dysfunctional family from the stereotypical success stories? First, we assess why the family is before us. Usually, the presenting problem in "alcoholic" families is the substance abuse. Referred by a family physician or the court, the family is in therapy to remove the denial that has attended the drinking and maintained the alcoholic's lifestyle. Although Alcoholics Anonymous contends that alcoholism is a disease, whatever the definition, family members share in this malady's disastrous consequences.

Alcoholic families differ in detail and each one has a unique story to tell. However, alcoholic families share many similarities. The guilt, blame, denial, shame, losses, and tragedies experienced during the alcoholic's substance use are all pieces of the story. In the Alcoholics Anonymous meeting process, the telling of the story (sometimes referred to as a drunk-a-log) is a large part of the therapy. Breaking the denial and admitting powerlessness over alcohol's control is called the first step toward recovery. In family therapy, the recovery is for the victims of the alcoholic's substance abuse. Recognizing the alcoholic's effect on the family is one the goals of family therapy and the assessment is very much a part of the treatment (Jesse, 1989). Honestly confronting the issues of alcohol abuse reflects openness to the therapy. Denial of the effects of alcohol on the family is indicative of the need for stronger intervention.

Next to the spouse, the children are the biggest victims of the alcoholic's behavior. Being under the care of an irresponsible and incapacitated adult is one of the worst scenarios a child can endure. "In dysfunctional families, the parents rarely acknowledge the positive contributions of their children; they focus instead on what is painful, wrong, and hopeless" (Hoopes & Harper, 1987, p. 79). Having to experience the loss of the parent to alcohol, children develop unique styles of behavior and create their own coping mechanisms. The children of alcoholics (COAs) often exhibit marked and identifiable personality characteristics. These personality types have been given labels to identify their unique attributes: the rebel, the loner, the hero, and the joker. Just as behavior in nonalcoholic families, each of these roles or behavioral sets fulfills a function within the alcoholic family. The point is not to label the child but to identify patterns of behavior and to understand the child's communicative intent.

Within alcoholic families, the rebel is often the provocative communicator and the one frequently referred to as the identified patient. As psychologists, the rebel is a type we see very often because of this individual's oppositional and defiant behaviors. These individuals are angry, and the rebellious are not afraid to show it. Having been raised in an alcoholic family, these youths are not convinced that anyone in authority has any right to their respect and, in fact, their distrust of authority figures leads them to attempt to dismantle any adult's superior position. The oppositional-defiant child's reaction to most rules is summed up with the expression, "Fuck that shit!" Tracy Chapman's song *Fast Car* recounts the life of a young girl, her lover, and her alcoholic father. Her wish is to get a fast car and ride out of her family's grueling grip to a place where she feels she "belongs."

More extreme reactions to parent's alcoholism are identified with conduct disorder, a personality disorder. Although we will describe the identification of personality disorders in chapter 7 (assessment in mental health settings), conduct disorder and the milder oppositional-defiant disorder are frequently a part of the rebel's personality. This rebel is antiauthority and can be dangerous. Conduct disorder "rebels" frequently end up incarcerated for taking their anger out on others. It is easy to see why they could be the identified patient. Your assessment may reveal why they are so rebellious.

The loner is the child who internalizes all of the family's alcoholic woes. Most often depressed, the loner may cut school and stay home. She/he avoids conflict and keeps in the shadows. These individuals have found that the best way to cope with mom or dad's drinking is to stay in their room or to hide inside a novel. The loner can also choose to hang around the house because they fear their parents' demise. Staying home and taking care of the parent is preferable to coming home and finding her/his mother or father passed out on the floor or worse. The loner, through their silent suffering, waits for the problem to resolve.

The loner is often underidentified for therapy. Because of the loner's quiet coping strategy, she/he is easily overlooked. Many adult caregivers wrongly assume that a quiet person is content or satisfied. They may not know that within the loner's family, the unspoken rule is, "Don't do anything to make your father mad." Talking with loners in the counseling office can be challenging because their feelings have been stuffed for so long, they have difficulty articulating their position within the family.

A more animated and colorful family member, the joker is trying to refocus the attention away from the parent and make humor the balm for everyone's pain. Rather than let the alcoholic parent sit in her/his chair and bring everyone down with tired ranting "something about Republicans" (Soto, 1999), the joker can provide an endless entertainment for the family. Practical jokes, stand-up routines, and the provision of chaos are the tools of the joker. Whatever the joker does, it keeps the focus away from the alcoholic. Family members and outsiders are so entertained by the joker that the miserable situation of the parent's substance abuse is masked.

The joker is, in many ways, a lost child, too. Frantic attempts to provide comic relief for the family often leave her/him in despair over her/his own situation. The clown in the classroom, the joker continues to seek attention in other venues. Being stuck in the joker role can be vexing for adults outside of the nuclear family. Not knowing that this behavior is lifesaving within the child's family, the joker is often blamed for spreading her/his chaos outside the home.

The polar opposite of the joker, the hero is trying to fix the family by demonstrating an endless stream of good works. By bringing honor to the family, the hero disproves that there is or could ever be anything wrong. Why? There could not be a product this fine coming from a dysfunctional family. Heroes work to create the myth that everything is great. The hero is often captain of the school's football team, president of the class, a member of the National Honor Society, or all of the above.

This child can be one of the most hurting, because she/he is working double-time to hold up the image of perfection. The heroine/hero is lonely in her/his achievement because her/his parent cannot share in the experience the joy of their child's accomplishments. Very often, this child would rather that her/his parent stay away from the awards banquets, too. Showing up drunk and making the child embarrassed or humiliated would ruin the hero's cover-up and illusion of the "perfect family." For all of the children of alcoholics, there is tremendous pain and suffering.

## Genograms and Family Mapping

One of the best assessment tools for a family therapist is a genogram. Initially labeled a "family diagram" by Bowen (Kerr & Bowen, 1988), the process is essentially the same. Standardized by family therapists in the 1980s, genograms provide the therapist with a concrete tool with which to examine the changing structures of the family. The genogram is a representational map of the family. Its use and function is to delineate "structural, relational, and functional information about a family" (McGoldrick, Gerson, & Shellenberger, 1999, p. 2).

The genogram is an excellent example of Ubiquitous Assessment. The gathering of factual information and the stories of the family comprise both assessment and therapy simultaneously. In the telling of the stories, understanding of current dynamics naturally unfolds. According to McGoldrick et al. (1999), "clinicians typically do not compartmentalize assessment and treatment. Each interaction of the therapist with the family informs the assessment and thus influences the next intervention" (p. 2). As mentioned earlier in this chapter, the process is circular.

Genograms are an effective tool for teaching clients about the systematic nature of families. Families tend to create patterns of behavior that repeat and resurface in multiple generations. Families are comprised of many ingredients that make this repetition inevitable: genetics, culture, environment, religion, social status, and behavioral styles. Being able to construct a map depicting the flow and changes within the family can assist the therapist and the family members understand their current situation. Although the maxim "the best predictor of future behavior is past behavior" is not reflective of changes in systems and personalities, the truth of the statement bears evaluation. Often, family moves and actions are in opposition to the family "traditions" and that is grist for the psychologist's mill, too. Many people will never enjoy a glass of wine because their parent's alcohol abuse ruined the taste for them.

The essential element of the genogram involves the telling of stories. How we link and separate are the essence of family life and function. From the facts of births, deaths, marriages, divorces, moves, and other major life events, the secrets behind the occurrences can be comprehended. This is essentially the same philosophy as we earlier recounted: behavior serves a function and holds a communicative intent. Stephanie Dowrick (1991) sensitively revealed the feeling by hearing Alexandra's story:

> Alexandra is a landscape painter living in the South of England, a courageous woman who has managed with years of effort to overcome a pattern of emotional blindness and inadvertent neglect. This has allowed her to become wise and generous not only to herself, but also to the mother who was far from ideal.
>
> Alexandra knows that when she was a baby her mother "chose" to leave her right at the bottom of the family's large garden where her crying wouldn't disturb anyone. The pain of this knowledge is not lessened but is made more bearable by also knowing the circumstances of her birth.
>
> "About two years ago my mother became very angry with me. It was one day when I was visiting her. I think that in some way I was

> threatening her sense of our fusion. Anyhow, she became so angry that she embarked on the story of my birth. It was the first time that she had told it to me and as she told it I understood that of my mother's hatred for me, this was the deepest part (I don't mean that she doesn't have other feelings), and that nothing she could ever say to me would be worse than this. It may sound awful but it was terribly real and so ultimately freeing. She said that the pain of my birth was the worst thing she had ever experienced and that even now she remembers it as vividly as when it was happening. (In fact, she had a quick labor with me.) I caused such intense pain in the process of my birth that she was convinced that I was going to kill her. She said to the doctor that she felt she was going to die, over and over. He said that people did not die in childbirth these days, but that made no impression on her.
>
> "Then, somehow, she got the idea she could prevent me being born. Mum said, 'I thought to myself, no, this child has a right to live. I must allow her to be born.' So I was born amidst her fear and anger. Well, when I came out I looked at her, and Mum said that with that look she felt I could see right through her, and that I saw into her soul, and that nothing escaped me. I seemed to be detached, observing, and seeing. (Which seems to be the source of some of her paranoia about me.) I suppose she felt I could see her anger." (p. 145)

In the genogram, the connection between Alexandra and her mother is represented by a line; however, the meaning is drawn from the map through the involvement and engaging of the entire family in the process (Alexander & Clark, 1998). The process of discussing the interrelationships is where the richness of the genogram lies. Opening up and telling the stories of the relationships is the genogram's genius.

Genograms have many varied applications. Because of the wealth of research and interest in genograms, their use has become diversified. "A wide range of uses and modifications have been proposed: family sculpting of genograms (Papp, Silverstein, & Carter, 1973; Satir, 1972), culturegrams (Congress, 1994; Hardy & Laszloffy, 1995), gendergrams (White & Tyson-Rawson, 1995), sexual genograms (Hoff & Berman, 1986), genogrids emphasizing the social network developed to facilitate work with lesbians (Burke & Farber, 1997), family play genograms (Buurma, 1999; Gill & Sobol, 2000); and genograms with many age groups and different symptoms and life situations" (McGoldrick, Gerson, & Shellenberger, 1999, p. 149). As is evident from the work of McGoldrick et al., there are numerous sources for genogram information. There are even computer-assisted programs that generate genograms (Gerson & Shellenberger, 1999). Clearly, genograms are a valuable tool for the marriage and family therapist.

**Ubiquitous Assessment of the Family System**

In the process of family therapy it is easy to see that the assessment process is ubiquitous. The distinction between assessment and therapy is nonexistent when the therapist is able to achieve an integration of the two processes. As the conversations in therapy continue and deepen, the therapist is accumulating more and more information about the client's history, experiences, and feelings. In many respects, it is the goal of the therapist for the client to do some self-assessing as the process unfolds. This is not to say that the therapist does not assess. However, the client's assessment of her/his own problem is of greater therapeutic value than being told that the problem is, whatever diagnosis is concluded by the therapist. "Therapy based on systems theory is guided by the assumption that it is not necessary for a therapist to diagnose the family's problem. If the therapist is reasonably successful at maintaining a systems orientation, the family will begin to diagnose their own problems and to develop their own direction for change. It is important for the therapist to make his own assessment of the nature of the family problem, but he does this primarily to maintain his bearings in the family and to plan productive areas for inquiry" (Kerr & Bowen, 1988, p. 293).

Although these authors believe that family systems theory contributes greatly to our understanding of the family, we believe that each family is a unique amalgam of the individual ingredients of culture, genetics, environment, emotion, and personality characteristics possessed by the family and its individual members. The family comes to therapy motivated to find a solution to their problems and, concomitantly, relief from their pain. As therapists, it is our job to help the family grow to better know themselves and to empower the family to be able to solve their own issues. Through the process of our becoming one of the family for the length of the therapy, we can participate fully in the discovery of the solution with the family. Through the exciting and intimate experiential process of family therapy, there is tremendous potential for learning, growth, and change.

# Chapter Six

# Assessment in School Psychology

When people think about what school psychologists do, the first thing that comes into their minds is "testing." Unfortunately, school psychologists have gotten this reputation from what they most often do and while there have been widespread calls for reform within the profession, many school psychologists have been unwilling or unable to heed the call for change.

School psychologists, however, have a much broader range of training than simply testing and are well equipped to provide Ubiquitous Assessment in the school setting. Fagan and Wise (2000) define a school psychologist as "a professional psychological practitioner whose general purpose is to bring a psychological perspective to bear on the problems of educators and the clients educators serve" (p. 4). They are trained to work with children from preschool through the college level, and serve regular education students, students at risk for school failure, and special education students. Special education students can include children with severe or profound handicapping conditions; learning disabilities; mental retardation; visual or hearing impairments; health problems, including children who have chronic (asthma) and or severe (cancer) medical issues; emotional disturbances; attention deficit disorders; and autism. School psychologists have training in both psychology and education and should use those skills to work closely with children, parents, teachers, administrators, other school personnel, mental health professionals, and community members when appropriate. In addition to assessment (as differentiated from testing), school psychologists are also trained in consultation; counseling; developing, implementing, and evaluating interventions; engaging in the development, implementation, and evaluation of prevention programs for children; conducting in-services and other educational services to the school, family, and community members; and conducting research and program evaluations (National Association of School Psychologists, n.d.).

### Consultation

The primary role of the school psychologist involves consultation. Consultation should be the first service provided to those individuals making referrals and should be ongoing throughout the assessment-intervention/treatment process. Consultation as defined by Zins and Erchul (1995) is "a method of providing preventively oriented psychological and educational services in which consultants and consultees form cooperative partnerships and engage in a reciprocal, systematic problem-solving process within an ecobehavioral framework" (pp. 609–10). Consultation is an indirect service delivery model whereby the consultant (e.g., school psychologist) provides services to the consultee (i.e., the teacher or parent), and the consultee provides the direct services to the student or client. School psychologists generally serve several schools so they are not always available. By providing indirect services to teachers and parents, they are able to provide input and assist in developing intervention/treatment plans to those persons who will be directly responsible for implementing the plans.

There are three major models of consultation used in the schools depending on the orientation of the school psychologist: (1) mental health consultation, (2) organizational-development consultation, and (3) behavioral consultation. Other types of consultation described in the literature include collaborative consultation (Gutkin & Curtis, 1990) and instructional consultation (Rosenfield & Gravois, 1999). All of the models have two goals in common. The first is to provide the consultee with assistance in changing a child's academic, behavior, or social skills problems. This is directly relevant to Ubiquitous Assessment. Using consultation techniques provides the means by which the school psychologist, working with teachers and parents, can ensure a seamless process from assessment through the problem-identification interview to the development, implementation, and evaluation of intervention and treatment plans for use with clients/students. The second goal is that the consultee will learn to enhance his/her skills and be able to intervene or prevent such problems from occurring with other children in the future (Kratochwill, Elliott, & Carrington Rotto, 1995). School psychologists engaging in consultation believe that it is in their best interests to be "giving psychology away" to those with whom they work (Miller, 1969). There is simply not enough time in the day for school psychologists or other mental health professionals to provide all of the services needed to all of the students at risk. Through consultation, school psychologists can assist, teach, and model practices that will aid consultees throughout their teaching or parenting careers.

Viewed in this way, consultation should be the basic framework for any services provided, including Ubiquitous Assessment. Through consultation, the students with whom school psychologists work are immediately provided with the services they need rather than waiting for traditional tests to be given and reported on. This process of consultation to intervention is consistent with the proposed changes in the reauthorization of IDEA.

Consultation is a cooperative, collaborative process between two (or more) people with expertise in particular areas. The school psychologist has expertise in the fields of learning and behavior; teachers have expertise in the day-to-day functioning of their classrooms, in curriculum, in their understanding of other students for whom they are responsible, and in their knowledge of the student in question; and parents have knowledge about their home lives and how they live their lives, and are the individuals most intimately connected to the student in question. By working together on an equal level and contributing different knowledge to the problem, the consultant and consultee can solve the problem and prevent future problems.

All school psychologists should be knowledgeable about the process of consultation and should be able to engage in consultation "on-the-fly." Most often, school psychologists must consult while walking in from the parking lot, while walking down a hallway, or in the teachers' workroom. School psychologists do not have the advantage of meeting with consultees for hours at a time to work on a problem; they must work efficiently and effectively throughout each day. The stages of consultation (described below), then, are often conducted quickly during brief interactions between the consultant and consultee.

Problem identification is the first stage of consultation and often takes the most time. A problem presented by a teacher or parent may not be identified as the actual target behavior during the initial steps in stage one. Through the problem-identification interview, the specifics of the dilemma facing the teacher or parent can be acknowledged, allowing for the initial development of an intervention/treatment plan. Once the problem has been identified, the consultant moves on to the next stage, called problem analysis, whereby the situation is further examined in terms of resources available and other relevant environmental factors that will impact the development of the intervention plan. The third stage is the identification of a treatment or intervention plan. Together, the consultant and consultee brainstorm solutions to the problem, evaluate the possible solutions, and then select one of the possible solutions. They then develop the plan and write down the specific steps that will be followed during implementation to make sure that all participants understand and agree on the particulars of the intervention plan. At this time, the consultant and consultee also identify responsibilities, as both parties should have specific roles for intervention implementation (not just the teacher or parent). Once these important decisions have been made, the plan should be implemented. Over time, both the consultant and consultee will need to work together to evaluate the plan and determine the effectiveness of the outcomes. Only by doing so can treatment integrity be ensured, resulting in the best outcomes for the student. Unfortunately, the last step, evaluating the plan, is often overlooked. All interventions should be evaluated via data collection and analysis. When a plan is not evaluated, there is no way of knowing whether the plan was actually successful and whether the student was able to generalize to other settings the skills learned during the intervention.

## Counseling Psychology

Issues related to school counseling covered in chapter 3 of this volume apply to the school psychologist as well as the school counselor. Many schools at the elementary level do not have school counselors, and at the secondary level schools often do not have counselors who are able to engage in personal counseling. The role of counselor may be relegated to the school psychologist in these situations.

The ideal situation, however, occurs when both a school counselor and school psychologist are assigned to the same school. Working together, they can designate the types of counseling each will provide in order to make the best use of their theoretical orientations and provide the best services to students. School psychologists, depending on their training, will have different theoretical perspectives related to counseling. However, following the model of Ubiquitous Assessment, all school psychologists should adopt a philosophy of "child-school-family" when engaging in counseling (Tharinger & Stafford, 1995).

The types of counseling that are most often provided by school psychologists include individual and group counseling. Including issues such as suicide intervention, divorce, social skills, grief, anger, and self-esteem, the school psychologist may be required to offer any type of counseling a student might need in order to be successful in the academic environment. What school psychologists do not do is engage in long-term therapy with students and families. School psychologists can provide brief, solution-focused counseling and should be a referral source for students and families needing more intensive treatment.

In order to successfully engage in counseling from a Ubiquitous Assessment perspective, the school psychologist should begin his/her evaluation immediately when the referral is made. This is done through consultation with the teacher and parent. Following this problem-identification interview, assessment and intervention plans should be developed. Often this will include clinical interviewing and/or counseling with the student. A plan for the counseling sessions should be established with specific goals identified for the student receiving counseling. "The general goals of counseling can include alleviating the child's emotional and cognitive distress, changing the child's behavior, assisting with self-understanding, helping the child meet current developmental tasks successfully, supporting needed environmental changes, and promoting a more positive fit between the child and the systems in which she or he resides (e.g., school and family)" (Tharinger & Stafford, 1995, p. 896). Too often we have seen situations where a teacher has requested counseling and the student meets with the school psychologist (or counselor) and no goals are identified or plans made, resulting in minimal or no progress from the "counseling." Within Ubiquitous Assessment, counseling should be viewed as an integrated part of the assessment process. As the school psychologist interacts with the counselee, information is gathered that helps the student to identify possible changes that need to be made in his/her world.

The stages for counseling in Ubiquitous Assessment can be delineated in the following manner:

1. Problem-solving consultation with referral source
2. Problem analysis and brainstorming with referral source
3. Interviews with important individuals in the student's life
4. Interviews and observations with the student
5. Identification of the goals for counseling
6. Determination of methods to be used
7. Begin counseling (including discussions of confidentiality and rules)
8. Establish the counseling relationship
9. Evaluate the treatment/intervention plan as time progresses
10. Reevaluate the methods and treatment/intervention plan.
11. Continue consultation with teacher(s) and parent(s)
12. When goals achieved, plan termination of counseling
13. Terminate counseling
14. Continue with follow-up and evaluate outcomes
15. Write up counseling report

Every step is important to ensure the best long-range outcomes for the student. Counseling can provide exactly what the student needs to be successful and to reach his/her potential.

## Intervention and Treatment Plans

The main premise taken in Ubiquitous Assessment is that assessment is not something unique and apart from intervention/treatment but a seamless process whereby assessment leads directly to the intervention plan. This theoretical perspective should not be foreign to school psychologists as it has been discussed by many leaders in the field over the last two decades (e.g., Fagan & Wise, 2000).

Intervention/treatment should be guided by problem-solving consultation, interviews, and observations. Instead of spending time and money engaged in administering time-consuming traditional standardized tests, school psychologists should be engaged in these other functions. Through the use of these techniques, school psychologists should develop knowledge and understanding about the student that others may not be aware of. They should be intimately knowledgeable about the student in question and have an understanding of the factors that result in the student's troubling behaviors. Only by doing so can effective intervention/treatment plans be developed that will serve the student well.

Interventions and treatments can include counseling (as discussed above); classroom-based programs for academic problems, social skills problems, and behavior problems; home-based programs for homework completion and completing chores; and community-based interventions for riding the bus (for students who are mentally challenged) to vocational programs for students wanting to work. Intervention and treatment plans should be "(a) generalized from developmental studies and intervention research, (b) founded on the realities of settings determined through problem analysis, and (c) based on the predicted success of the least-intrusive intervention likely to accomplish the goals of change" (Barnett, 2002, p. 1253). Interventions and treatment plans should be selected based on their validity for the particular student and the problem that particular student is having. Single-case research designs are most effective as they allow for the comparison of effects across interventions/treatments, individuals, and environments. By using the single-case designs, we are able to evaluate our interventions/treatments across time and have an ongoing record of our success/failure by graphing the results.

Our interventions/treatments also must have treatment integrity. Treatment integrity refers to the degree to which an intervention/treatment is carried out as planned (Yeaton & Sechrist, 1981). Factors that affect treatment integrity include the complexity of the intervention, the time involved to implement the intervention, the materials and resources needed to implement the intervention, the number of persons needed to implement the intervention, the perceived and actual effectiveness of the intervention, the competition of other demands on the individual(s) carrying out the intervention, and the motivation of those individual(s) implementing the intervention. These all must be evaluated when we develop, implement, and evaluate our interventions/treatments. Many intervention and treatment plans that are developed and implemented are never implemented in the manner identified during consultation because of the potential for the above factors to interfere. So while we may be told that the intervention/treatment was not successful, the reality may be that the intervention was simply not implemented as planned.

Intervention and treatment plans need to be developed for use in the natural environment and be realistic for that environment. Again, only by engaging in Ubiquitous Assessment and becoming extremely knowledgeable and developing an understanding of the student and his or her life circumstances can we develop interventions and treatments that will be successful.

## Prevention Programs

An important area for school psychology practice is that of prevention. Rather than wait until a time students are in desperate straits and need counseling or treatment/intervention plans, school psychologists should spend their time focused on how to prevent future problems from occurring for students. Areas of prevention that school psychologists engage in include crisis, violence, teenage pregnancy, drug and alcohol abuse, academic failure, and, of course, suicide prevention, to name a few.

There are three types of prevention identified in the literature: primary prevention, secondary prevention, and tertiary prevention. Primary prevention refers to efforts to halt the development of new cases of a problem long before it occurs (Zins & Forman, 1988). Primary prevention may focus on "(a) competencies [that] may be increased through education; (b) training [that] may be provided to help people develop coping strategies to short-circuit negative effects of stressful life events and crises; (c) environments [that] may be modified to reduce, or counteract, harmful circumstances, or (d) support system [that] may be developed more fully" (Hightower, Johnson, & Haffey, 1995, p. 311).

Secondary and tertiary prevention are not true prevention. Secondary prevention refers to the early identification of problems in order that intervention/treatment can be provided. Through early intervention, problems may be solved more quickly without long-lasting effects. Tertiary prevention is actual intervention and/or treatment for a problem that is identified. A problem such as substance abuse, in which all persons in an individual's life are well aware of the problem, would be provided with a treatment program rather than a prevention program.

In order to develop a prevention program in the schools, school psychologists first need to develop a needs assessment survey to determine the most important area for which a prevention program could be implemented. Administrators, teachers, parents, and students may have differing ideas about what potential problems students face and whether or not a special program is needed. The school psychologist should work closely with school personnel, families, and community constituents in order to develop a meaningful, cost-effective program with the potential for positive outcomes. As with other areas of service delivery, the evaluation of the prevention program is essential. Too often, programs are maintained even though there are no data to indicate the effectiveness of the program. The resources wasted and, more importantly, the students' lives ignored through ineffective prevention programs, can be avoided through evaluation.

Prevention goes hand in hand with Ubiquitous Assessment. Making ourselves available to those with whom we work, looking at the seamless process from assessment to intervention, and developing the commitment and attitude to provide the best services at all times are the bases for Ubiquitous Assessment.

## In-services and Educational Services

Another service school psychologists can provide is in-service training or staff development. Such educational services fit nicely with Ubiquitous Assessment as the psychologist attempts to assist others working with students to provide the best services possible. "Staff development is a serious and systematic effort to engage a group of professional educators who work together, a staff, in activities designed to increase the power and authority of their shared work" (Griffin, 1991, p. 244). School psychologists are in a unique position to provide such training to school personnel as they have training in effective instruction and teaching, knowledge about the increasing problems evidenced by students in our schools, and positive interventions and treatments.

As in prevention, staff development should begin with a needs assessment survey conducted with the teachers at a school site. Identifying the areas in which they feel they can benefit from additional training will assist the school psychologist in developing a program that will be attended as well as one that will provide skills to the participants. After the needs assessment survey is conducted, the school psychologist should develop goals for the in-service program, paying careful attention to the cultural values and organizational climate of the school. Every school staff differs in minor ways and understanding such differences can enhance the training provided. The training should then be implemented along with practice activities for the participants. Following training, both short- and long-term evaluations should be conducted to determine the effectiveness of the training.

Staff development training can enhance the professional roles of all members of school staff and can have positive effects for the students in that school. By being the catalyst for such activities, school psychologists can help teachers and other school staff members enhance their tools and techniques for ensuring success for all students.

**Research and Program Evaluation**

School psychologists also have training in research and program evaluation. As related to Ubiquitous Assessment, these are essential skills if school psychologists are to demonstrate their understanding and knowledge of their field in order to provide the best possible services to all of the students with whom they work.

Whether or not they conduct research, school psychologists should be consumers of research. Those people requesting services assume that a practitioner's knowledge base will be up to date and current with best professional practices. As the world changes rapidly, school psychologists need to keep up with the research discoveries and make decisions about the usefulness of such for their everyday work.

The training school psychologists receive provides them with the skills for evaluating research and determining its applicability for use in the school setting. Some "research" is unimportant, irrelevant, and badly designed. Many times someone will come to us with a "new" technique that she/he is excited about it. However, when an analysis of the data collection methods, individuals participating, or statistically procedures utilized are examined, significant flaws are apparent. School psychologists have the knowledge to identify these problems with research and should always be questioning the "latest, newest, practices." These practices may be neither new nor important. Again, from the perspective of Ubiquitous Assessment, school psychologists need to be cognizant of their contributions to the school setting and the students they serve.

**Assessment**

School psychologists have extensive training in assessment. Assessment is much more than testing and includes the seamless process from referral to intervention/treatment evaluation. According to Fagan and Wise (2000), assessment refers "to a complex problem-solving or information-gathering process" (p. 119). They further state, "The reason that school psychologists assess individual students it to understand the difficulties a child is experiencing in order to intervene and ultimately help the child" (p. 119). This philosophy is consistent with Ubiquitous Assessment.

## Laws

How did school psychologists get a reputation for testing? In 1975, the Education for All Handicapped Children's Act (EHA), known as Public Law 94-142, was passed by Congress. This law became the full employment act for school psychologists. The law specified that every child, regardless of handicapping condition, had a right to an education in the least-restrictive environment; with the creation of many special classes, children with every problem and disability were tested to determine the most appropriate setting for them. School psychologists were hired in increasing numbers across the country to assess students for special education. In addition, the law outlined the requirements needed for children with achievement deficits to be diagnosed as learning disabled and mainstreaming programs were developed for these children to take the burden off regular classroom teachers.

The federal government outlined the law, but each state that wanted to receive funds from the government had to develop its own policies and procedures to meet the letter of the law. Almost every state department of education developed statewide regulations for determining what children would qualify for what services and how each handicapping condition would be assessed. For example, the law specified that children considered to be learning disabled had to have a significant discrepancy between ability (most often defined as intelligence) and achievement, in one or more of seven categories: reading decoding, reading comprehension, math calculation, math reasoning, listening comprehension, written expression, and oral expression. While these terms may seem straightforward, the problem arises when trying to determine the definition of a "significant discrepancy." Different states decided to define the term in different ways. In general, states have defined significant discrepancy as having to do with a difference in standard deviation units between the IQ test and the achievement tests. In California, for example, a significant discrepancy was defined as 1½ standard deviation units. In Nevada, the state department of education defined the discrepancy as one standard deviation unit, or 15 points. So children residing in Nevada who move to California might no longer be eligible for services.

By 1976–1977 when the law was implemented and state departments of education had defined their policies, school psychologists began to test children by the dozens. Since programs had been developed for these children, the general consensus at the time was that special education would aid these children in some way, allowing them to "catch up" to their peers and return to the regular classroom.

What school psychologists "taught" administrators, teachers, and families was that problem students could be dealt with through testing and such students removed from the regular education classroom to a "special" setting, where they would get the help they needed. (Unfortunately, for many, this has continued to be daily practice, although it is certainly not considered to be best practice.)

In 1990, Public Law 94-142 was amended and retitled the Individuals with Disabilities Education Act (IDEA). This was Public Law 101-476 and the rights of parents and children were enhanced by an increased focus on transition services. From the initiation of P.L. 94-142, it had become apparent to some (and, over the years, to many) that "special education" was not that special. Many children who received special education services while in the elementary and secondary school years did not get jobs upon completing high school and were unable to contribute to society in a meaningful or valuable way. Thus, the law was amended to require schools to develop transition plans for students sixteen years old and older receiving special education that addressed the development of employment, options for employment, and daily living skills.

Public Law 105-17 was the next amendment to P.L. 94-142 and was passed in 1997. The amendments to this law focused again on transition planning for students and expanded the services to students fourteen years old and older. Every special education student at the age of fourteen must have an Individual Education Plan (IEP) that includes information related to functional vocational skills, and the IEP determines the student's future course of study, whether it be academic or some alternative curriculum.

Currently, the law is under discussion in Congress for another reauthorization. Titled "The Improving Education Results for Children with Disabilities Act," the preliminary bill will reduce paperwork; place an emphasis on ensuring that students make academic progress, rather than the current focus on compliance with rules; emphasize the improvement of early intervention; reduce the overidentification and misidentification of students; support general and special education teachers through professional development programs; increase the use of mediation to solve school district and parental disputes; and encourage schools to discipline all students in a like manner (Boehner, 2003). It is unknown when the bill will actually appear before

Congress, but highly likely that it will be discussed sometime during 2005. As a school or mental health practitioner, we strongly recommend that you keep current on changes to this law. School districts are required to comply, as school psychologists are certainly aware, and for other professionals, such knowledge can enhance the operation and increase cooperation at all levels within schools.

These laws have always called for the involvement of school psychologists; school psychologists have, for the most part, responded by testing students to ensure school district compliance with the laws. However, none of the laws has ever mandated testing to the extremes it has been taken and many school psychologists have lost sight of the original reasons they wanted to work in schools. As university instructors we continually hear from undergraduate students exploring career options at the graduate level that they want to help children. These individuals are admitted to school psychology programs, learn a myriad of techniques for "helping children," but once employed in the schools continue or are forced by the powers-that-be to test, test, test. However, testing does not "help" children. Testing, as done by many school psychologists, labels children and places them in dead-end programs, with no hope of ever returning to the mainstream.

## IQ Tests

What kinds of tests do school psychologists generally administer? The primary test they are known for administering is the intelligence test. There are a number of different intelligence tests available and the most common ones will be very briefly reviewed and analyzed here, in order that the reader can get an idea of the problems encompassing this type of testing.

Some points of information, however, are needed. First, intelligence has never been able to be adequately defined; generally, each test author defines what he/she means by intelligence, but in no way are the definitions similar. Second, many believe that an IQ score is somehow written in stone, and that once an individual obtains a score, that IS his/her score. This is simply not the case. IQ scores can fluctuate and often do between one testing situation and the next with the same individual. It is not unusual to see a difference between scores over time of one standard deviation (15 to 16 points, depending on the test used). Third, IQ tests are merely structured observations to determine how an individual performs in a structured situation and are merely samples of behavior. When parents and teachers refer students for assessment, they do not ask what the students' IQs are. They are far more interested in what can be done to help a student succeed. Fourth, and most importantly for Ubiquitous

Assessment, is that the information obtained from IQ tests or the scores obtained do not lead us to treatment/intervention decisions or options. They do not provide us with a picture of the whole child and his/her specific needs to excel in school or the world. They simply provide us with one number in a brief span of time.

### Wechsler Scales

The most recent revision of the Wechsler scales (the most common intelligence test used with the school age population) is the Wechsler Intelligence Scale for Children-IV Edition (WISC-IV), which will be discussed here. This test is designed for children ages six years through sixteen years of age. Other tests in the Wechsler series that a school psychologist might use are the Wechsler Preschool and Primary Scale of Intelligence-III Edition (WPPSI-III) designed for children between the ages of three and seven, and the Wechsler Adult Intelligence Scale-III Edition (WAIS-III) designed for individuals sixteen years old and older.

The Wechsler scales are individually administered norm-referenced tests and the concept of intelligence was defined by David Wechsler as "the overall capacity of an individual to understand and cope with the world around him" (Wechsler, 1974, p. 5). He further stated that intelligence is "multidetermined and multifaceted entity rather than an independent, uniquely defined trait," and that general intelligence cannot be equated with intellectual ability (Wechsler, 1974, p. 5). The WISC-IV subtests consist of ten core subtests and three supplemental tests. Four composite scores can be derived from these scores as can the full-scale IQ score.

While the Wechsler scales are relatively free from bias and the technical adequacy of the scales is very good, with reliabilities above .90, the test has little treatment validity. Treatment validity refers to whether or not an instrument leads to effective educational interventions. Witt and Gresham (1986) in a review of the WISC-R, which also holds true for the WISC-IV, stated "the WISC-R lacks treatment validity in that its use does not enhance remedial interventions for children who show specific academic skill deficiencies" (p. 1717). Thus, the Wechsler scale holds little promise for use in Ubiquitous Assessment.

### Woodcock-Johnson Psychoeducational Battery-III

Another commonly used test of general intelligence is the Woodcock-Johnson Psychoeducational Battery-Third Edition (Woodcock, McGrew, & Mather, 2001). This instrument is designed for individuals from preschool to adulthood. The WJ-III is composed of ten subtests in the standard and the overall score is referred to as the General Intellectual Ability or GIA. Reliability and validity appear adequate, with the GIA reliability above .90, but again, as with the WISC-IV, while the scale may be technically adequate, it does nothing for us if we want to engage in the seamless process of Ubiquitous Assessment, from assessment to intervention.

### Differential Abilities Scales

Another instrument that has become popular with school psychologists is the Differential Abilities Scales (DAS) (Elliott, 1990b), for use with preschool and school-age children. There are two preschool batteries and one school-age battery that result in a General Conceptual Ability (GCA) score. The school-age battery is designed for children from six years old to seventeen years eleven months and consists of six core subtests. According to Sattler (2001), the school psychologist should "carefully consider whether you want to use the DAS for repeated evaluations, especially if you plan to use the results obtained on the retest for placement, eligibility, or diagnostic decisions" (p. 515) because of problems with test-retest reliabilities. Thus, again, the question becomes: What use does such a tool have when engaging in Ubiquitous Assessment? Obviously, if one is concerned with long-term growth and adjustment, it would seem the DAS lacks usefulness for treatment or intervention.

## Ubiquitous Assessment

So what should a school psychologist do in terms of assessment? First, the school psychologist should understand the definition of assessment. According to the National Association of School Psychologists (NASP) (2003), assessment is defined as "the process of gathering information from a variety of sources, using a variety of methods that best address the reason for evaluation" (p. 1). Testing is "limited to administration and scoring of tests" (National Association of School Psychologists, 2003, p. 1). NASP furthers delineates assessment as

> practices that are: scientifically based; multidimensional and based on the needs of the student; relevant to a variety of scientifically based interventions; inclusive of an examination of family and educational systems, and home environments, in addition to the student; initiated by efforts to resolve the problem through early intervention; nondiscriminatory in terms of ethnicity, gender, native language, family or socioeconomic factors; comprehensive and address the educational, cognitive, and mental health needs of the student; not limited to any single methodology or theoretical framework; technically appropriate and

> used for the purposes for which they were developed and/or validated; conducted so that ethical standards are maintained; and used only by qualified personnel. (pp. 1–2)

In addition, the school psychologist should utilize the information contained in other chapters within this volume to ensure they are engaging in best professional practice, which is Ubiquitous Assessment.

We recognize that for some school psychologists testing may be unavoidable in order to keep a job. Many school psychologists are pressured to determine eligibility for children under state and federal requirements, primarily in order for the school district to obtain additional funds to educate children experiencing difficulties at school. However, Barnett and Carey (1992) commented on this problem: "What could be more descriptive that Galagan's (1985) title: 'Psychological Testing: Turn Out the Lights, the Party's Over'" (p. 39).

Barnett and Carey (1992) go on to discuss what the practitioner should do if he/she is required to use individual intelligence tests or other scales. First, testing is viewed by many as an "accepted professional function" (p. 40). While many of the tools used by school psychologists and others are technically adequate, they do not provide sufficient information about individual children and what these children actually do in the "real" environment, nor do they assist us in Ubiquitous Assessment.

Second, if a practitioner must test, he/she should use the scales in "reasonable manner" (p. 40). The user has the responsibility of ensuring that any tools he/she uses be technically adequate for the purposes for which such tools are being used. School administrators, teachers, parents, and others who are often pressuring for some type of testing often do not understand the limitations of testing, and they do not understand that these tools will not lead to treatment/intervention. As practitioners, we have a responsibility to educate those persons asking for testing to make certain that they understand what information can be obtained and what cannot. Most importantly, we must make certain that they understand that tests have no real place in Ubiquitous Assessment.

Third, according to Barnett and Carey (1992), "do not test unless you have to" (p. 40). Practitioners often fail to take the time to develop the reason for the student being referred. Only by conducting problem-solving interviews (see chapter 4) can the referral question be truly understood. However, many practitioners simply grab one test or another and race in to test the student presented by the teacher or parent. Unfortunately, such haste leads to poor judgments and certainly does not contribute to the design of treatment or intervention plans.

Fourth, the practitioner should consider what we are discussing in this book—Ubiquitous Assessment—and "consider alternative assessment frameworks" (Barnett & Carey, 1992, p. 40). Alternative-assessment frameworks in this context refer to testing adaptive behavior (skills needed for daily functioning), testing of limits (whereby items a student misses on an IQ test are readministered at the end of the test in order to determine how the student reached his/her conclusion or answer), and comparing results of different tests given at different times.

Fifth, the practitioner wishing to work from a Ubiquitous Assessment model should develop "intervention-based questions" (Barnett & Carey, 1992, p. 41). If the tests are unreliable and invalid for the development of treatments/interventions (which is our goal), why would we want to spend hours and hours engaged in a dead-end process? We should be exploring all facets of the student through consultation, direct and indirect observations, and interviews with significant others. Barnett and Carey (1992) offer questions that can help practitioners using tests to develop recommendations for short- and long-terms goals:

1. What is the range of skill development?
2. What component skills did the child demonstrate?
3. What skills are necessary in solving inadequately performed tasks?
4. What problem-solving steps or knowledge did the child seem to be missing?
5. How could these be adequately assessed?
6. How do children acquire those skills?
7. What learning difficulties seem to exist (attentional, retentional, productive, motivational)?
8. Are there deficits in related skills (such as language) that affect the level of performance?
9. How did the performance in testing compare with the child's performance with other materials, test questions, in other environments, or at other times?
10. What are the child's current optimal performance levels? (p. 42)

Sixth, according to Barnett and Carey (1992), the practitioner should "consider aids for decision making" (p. 42). Importantly, strategies other than tests are needed in Ubiquitous Assessment, including observations, interviews, and actual intervention plans that have been implemented and evaluated. Only by using a multitude of data garnered from observations, the student's interactions with others, and actually implementing and analyzing the effectiveness of interventions can we be certain we truly *know* the student.

The idea of school psychologist as tester is outdated, outmoded, and will soon be outsourced, if individual school psychologists do not change their practices. There are many roles for school psychologists and they are a vital part to every school. However, this can only be true if school psychologists embrace reform and work with each and every student from a Ubiquitous Assessment frame.

THE FAR SIDE® By GARY LARSON

**"It's just a simple Rorschach ink-blot test, Mr. Bromwell, so just calm down and tell me what each one suggests to you."**

# Chapter Seven

## Assessment in Mental Health Settings

Assessment within the field of mental health has traditionally been conducted through formalized methods and techniques, and its use has been viewed as a distinctly differentiated process and procedure than therapy. This role of assessment follows the medical model and has been conceived according to the precepts similar to a general physical examination (Zimmerman, 1994). Generally referred to as the mental status examination, the initial assessment process has traditionally directed the therapy. "Since its [the mental status examination] introduction into American psychiatry by Adolf Meyer in 1902, it has become the mainstay of patient evaluation in most psychiatric settings. Most psychiatrists consider it as essential to their practice as the physical examination is in general medicine (Rodenhauser & Fornal, 1991)" (Groth-Marnat, 2003, pp. 84–85). For purposes of this book, we include within the realm of mental health all public and private mental health organizations including psychiatric hospitals, psychiatric assessment departments in local hospitals, county and state mental health facilities, mental health units of the criminal justice system, drug and alcohol treatment organizations, and any other venue where MFTs and LCSWs (Licensed Clinical Social Worker) would be practicing as members of a comprehensive psychiatric treatment team.

For individual patients entering the mental health system or any other agency or hospital setting providing mental health services, the process of assessment is critical for the prescription of therapy and the provision of services. In many cases, the assessment will be conducted by a treatment team and will include the intake interview by the MFT or LCSW, a clinical interview by a staff psychologist, and a medication review by the medical director, psychiatrist, or clinical psychologist. Depending upon the requirements of the agency, there may be a need to write a treatment plan, including clear goals and objectives of the therapy. Following specific guidelines for clinical evaluation within the agency, the MFT or LCSW may be using a combination of formal psychometric and informal assessment procedures. This chapter will outline some of the most common of those procedures and review their use in concert with the multiaxial diagnostic system outlined in the mainstay of mental health assessment, the *Diagnostic and Statistical Manual of Mental Disorders, Fourth Edition-Text Revision* most commonly referred to as the *DSM 4-TR* (APA, 2000). Multiaxial is a term used to define the combination of mental, environmental, and physical processes that would affect an individual's life functioning and experience. This system concludes with an overall assessment of the individual's risk of causing harm to himself/herself or others.

## The Multiaxial Diagnostic System

The multiaxial diagnostic system is a method of conceptualizing an individual according to a multimodal process. This process views the person as a complex and multifaceted being comprised of mental wellness, physical health, psychosocial status, and environmental issues (APA, 2000). This multiple or multiaxial approach is consistent with current applications of biopsychosocial research in medical and educational settings (Gregory, 2004). Rather than focusing upon one aspect of individual functioning, the multiaxial approach can guide the clinician to create a comprehensive assessment of the client's condition. The method of multiaxial assessment is designed to emphasize that the assessment process is multifaceted. This is to suggest that the clinician needs to evaluate or assess more than the client's presenting problem. According to the manual (APA, 2000), "The use of the multiaxial system facilitates comprehensive and systematic evaluation with attention to the various mental disorders and general medical conditions, psychosocial and environmental problems, and level of functioning that might be overlooked if the focus were on assessing a single problem" (p. 27). This multiaxial and clinical foundation of mental health assessment is delineated within the *DSM 4-TR* (APA, 2000). The *DSM 4-TR* is one of the most comprehensive and continuously updated collections of assessment criteria compiled for the clinician's aid in client evaluation.

According to the *DSM 4-TR* (APA, 2000), the axes include:

1. Axis I Clinical Disorders—Other Conditions That May Be a Focus of Clinical Attention
2. Axis II Personality Disorders—Mental Retardation
3. Axis III General Medical Conditions
4. Axis IV Psychosocial and Environmental Problems
5. Axis V Global Assessment of Functioning

The most efficient way to conceptualize Axis I is to list the disorders encompassed by this axis:

1. Disorders Usually First Diagnosed in Infancy, Childhood, and Adolescence (excluding Mental Retardation, which is diagnosed on Axis II)

2. Delirium, Dementia, and Amnestic and Other Cognitive Disorders
3. Mental Disorders Due to a General Medical Condition
4. Substance-Related Disorders
5. Mood Disorders
6. Anxiety Disorders
7. Somatoform Disorders
8. Factitious Disorders
9. Dissociative Disorders
10. Sexual and Gender Identity Disorders
11. Eating Disorders
12. Sleep Disorders
13. Impulse-Control Disorders Not Elsewhere Classified
14. Adjustment Disorders
15. Other Conditions That May Be a Focus of Clinical Attention (APA, 2000)

Essentially, Axis I disorders include all of the major psychological disorders and substance abuse-related conditions with the exception of personality disorders and mental retardation. Axis I disorders are most likely to include major depressive disorder, bipolar disorder, dissociative disorder, and schizophrenia. However, more obscure or less frequently identified disorders may also be included within this axis. For example, individuals with Korsokoff's syndrome would be considered as having a Mental Disorder Due to a General Medical Condition (APA, 1987; Missouri Department of Mental Health, 2003). Korsokoff's syndrome is an alcohol amnestic disorder believed to be associated with a thiamine deficiency. This neurologic disease is characterized by mental confusion and other neurological dysfunctions such as memory loss.

Most commonly, Axis I disorders encompass the most severe mental health disabilities such as schizophrenia and other psychotic disorders (bipolar disorder, anxiety disorders, and mood disorders). Quite frequently, individuals will present with multiple or dual diagnoses. Comorbidity of depression and substance abuse is frequently diagnosed within many individuals referred by the criminal justice system and other health agencies such as hospitals. Diagnosis of Axis I disorders generally require extensive assessment and use of multiple professional or treatment team approaches.

The Personality Disorders and Mental Retardation are reviewed in Axis II. Axis II disorders include all of the eleven personality disorders and Mental Retardation:

1. Paranoid Personality Disorder
2. Schizoid Personality Disorder
3. Antisocial Personality Disorder
4. Borderline Personality Disorder
5. Histrionic Personality Disorder
6. Narcissistic Personality Disorder
7. Avoidant Personality Disorder
8. Dependent Personality Disorder
9. Obsessive-Compulsive Personality Disorder
10. Personality Disorder Not Otherwise Specified
11. Mental Retardation (APA, 2000)

Axis III includes phenomenon articulated as General Medical Conditions. This axis includes medical conditions not usually directly related to Axis I Clinical Disorders. However, there are times when a medical condition such as chronic heart disease or lymphoma can be a cause of Axis I manifestations of the illness, such as Adjustment Disorder with Depressed Mood (APA, 2000). General Medical Conditions may include:

1. Infectious and Parasitic Diseases
2. Neoplasms
3. Endocrine, Nutritional, and Metabolic Diseases and Immunity Disorders
4. Diseases of the Blood and Blood-Forming Organs
5. Diseases of the Nervous System and Sense Organs
6. Diseases of the Circulatory System
7. Diseases of the Respiratory System
8. Diseases of the Digestive System
9. Diseases of the Genitourinary System
10. Complications of Pregnancy, Childbirth, and the Puerperium
11. Diseases of the Skin and Subcutaneous Tissue
12. Diseases of the Musculoskeletal System and Connective Tissue
13. Congenital Anomalies
14. Certain Conditions Originating in the Perinatal Period
15. Symptoms, Signs, and Ill-defined Conditions
16. Injury and Poisoning (APA, 2000)

Axis IV includes psychosocial and environmental problems. Generally, Axis IV includes problems that have occurred within the last year. Axis IV, Psychosocial and Environmental Problems, is comprised of the following:

1. Problems with primary support group
2. Problems related to the social environment
3. Educational problems
4. Occupational problems
5. Housing problems
6. Economic problems
7. Problems with access to health care services
8. Problems related to interaction with the legal system/crime
9. Other psychosocial and environmental problems (APA, 2000)

Axis V is the Global Assessment of Functioning (GAF). This scale is a continuum that asks the clinician to give an overall composite score to the client. This scale runs from 1 to 100. One (1) on the scale places the client at extreme risk for hurting himself/herself or others. As the scale moves toward 100, the next steps are moderate risk for hurting oneself or others, delusionary behaviors or hallucinations, impairment in reality, suicidal ideation, difficulty functioning, slight impairments in daily functioning, minimal impairment with daily function, and, lastly, no symptoms (APA, 2000).

Diagnosis of Axis I (clinical disorders and other conditions that may be a focus of clinical attention) and Axis II (personality disorders and mental retardation) (APA, 2000) are the major diagnostic categories most often addressed by MFTs and LCSWs within the mental health setting. Although the complete system of multiaxial assessment will be covered, a large part of this chapter is focused upon Axis I and Axis II diagnostic criterion.

## The Mental Status Examination

As we have mentioned earlier, formalized testing and assessment have traditionally existed as distinctly different procedures from therapy and this evaluation contains the specific goal of developing a diagnosis. Within many agencies, treatment follows assessment and diagnosis. Because of this mandate, most MFTs and LCSWs begin their work with a mental status examination. If the initial interviews and clinical history do not yield an immediate conclusion, further assessment may be indicated. To assist in this process, formalized testing is generally conducted by psychometrists (or clinicians trained in formalized assessment) and their goal is to evaluate specific areas of individual functioning. Psychometrists conduct individual tests to determine IQ, learning disabilities, or other specific problems.

As we have mentioned earlier in this text, assessment is more global in its goals and processes. Whereas specific tests such as IQ tests measure a particular area of functioning, assessment seeks to develop an understanding of the whole person and the client's psychosocial status. As referenced earlier, this is most commonly identified as the Global Assessment of Functioning (APA, 2000). Assessment's aim is to comprehensively evaluate the individual's psychological, social, and occupational functioning along a continuum ranging from positive mental or biopsychosocial health to its inverse.

Individuals enter the mental health delivery system for diverse reasons. Ranging from self-referral to referral from outside agencies such as schools, courts, and other community agencies, individuals coming to mental health represent extreme differences of motivation for therapy, knowledge of the processes, and sense of what will be the outcome of their efforts and participation. The client's sophistication and knowledge of mental health practices and procedures can have a large effect on the outcomes each individual achieves. Regardless of the client's previous experiences, the initial contact between the therapist and the client can be critical in establishing rapport and in being able to conduct a valid assessment of the counselee or client. According to Zimmerman (1994),

> The patient is probably more nervous than you are. Anxiety, which may be a symptom of their illness or due to their concern about speaking to a mental health professional, is the rule. The patient may be suspicious of an unfamiliar doctor. They may also be angry because they are not there willingly. Perhaps they have been involuntarily committed, or perhaps a friend, family member, or boss strongly encouraged them to be evaluated. Thus, it is important to realize that an important purpose of the initial evaluation is to provide support and understanding to the patient, establish a trusting doctor-patient relationship, a by-product of which will be the information necessary to derive a diagnosis and treatment plan. (p. 6)

Even though mental health has held a traditional view that the processes of assessment and therapy are distinctly differentiated, we believe that they are enmeshed, and we support the use of ubiquitous techniques within this field. The more the client feels that she/he is in a therapeutic relationship rather than under some form of assessment, the easier it will be to develop rapport. In the bailiwick of an experienced therapist, developing the trust necessary to begin the process of assessment can be therapeutic for the client. The same is true for overcoming resistance to participate in recovery or to enter into a process of self-discovery. From the outset of contact with the client, assessment and therapy need to be undifferentiated by the client and inseparable components of mental health practice.

Having had the privilege of sitting on both sides of the couch, we empathize with both the clinician and the patient concerning the intricate issues of the initial assessment. Although much of the process of the initial interview will be determined by the agency requirements, the setting, and, essentially, whether the client is voluntarily seeking help or is an involuntary participant, the goals of the initial interview are to forge an appropriate client-therapist relationship and to develop trust and rapport worthy of a therapeutic experience. "The first principle of interviewing is to forge a warm, trusting environment" (Yalom, 1996, p. 4). Beginning the therapy process with a standard administration of the mental status examination does not allow the client and the therapist an opportunity to develop mutual respect or for deep feelings to be shared concerning the client's problem. The mental status examination needs to be embedded in the initial interview and take a tone of openness and relaxed conversation (Zimmerman, 1994).

The initial interview should attempt to balance the therapist's orientation for the client concerning confidentiality and a brief explanation of the processes of the assessment/therapy. Following that brief introduction, the initial interview attempts to create a structure within which the client can express all of the feelings, facts, and information necessary for the therapist to begin to understand the dilemma the client confronts. Throughout the process, the role of the clinician is consistent: listening for the feelings and the facts (or content) the client is expressing. As the client shares her/his feelings and facts about her/his experience, the therapist is assessing, building rapport, and providing therapy through use of Ubiquitous Assessment technique.

Because of the time constraints of most attending psychiatrists and clinical psychologists within the clinical setting, the comprehensive mental status and other related intake information is generally obtained by the MFT or LCSW (Groth-Marnat, 2003) in an initial interview. This can provide some significant therapeutic opportunities for the MFT or LCSW. We believe that the initial interview should focus on trust and rapport, and, therefore, the position of the MFT or LCSW is situated perfectly to communicate the mental health agencies concern for its clientele. "Without concern, respect, and interested listening on your part, there will be no therapy" (Lukas, 1993, p. 172).

The mental health agency's concern for the well-being of the client is reflected throughout the entirety of the treatment of the client from the initial contact with the receptionist to the meeting with the psychiatrist. In most instances for the client, there is no distinction between a warm and welcoming MFT or LCSW and a caring and concerned PhD or MD. For our purposes, the MFT or LCSW is the focus of discussion. Whether this mental status assessment will be used by another clinician providing therapy or by the MFT or LCSW as therapist, the process of the mental status examination is open and needs to fit the individual client. This is to say that there are wide variations in the use of this assessment, and each clinician adapts the basic evaluation to meet the needs of her/his client and the agency the therapist represents.

The mental status examination is more a collection of observations than a complete biopsychosocial assessment (Lukas, 1993). Although it may be included within a comprehensive biopsychosocial assessment, its use is for initial screening and parallels the physician's physical examination (Groth-Marnat, 2003). The mental status can be a standalone assessment when the assessment of global functioning discloses high risk for personal or other's injury. In this case, the client may be "51–50"-ed (the police radio code for psychiatric emergency) or committed to a hospital for seventy-two-hour observation and further assessment.

The mental status examination is primarily an observational assessment. The observations take place while the clinician is interviewing the client. The clinician is observing the client to evaluate the client's current psychological status or condition. The observations seek to identify distinct areas of client functioning. Lukas (1993) gives an excellent rubric for the assessment:

- Appearance: How does he [she] look or behave?
- Speech: How does he [she] speak?
- Emotions: What is his [her] predominant mood? What is his [her] predominant affect? (Mood = How does the client feel most of the time? Affect = How does the client appear to be feeling while he [she] is with you?)
- Thought processes and content: (Process = How does the client think? Content = What does he [she] think about?)
- Sensory perceptions: Are there any indications of illusions or hallucinations?
- Mental capacities: Is he [she] oriented X 3? [Is the client able to articulate the current time, his/her location, and his/her name?] What is your estimate of his [her] intelligence? Can he [she] remember and concentrate? How are his [her] judgment and insight?
- Attitude toward the interviewer? How does the client behave toward you? (p. 15)

General appearance and behavior of the client is logically the first step in the mental status examination. This follows from the first encounter between the client and the clinician. Very much like a behavioral observation, the assessment of general appearance and behavior attempts to discern attributes based upon the client's outward manifestations. Items such as style of clothing, appropriateness of clothing, condition of physical self, grooming, and hygiene all deserve the attention of the clinician. Behaviors could include openness, quick-temperedness, hostility, defensiveness, humorousness, cooperation, languidness, boisterousness, or other possible manifestations of feelings. Clinicians look for behavior that may be inappropriate or bizarre or, conversely, actions that are in accordance with good manners and socialization skills. Analysis of speech speed—slurring, slowness, or other deviations from normal patterns—is noteworthy.

In the assessment of general appearance and behavior, it is important to guard against stereotyping and prejudice toward the client. The appearance of tattoos, body piercing, or other unusual accoutrements could cause the clinician to make assumptions concerning the client's social appropriateness. The appearance of unusual dress or accoutrements should lead the clinician to inquire further into the client's motivation for choosing the particular outfit or dress. Questions of what, who, where, when, and how are appropriate. The question "why?" is never appropriate in psychology. Why is considered an intrusive question because it seeks the client's revelation of feelings and possibly internal motivations. This question's answer is the work of therapy and not appropriate for interview within the mental status examination (Lukas, 1993).

Feeling (affect and mood) is the next component of the mental status examination. Mood is characterized as the dominant emotion or overall emotional condition of the client. Affect means the way the client expresses her/his emotions. Clinicians observe the changes or lack of changes in affect as the client shares information concerning the problem that brought her/him to therapy. Expressions of extreme grief or flat emotionless talk of one's loss are the clues for the therapist concerning the client's condition: depressed, hostile, anxious, or emotionally labile.

Thinking is the next component of the mental status examination. The two major elements of thinking include how a person thinks (process) and what a person thinks (content) (Groth-Marnat, 2003). Clear, cogent thoughts are distinguishable from scattered, chaotic thinking. The clinician's role in this part of the assessment is to observe the client's ability to logically and sequentially process the information necessary to complete the interview. Rambling, chaotic, or nonsequential skipping about are indications of possible thought-process difficulty. The continuum of articulate to incoherent is what the clinician uses to assess thinking process.

Thinking content covers a wide array of possible themes, including possibly causing harm to oneself or others. Suicidal or homicidal thoughts may surface if the client is agitated, under the influence of alcohol or other drugs, or is honestly expressing anger toward herself/himself or others. Thought content can also include expressions of phobias, delusions, obsessions, paranoid ideations, or other strange references or mental constructions (Zimmerman, 1994).

Next, the mental status examination focuses on thought processes. Process is differentiated from content by the manner in which the thoughts are expressed. Are the thoughts logical or illogical? Does the client perseverate or repeat content over and over? Is the speech coherent? Does the client show good attention and concentration? Do the words link to make sense or is this verbal salad? Are the ideas flowing together to make a cogent story or series of events? Is the speech rapid or slow? "Thought processes such as the presence of rapid changes in topics might reflect flighty ideas. The client might also have difficulty producing a sufficient number of ideas, include an excessive number of irrelevant associations, or ramble aimlessly" (Groth-Marnat, 2003, pp. 89–90). The key to mental status evaluation of the client's thought process is to pay attention to the overall flow and to holistically evaluate the conversation.

Related to thinking, the perceptions of the client are also critical to the assessment of mental status. In assessment of perception, the clinician is questioning or investigating for possible hallucinations or the presence of illusions in the mind of the client. Auditory hallucinations may be related to a diagnosis of schizophrenia, and visual illusions or hallucinations may indicate the possibility of organic cognitive dysfunction (Groth-Marnat, 2003). Perception is matched with misperception and can include compartmentalized thinking such as depersonalization or derealization. Even nonperception—for example, blackouts associated with alcohol abuse—are strong indications of potential diagnostic considerations (e.g., alcoholism).

Typical of many mental status evaluations is a brief intellectual or cognitive functioning assessment. For this evaluation, the clinician is simply trying to estimate the client's overall intellectual aptitude along a continuum from above average to below average. Simple mental arithmetic problems such as asking the client to count backwards from 100 by 7s may assess cognitive facility. Questions such as "What does this expression mean to you: 'One swallow does not make a summer,' 'Don't put all your eggs in one basket,' or 'Don't judge a book by its cover'" are sometimes useful. Other areas of assessment may include comprehension of social norms or mores. For example, "Why do we use juries in the legal process?" or "What are some of the reasons taxes are collected?" Answers to these questions can also shed light on the client's insight and other higher-level thinking abilities. Insight can also assist the client in understanding her/his reason for being in therapy and enable her/him to benefit from the process.

The final component of the mental status evaluation includes the attitude of the client toward the therapist and the overall process from the client's perspective. Does the client seem available for therapy? Is the client interested or disinterested in the process? Is the client willing to disclose personal information or is she/he leery of interaction with the therapist? Is the client easy to engage in conversation or does she/he withhold important information from the therapist? Do you feel comfortable sitting and interacting with the client? Is this comfortable for both the client and the clinician? Does this experience bode well for further psychological or therapeutic intervention?

## Interpreting and Summarizing the Mental Status Examination

One of the most challenging activities of the novice therapist is interpreting and integrating the assessment information in a summary of the client's mental status. Developing clinical judgment sufficient to give a valid interpretation of the client's mental status takes considerable knowledge and experience. For emerging practitioners, it is best to report factual information and to use this to draw possible diagnostic considerations. The salient concept is to minimize evaluator error. The practice of psychology is a combination of the use of clinical knowledge and experience in the application of those two components. Developing the clinical judgment to give valid interpretation to mental status evaluations can take years, hence the 3,500-hour internship.

The best practice for beginning therapists is to describe the results of the mental status evaluation in clear, objective, and nonjudgmental language. An effective reporting method is to use direct quotes from the client. The report can follow the order of the clinical interview. At the end of the report, the therapist can give some possible diagnostic considerations. The emphasis is on the word "possible." Because of the chance that the diagnostic consideration is inaccurate, use of expressions such as "may be associated with" or "sometimes related to a diagnostic consideration of" are best advised. This language clearly states that the clinician is open to other possible diagnostic considerations, and the client is not labeled.

The following is an example of a mental status examination summary. The example is taken from an examination conducted at the Seacoast Regional Counseling Center in Portsmouth, New Hampshire. Ernest had been referred to the mental health clinic by his family physician because of a long history of complaints of vague pains that were not medically corroborated.

**Appearance:**

Ernest F. presented as an appropriately groomed and cleanly attired 65-year-old Caucasian male. Ernest's flannel shirt and work trousers reflected the attire of a man who worked with his hands to make a living. A large man, it was easy to imagine Ernest in his career as a longshoreman working for the Merchant Marine.

Ernest's craggy face and ruddy complexion further reinforced an image of the retired dockworker. Eye contact was appropriate throughout the interview. Ernest appeared comfortable with the interview process and his body language reinforced his eagerness to discover the etiology of his complaint.

**Speech:**

Ernest's speech was clear and easily comprehensible. Other than a slight New England accent, his speech was appropriate and cogent. The vocabulary level was consistent with his high school education and completion.

**Emotions:**

Ernest appeared anxious to discover why his doctor referred him to the mental health clinic. He appeared insecure concerning his current health condition, and he seemed to require reassurance for his decision to pursue further medical attention. Ernest appeared quite submissive in his demeanor, and his overall affect seemed to reflect a sense of helplessness.

**Thought Process:**

Ernest seemed to be confused about his referral to mental health. He was compliant with the doctor's referral; however, he was not sure why his physician referred him for psychological help. He was willing to participate in therapy. He stated that he had been in either the hospital emergency room or in the office of his family physician on a weekly basis for at least two years. Although no source of his discomfort was located or identified, he felt better upon examination and was released to return home after each visit.

**Thought Content:**

Ernest spoke continuously about his health history. He appeared obsessed with his doctor and the need to obtain validation from the doctor for his every physical need. Even following through with the referral to mental health appeared to be a compliant move to appease the doctor's desire for Ernest to receive therapy rather than a desire he owned. "I hope the doctor likes it that I came to see you." "I really need to convince Dr. S that this is not just in my head."

**Mental Capacities:**

Ernest was oriented X3. He could remember a great deal of his history and recalled facts with relative ease. Ernest appeared to possess at least average intelligence. His cognition was more characterized by preservation concerning his medical history and condition. Although his visits to the doctor and emergency room were very frequent, he did not feel that his needs were being met by the medical community. He also seemed to lack self-esteem with regard to his ability to care for his own needs. Overall, Ernest did not seem to comprehend that his doctor concluded that his obsessive medical needs were related to a psychological problem. However, he wanted to comply with the doctor because he didn't want his doctor to refer him to another physician as had previous doctors.

**Attitude Toward the Examiner:**

Ernest seemed to have a genuine desire to please this examiner. Moreover, he seemed to have an excessive desire to develop a relationship and was curious to know the projected course of the therapy. Several times during the interview, Ernest interjected that he liked talking about his condition and that he felt better being able to talk with someone about his health. Ernest showed an eagerness to participate that appeared excessive. He concluded the interview by thanking this examiner profusely and expressing excitement about the next visit. He asked if he could have a home phone number if he needed to contact this examiner with questions when the clinic was closed.

**Summary:**

Because of the possibility that a general physical condition may not be completely ruled out, there may be reason to refer this client back to his physician for further study. Because of the referral from the family physician, consultation with this doctor may provide insight regarding the current referral and possible future direction regarding physical or mental therapy. In the client's psychosocial status, there is a possibility of somatization, mild depression, and or dependent personality disorder. Further conversations with this client may focus upon relationship history, general affective responses, and health history.

## The Personal Data Form

The Personal Data Form is an interview protocol effective for the completion of a moderately comprehensive adolescent client history. This general form has been modified by these authors over the past ten years to obtain salient client information through a structured interview format. This interview is presented here for the MFT or LCSW to copy or re-create to meet her/his specific agency requirements. The process for conducting this interview will vary greatly from client to client. Some clients will need to be led through this interview in a slow and methodical manner. Other clients will balk at one or more sessions of such a structured interview. For these clients, taking the form home to complete outside the agency is most appropriate. Just how this interview is implemented will require therapist's judgment and assessment of the client's motivation for participation. This specific personal data form was designed for use with parents or guardians of adolescents (see appendix).

An additional advantage of the Personal Data Form is that it does not require formalized training. The form can even be completed by the client without the assistance of the MSW or LCSW if the individual is compos mentis (sane or, literally, mentally sound) (Flexner, 1993). This interview may also be adapted for use with adults or young children. The value of using a structured interview is to aid in gathering a comprehensive social and personal history.

For those clinicians seeking a more structured interview, the Schedule for Affective Disorders and Schizophrenia (SADS) (Endicott & Spitzer, 1978) provides one of the most comprehensive and detailed structured interviews available. The SADS's main use is for differential diagnosis of schizophrenia from other affective disorders. Differential diagnosis is the term most commonly used to distinguish factors of a particular psychiatric condition from other and often similar psychological disorders. The SADS is especially well suited for differential diagnosis because of its comprehensive and "unparalleled coverage of the subtypes and gradations of the severity of mood disorders" (Groth-Marnat, 2003, p. 96). One of the limitations of this interview is that it requires extensive training.

Additional examples of other excellent interview protocols to consider for mental health assessment are: (1) the Structured Clinical Interview for the DSM-IV (First, Spitzer, Gibbon, & Williams, 1996) known as the SCID; (2) the Renard Diagnostic Interview (Helzer, Robins, Croughan, & Welner, 1981) known as the DICA; (3) and the Diagnostic Interview Schedule (Robins, Helzer, Croughan, & Ratcliff, 1981) known as the DIS. This last interview protocol was designed for use by both nonprofessionals and professionals alike. All of these interviews are effective for assisting the MFT or LCSW in determining appropriate diagnostic considerations corresponding to *DSM 4-TR* criterion. Used in conjunction with other professional decision-making techniques, a clinician will be able to follow best practice in the determination of valid clinical judgments.

Although most MFTs and LCSWs rely heavily upon their clinical experience, knowledge, and intuition skill in the development of diagnoses, there is a significant body of research to support the use of tests because of their reported superiority in achieving valid diagnostic conclusions. Examples of popular psychometric assessments include the Minnesota Multiphasic Personality Inventory–2 (Hathaway & McKinley, 1940), the Millon Clinical Multiaxial Inventory (Millon, 1983), and the California Psychological Inventory (Gough, 1987). All of these assessment techniques are effective, and reasonably reliable and valid measures of personality and psychopathology. Keyed to specific diagnostic criterion, these tests are widely used by clinical psychologists with specific training in the effective use of these instruments.

## Ubiquitous Assessment in Mental Health Settings

In reviewing the role of the MFT or LCSW, we have focused on the role of the multiaxial assessment system, the intake interview or mental status examination, the use of psychosocial history, the Diagnostic Interview Schedule (Robins, Helzer, Croughan, & Ratcliff, 1981), and the applicability of these processes within mental health's medical model. From this point, we would like to explore the role of Ubiquitous Assessment within the practice of the mental health clinician. Although much emphasis is placed upon the initial mental status and other interview data, we believe that the true therapeutic value of the mental health experience is within the relationship between the therapist and the client. Whether the therapy is long term or brief and strategic (Morawetz & Walker, 1984), assessment and therapy can begin to occur from the first encounter between the therapist and the client. Over the course of this professional relationship, deeper and more significantly valid appraisal of client's conditions can be conducted as the therapy progresses and grows. For the client, the need for therapy is immediate and to acknowledge that reality is to validate the client's experience.

For most individuals entering the mental health system, there is not so much an eagerness to discover the etiology of their condition as there is to proceed with the therapy. Often individuals arriving for therapy will be in a rush to get to the bottom of their problem, get a quick fix, and get on out the door. Many times, individuals referred to mental health are there to appease a boss, spouse, or significant other. For some clients, they have personally exhausted their repertoire of coping mechanisms, and they have asked everyone close to them for suggestions, too. As opposed to the client seeking long-term, private psychoanalysis, coming to mental health is often a last resort to seek relief.

Because the client is eager to resolve her/his issues, it is important to remember that the therapy begins with the first step: admitting she/he has a problem and consenting to participate in some form of treatment. Very often, these individuals do not want to spend three sessions on the mental status, MMPI, or other assessments that they consider vexing. The typical client of mental health will need and want relief immediately. As the first session may be their only session, it is important that the client leaves the therapy session with hope and a good impression of their therapist. If ever "bedside manner" were salient, it is in the initial contact between therapist and client.

Because of the urgency, anxiety, and insecurity that the client brings to the initial interview, the therapist and client both may benefit from the techniques of brief strategic therapy (Zimmerman, 1994). Since the therapy may be as brief as one session, the therapist will want to be sure not to leave the patient or client empty-handed. Because it is often of great significance that the client even followed through to make and keep the appointment, this initial session needs to be treated as sacred. Given the cultural taboos of certain groups, it can be profound to have the patient even appear. All that occurs in the here and now is of utmost importance.

Although Gestalt therapists see the here and now as a metaphor for all of the individual's experience, factors of anxiety, an unfamiliarity with the therapist and the awkwardness of being in a new environment may negatively influence the client's response set. Fear of the outcomes of the initial interview or the intrusion of other affective responses, such as anger or resentment regarding the time spent in therapy, can negatively affect attempted outcomes of the evaluation/therapy process. One of the primary objectives of the therapeutic experience continues to be the development and maintenance of relationship qualities that facilitate the client's psychological growth and promote positive outcomes.

In the Ubiquitous Assessment of individuals presenting voluntarily or otherwise referred to mental health, the evaluation begins with the initial client contact and continues throughout the process of therapy. From the first conversation through to the completion of a mental status evaluation, the MFT or LCSW needs to proceed with more structured interviews and activities to conduct the most valid assessment of her/his clients. Structured interviews are very effective with reticent or laconic clients because they give the therapist a comprehensive frame upon which she/he may conduct valuable and, quite possibly, therapeutic conversation. According to Groth-Marnat (2003), "The interview is the primary instrument that clinicians use to develop tentative hypotheses regarding their clients" (p. 90). Interviews and the data they generate can be organized to feature relevant psychological, vocational, familial, and other personal information for the purposes of achieving a valid diagnostic consideration for the client.

By allowing the client the opportunity to tell her/his story, the therapist is conveying a trust in the individual's ability to comprehend and convey her/his own situation. This validation of the client's perspective contributes to the establishment of the phenomenon Carl Rogers (1961) called unconditional positive regard. Of this phenomenon, Rogers stated:

> I hypothesize that growth and change are more likely to occur the more that the counselor is experiencing a warm, positive, acceptant attitude toward what is in the client. It means that he prizes his client, as a person, with somewhat the same quality of feeling that a parent feels for his child, prizing him as a person regardless of his particular behavior at the moment. It means that he cares for his client in a non-possessive way, as a person with potentialities. It involves an open willingness for the client to be whatever feelings are real in him at the moment—hostility or tenderness, rebellion or submissiveness, assurance or self-deprecation. It means a kind of love for the client as he is, providing we understand the word love as equivalent to the theologian's term agape, and not in its usual romantic and possessive meanings. What I am describing is a feeling which is not paternalistic, nor sentimental, nor superficially social and agreeable. It respects the other person as a separate individual, and does not possess him. It is a kind of liking which has strength, and which is not demanding. We have termed it positive regard. (p. 94)

After completing the introductions and invitation to the client to disclose her/his reason for presenting for therapy, it is incumbent upon the therapist to describe to the client the process of therapy and their rights as an individual participating in a therapeutic relationship. Although the requirements of each agency may exhibit some degree of variability, basic processes such as the length of each session, confidentiality, personal and professional boundaries regarding use of language, and other guidelines for conducting the therapeutic relationship merit review. Obviously, expressing the need to curtail the excessive use of obscenity is moot if there is no use of inappropriate language; however, the point of this is to reinforce the need for the creation and maintenance of healthy professional boundaries.

Confidentiality needs to be clearly and carefully explained to clients to assist them in understanding the limits of law and the requirements of the therapist. In many cases, clients will assume that everything that is shared with the therapist is in confidence. All general exceptions to confidentiality need to be explained to the client. In addition, when a therapist needs or is asked to communicate the progress of the therapy with another agency—for example, a school—the client needs to be informed of the request and written and informed consent must be obtained for the release of any information regarding the client. Even the fact that the client is attending therapy is confidential and cannot be released without the consent of the client (Lukas, 1993). This issue will be discussed further within the chapter concerning ethical responsibilities.

Ubiquitous Assessment within mental health settings involves being in a process of continuously evaluating the client's affect and cognition. Through this assessment, the therapist can direct the therapy to effect the greatest benefit for the client. Paying attention to the client's affect and the content of her/his thought, the therapist can work to direct the client's growth and insight into the individual's specific issues. The concern, respect, and understanding expressed by the therapist are directly related to the degree of therapeutic value the encounter between client and therapist will hold (Lukas, 1993). As the therapist listens and evaluates each contribution made by the client, the feedback can be tailored to demonstrate comprehension and understanding, and, in turn, this communication can lead to therapeutic outcomes.

# Chapter Eight

## The Written Report

One of the most difficult and time-consuming activities of any assessment is writing the final report. Oftentimes, reports are worthless in terms of the information they provide, and many consumers say they don't even take the time to read them. The primary reasons for the lack of perusal by those for whom they were written are the use of jargon, a tendency for the writer to sound as if only she/he could engage in such an activity, a tendency to focus on an individual's weaknesses without any mention of strengths identified, and the absence of "a distinctive prescription for educational practices…that leads to improved outcomes for students" (Heller, Holtzman, & Messick, 1982).

Reports for Ubiquitous Assessment focus on the totality of the individual, and not just the weaknesses identified from some traditional norm-referenced measure. Our goal should be, as Gopaul-McNicol and Thomas-Presswood (1998) state, "to write more culturally sensitive reports, rather than narrowly focused reports that are endemic to psychometricians" (p. 96). Having spent the time necessary to understand the individual's environment, circumstances, and situation, the report writer should describe the individual assessed as a whole person, and her/his unique talents and potential. Only by doing so can the report actually be useful to others attempting to develop or evaluate treatment/intervention plans for the individual assessed.

Ubiquitous Assessment reports need to be integrated from start to finish as related to the reason for referral. Our assessments should answer the questions raised about the possible problems the individual is facing with the primary emphasis on how to intervene or treat. Too often report writers overanalyze their assessment tools and identified problems that were never identified by those making the referral. The reality of any traditional assessment is that if we look long enough and use enough standardized, norm-referenced tools, we will find weaknesses in any person we assess. Why? Because each and every one of us has some weakness that can be identified. However, that should not be the point of our assessments. The report should be a "vehicle to convert the assessment data into faithfully designed and executed interventions that lead to improved student performance" (Surber, 1995, p. 161).

## The Basics

Psychological reports of all types are generally written not only to provide information about findings from an assessment but also to provide important information to other professionals working with the client, as well as for the client's parents and other family members. In general, all reports should provide detailed information regarding what was done during the assessment to ensure that others understand the findings and can use them to assist the client. In addition, reports provide historical information for those who might engage with the client later in her/his life (Surber, 1995). Results and interpretations can be compared to those obtained earlier, in order to determine client growth. Interventions and programs developed for the client described in the report can also ensure that past ineffective procedures are not repeated. Finally, the report provides documentation as well as accountability for what you do. The written document is a concrete representation of your daily activities and functions.

Reports can take many forms. We believe reports should be written for all types of assessments that one might conduct. Certainly, any educational or psychological/mental health assessment requires a report of how data were gathered and interpretations of those data. Counseling sessions should also be summarized. We do not want to break confidentiality, but we must provide a written summary of the concerns presented and the methods used in order to make certain that, should the problem reappear, we do not engage in activities that were previously deemed ineffective. Interventionists should also take the time to write up their results and actual client data should be included. Again, only by knowing what occurred in the past, what was successful and unsuccessful, can we design programs for clients that will meet the clients' needs as well as those concerned for the clients. Importantly, all reports should be written as soon as possible, as it is easy to forget important details that will help others in understanding the client.

Reports need to be written in a straightforward, concise manner. Wordy sentences, tired phrases, jargon, and long, run-on sentences should be avoided (Sattler, 2001). Grammar, punctuation, and spelling should follow accepted conventional rules, and the tense selected by the examiner (e.g., past, present) should be consistent throughout the report. The report should address and answer the reason the assessment was conducted. What was the reason for referral? If the reason for referral is, for example, reading problems, then to assess every other area in addition to reading is a waste of time and resources. Many school psychologists we know give the Beery Visual Motor Integration Test (VMI) to every client they assess. Why? Because someone has told them that according to the law you must assess a child in this area. The law generally referred is the Individual with Disabilities Act (P.L. 101-476), previously the Education for All Handicapped Children's Act (P.L. 94-142). However, this law says no such thing. The law only says a child must be assessed in all areas related to the *suspected* disability. If, after a thorough observation, there is no reason to suspect visual motor problems as related to the client's difficulties, giving more tests is, again, quite simply a waste of time. No additional information is provided and going on a search for problems is unethical. The hard fact is that if we give many tests or engage in other types of assessments we will find problems or weaknesses. Often, however, those weaknesses are irrelevant to the individual's actual performance in the world, and they learn quite efficiently to compensate for such weaknesses.

One of the most important issues related to report writing for Ubiquitous Assessment is the integration of information. If the information from background information, medical assessments, observations, and interviews (and tests if we are so unfortunate as to be in a situation where norm-referenced testing is required) is not integrated or the assessor does not take the time to truly interpret the findings but merely reports the data, then inconsistencies can occur across observations, interviews, and other tools. A truly integrated report discusses all strengths and weaknesses, making sure inconsistencies discovered across documents are reviewed and assessment situations are fully addressed. For example, if a client performs well in one setting and poorly in another, there often is no explanation in the report as to why this would occur. Is such a discrepancy due to differences between the two settings? Perhaps there is an issue of depravation affecting the client, such as hunger? Was there something going on with the observer, such as being in a hurry one day and not the next? Can we attribute the difference to changes in temperature, noise level, or interruptions? The counselor, psychologist, or mental health practitioner must take a close look at why such a discrepancy would occur for the individual they have come to understand and then analyze the reason for such differences in findings when interpreting the data.

Relatedly, differences between the current evaluation and an earlier assessment need to be described. Are differences in results related to changes in client history or maturation? History refers to those events that occur in the external environment that appear unrelated to events during the assessment situation. For example, a client experiencing a life-threatening illness may appear very differently from one observation to another. Information related to accidents and/or whether the client has experienced any psychological trauma need to be investigated as well, as she/he may respond and behave in seemingly uncharacteristic ways at different times.

Maturation refers to normal developmental changes that occur as an individual ages and time passes. Maturation is an especially important issue when working with young children because they can change quickly, or their growth may be significantly delayed. Specifically describing your hypotheses as to why differences between two observation sessions result in such discrepancies needs to be fully and completely described based upon your knowledge of the individual.

Furthermore, a summary of reports written by others (for example, a special education teacher or a doctor) and previous results need to be included in your written assessment. Oftentimes, psychologists will refer to reports written by others, but they may not be available or they may be lost. In addition, some reports need further interpretation so that the current reader(s) can understand what was said previously. This is especially true if the client has been evaluated by a medical specialist. Medical reports are not easily understandable to the novice reader, and may be difficult for the mental health provider to understand as well. Oftentimes, you will need to follow up with the specialist or engage another medical professional to interpret the information for you. In the school setting, school nurses can often serve this function very effectively.

Unfortunately, in many traditional reports, the individual assessed often gets lost in the language or rhetoric of psychometry. The assessor becomes so busy reporting technical information such as test scores that the client appears to become a series of unrelated numbers or observations. The IQ score is such and such, the achievement tests are thus and so, the behavior rating scales reveal that and this, the client responded this way in one setting and that way in another; but who the individual is as a whole person is ignored. The Ubiquitous Assessment report should be a description of the "whole" client and how she/he responds in different settings, with different individuals, and in different contexts. Imbedded within the information should be how the client functions in the natural environment as well as information provided by significant others related through interviews. By the time the reader reaches the end of the report, she/he should have a thorough view of the individual as an individual, not a series of numbers or unrelated observations.

Assessment writers need to evaluate their procedures and reports for evidence of bias. Bias can include not only ethnic and racial bias, but gender, sexual preference, age, political affiliation, religion, dress, and speech or dialectical bias. Surreptitiously, bias can creep into our reports. Bias and prejudice can often be seen through the stereotyping of clients, using tests with clients from different groups upon whom the tests are not standardized, and/or our own personal agendas. Making judgments within assessments based on biased beliefs is never in the best interests of clients. If we have personal agendas, we need to carefully evaluate them to ensure that we are objective in our dealings with our clientele. All mental health workers need to take the time to truly evaluate who they are and what they believe in order to be aware of any deep-seated bias or prejudice. Carefully attending to the issue of bias can ensure that our assessments and reports are conducted with the best interests of the client in mind.

How do we integrate reports to make them worthwhile and useful for the reader? First, prior to assessment, we take the time to actually determine what the reason for referral is. Simply taking the referral question on face value that a parent or teacher has verbally expressed or written down is not a reason for referral. We must take the time to meet with the parent or teacher and have him/her fully discuss the problem from his/her point of view. Consultation, discussed in chapter 2, is the primary means for fully exploring the problem. Only by engaging in collaborative consultation can we determine if the problem, as the referrer views it, is really the problem.

The result of consultation should be a definition of the problem behavior in terms that are measurable and observable, as the identified problem behavior will become our target behavior later when interventions are developed for the client. Defining the reason for referral in such terms allows us to know what to look for during our observations and determine the tools for measurement that we will want to use. Defining the behavior in measurable and observable terms provides us with a means for actually seeing the behavior, rather than assuming that the behavior exists. We can enter the home or classroom and know what behavior we are looking for and how to best record our observations of the problem behavior, as well as the techniques to use during assessment.

We also should determine who the readers of our report are going to be prior to writing the report. Is the report for the parent(s)? Teacher(s)? Other professionals? Administrators conducting an expulsion hearing? A court of law? We believe a report should be written in order that all readers will understand the complexities of the client assessed at a level they can comprehend. If terms or jargon must be used, those words or phrases should be defined within the report to avoid confusion and misinterpretation by the reader.

### Reason for Referral

The report should begin with the reason for referral. Providing information relevant to what was discussed during the consultation session can be an overview for the referral source to recall her/his specific concerns. Using the information from the consultation can help the writer elucidate the problem in concrete, definable, and measurable terms. Further, the reason for referral should have something to do with some difficulty a client is having in comparison to her/his peers. The reason for referral is not whether the client is eligible for services or special education, as such decisions do not assist in the development of intervention/treatment options, which should be the primary goal of our assessment.

**Background Information**

Following the reason for referral, information related to the client's background should be discussed and how such information relates to the reason for referral should be described. Irrelevant information or information that does not provide us with a better understanding of the client's problem should not be included. Such information might include a physical description of the client, her/his family living situation, or confidential information and/or rumors about the family obtained from other sources.

This section should include information about the client's developmental history and when important developmental milestones (i.e., walking, talking, etc.) were attained. The assessor or a health care provider must interview the parent to obtain this information in order to ensure accuracy. The report writer should be careful to attribute statements to the correct sources. Stating that the client attained developmental milestones at appropriate age levels begs the question of where the information came from. Certainly the assessor was not present while the client was attaining such milestones. Assuming development occurred at a normal rate can lead us to erroneous conclusions in our final analysis.

Information related to the client's current physical condition, including vision and hearing, should be included in this section. Medications the client is taking should be listed, along with the diagnosis for the prescription of the medications. Information related to accidents, illnesses, and injuries should be obtained as well. Taking the time to interview the parents or other caregivers will certainly pay off in the long run as the information obtained is integrated into the current levels the client is evidencing at the date of assessment. Again, noting who provided the information is necessary. Furthermore, it is important to summarize these findings. Simply referring the reader to some previously written report is not helpful.

Many view the educational/psychological/counseling/intervention report as the compilation of all information obtained during the assessment and at least a summary of information obtained from other sources. Making certain that the report is thorough, free from bias and jargon, and integrated throughout can help the reader develop a realistic view of the client.

Background information should also include information related to educational history. The number and location of schools attended, number of family moves, whether the client has resided in a group home, and any information relevant to the current referral question should be addressed. In addition, information related to prior assessments and school-districtwide testing should be included. Many child clients today are being referred to mental health professionals for scoring poorly on districtwide standardized tests. Reviewing cumulative files or confidential files that can be obtained from the school can provide additional information for gathering background educational information.

Most importantly in this section is a description of any interventions that have been tried to assist the client in the home, classroom, or community, and the outcomes of such interventions. Data from interventions should be summarized and reasons for their success or lack of success described. Generally, three interventions should be attempted prior to any traditional type of assessment. In addition, the interventions should be judged for treatment integrity. Treatment integrity is the degree to which the interventions were carried out as planned. If the interventions were not implemented in a consistent manner and data are not available, it is strongly recommended that the assessor move back a few steps before actually engaging in assessment.

**Behavioral Observations**

Observations of the client in the home or classroom, particularly at times when the client is evidencing the reason for referral, on the school grounds, at home, and during play should be conducted. Generally, classroom observations require several observations in order to develop a picture of how the client performs in the natural environment. Clients who are having difficulty often know that a stranger in the room is focused on them, and only by being present several times, and having the client be adjusted to our presence, will the client actually engage in her/his normal behaviors. Observations in the home can also be extremely useful. Seeing where the client lives, how she/he lives, and the resources available to the client can provide valuable information. With children this is particularly important as you can see how the child is treated in the home environment, the types of toys and books the child has available to him/her, and the interactions of the family within the home. Again, several observations may be necessary to get a true picture of the home environment.

Information related to the instructional environment of the classroom should be included in this section when appropriate. The instructional environment includes such areas as classroom configuration, the teacher's style of presenting tasks, how students are called on, scope and sequence of the assignments, pace of instruction, how and when feedback is provided, and how reinforcement and consequent programs used. This is not meant to be a teacher evaluation in any way, but a means to determine if the student/client is responding in the current classroom environment and whether that environment is appropriate for the individual.

To give a valid assessment, the client's behavior in the classroom should be described in terms of peer comparisons. Does the client appear significantly different from her/his peers in terms of age-appropriate social skills, positive interactions, and attention? Data from peers can be collected by using micronorms (see chapter 2). Additionally, the student's interactions in the classroom environment need to be observed. What does the student attend to? What is rewarding to the student? What tasks "capture" the student? How many prompts or cues does the student require from the teacher? How much practice does the student need to complete a task? Does the student respond to feedback? How much feedback is needed? Does the student ever experience success? When? For what activities? Are any unusual behaviors observed or are any other behaviors observed that would interfere with the student's academic or social functioning? These questions can help guide the observer in the classroom to get the most information possible while observing. Using the observation methods described in chapter 4 to collect these types of data can be most useful. Only by having actual data can valid judgments be made about the extent of a client's difficulty in the classroom.

In addition to classroom data, observations conducted of the client in her/his home and the relationships she/he has with siblings should be presented. Questions addressed in the report might include: Do the siblings interact at age-appropriate levels? Do they play together? What is the client interested in doing at home? Are rewards provided to the client and siblings for appropriate behavior? Is the setting loud and chaotic? Is the client ignored while other children are attended to? Describing client and sibling interactions, in addition to parent interactions, can give insight into what the child client experiences in the home on a regular basis and how these interactions carry over to other settings.

Observations of the client in the interview situation must also be described. How did the client enter the setting? Was she/he nervous, relaxed, and/or cheerful, and what actual behaviors led you to these assumptions? How was rapport with the client established and was it easy to do so? Was the client attentive? Able to respond to your questions? Or did the client engage in other behaviors that help describe who the client is? In addition, use the client's own words and behaviors to describe what occurred during the session(s).

As you go through these sections, are there areas you can tie together? Do you see evidence of early developmental milestone delays that may be evidencing themselves in the current situation? For example, a client who may have been delayed in fine motor skills earlier in life could be having difficulty with writing tasks or other visual motor activities. A good, solid, basic knowledge of developmental patterns across the human lifespan can be invaluable for determining if the client is engaging in age-appropriate ways and help as you integrate your data into the report.

**Evaluation Procedures**

A listing of all the assessment techniques used should be provided in this section with their accompanying abbreviations if they are used in the text of the report. Were all measures given in the client's primary language? Who was interviewed? Where were observations conducted? How many observations were conducted? Were other records reviewed? Were any alternative means of testing used during the process (e.g., sign language, interpreters, etc.)? Any method or tool used should be listed here.

**Results and Interpretation**

This section of your report will describe the actual assessment findings. Generally, in the traditional report, each test is described without any regard for integration of information. In other words, the assessor discusses results of cognitive, motor, social/emotional, academic, vocational, speech and language, and medical assessments.

### Traditional Assessments

As stated earlier, Ubiquitous Assessment does not promote the use of traditional norm-referenced tests. However, if you are in such a situation where some such tests must be administered, the following provides a brief description of how to include such information in your report.

Each tool used should be fully described. The name of the test and a description of what it measures should begin each section. What age ranges does the test cover? What is the mean (i.e., average) of the test and standard deviation? Are there additional scales on the test? What are they and what do they measure? Using the actual descriptions from the test manual can demonstrate that you have knowledge of the instrument you are using and know specifically the pros and cons of the tool. In addition, concrete descriptions of the reliability and validity of the instrument should be included. What was your rationale for using a particular instrument? Does the instrument used have anything to do with the referral questions raised? Can we be assured that results we obtain will hold true for the client tomorrow? Certainly, if you ever have the misfortune of being called as a witness in a court proceeding related to the client, the attorneys will question you about your knowledge of the reliability and validity of the tools you used (Ziskin, 1981). Furthermore, many traditional reports often "present[s] intellectual, educational, fine motor, and behavioral/emotional data in a compartmentalized format with each assigned its own heading. This format typically places the burden of determining what information is relevant on the reader, rather than the author" (Surber, 1995, p. 162). Therefore, you must always ensure that the referral question is addressed, all information is integrated, and most importantly, that you take the time to really interpret your data rather than just reporting scores. Reporting scores is not interpretation!

Describing this information in ways that the reader(s) will understand gives credence to your findings. Discussing the client's results and how those results compare to the standardization sample if an assessment tool is used is necessary. Standard scores should be the primary scores reported as they are the most valid and reliable, and they are transformations of raw scores. As raw scores tell us nothing about how a client actually did on a test as compared to her/his peers, standard scores indicate how far a particular score is from the test's average or mean and the standard deviation tells us the distance from the average or mean. Thus, standard scores allow us to make accurate comparisons of scores on one test to another. Percentile ranks should be reported as well, and these are often easiest to explain to those people unfamiliar with such testing instruments. Percentile ranks are the percentage of cases falling below a certain score. For example, if an individual obtains a percentile rank of 63, we would report that the individual with whom we are working scored as well as or better than 63 percent of people of her/his same chronological age.

Many tests report age and grade equivalents; however, there are important problems with reporting and using these scores. Grade and age equivalents are invalid and confusing. They do not represent equal intervals or units. The difference between first grade and second grade is not equivalent to the difference between tenth and eleventh grade, as growth is much more pronounced at younger age levels. In addition, grade and age equivalents are obtained by statistical procedures, not the actual scores individuals obtain on the test. For example, test publishers do not norm their tests on children at age levels of six years, two months; six years, three months; six years, four months, and so on. They instead engage in interpolation (i.e., Merriam-Webster's dictionary definition is to estimate values between two known values) or extrapolation (i.e., Merriam-Webster's dictionary definition directs us to infer values of a variable in an unobserved interval from values within an already observed interval). Furthermore, trying to compare grade and age equivalents from one test to another is error prone. Grade equivalents on one test may have a much broader band than scores on another test. For example, some tests may extend to four grade equivalents, while others extend only to three. Finally, grade equivalent scores on one test may be lower but indicate higher performance than on a second test. Again, this occurs because of how the test authors used interpolation or extrapolation.

Following the actual reporting of overall test results, and where appropriate, actual scores, subtest analyses should be reported along with the strengths and weaknesses noted for the individual evaluated. If previous tests or rating scales measuring the same domain (e.g., behavior difficulties) have been administered, it is appropriate and necessary to describe the similarities and differences obtained between the current administration and previous testing situations. Why would differences be obtained? Are they so large that something significant must be explored before continuing? How does the information obtained here "fit" with background information and observations? Are the results consistent? Are there discrepancies? Is a picture of the client as a total individual emerging? Again, the integration between background information, observations, and testing instruments is important to make clear to the reader, rather than a listing of discrete skills that never put the client together as an integrated individual.

Specific examples of the client's responses can be provided by "making up" equivalent questions without giving away the contents of the test. Such examples can help the reader(s) to see the unique strengths and weaknesses of the client, and how the client responds in specific situations.

Often assessors, in order to appear knowledgeable, will interpret tests in ways that are unfounded, and have no validity or reliability. Interpreting clinical or psychological problems using tools not designed for such purposes is unethical. For example, many assessors attempt to "read things" into a client's responses, without any basis in fact. These individuals seem to think that such interpretation makes them appear more professional and intelligent. However, such overinterpretation does nothing to help our clients, and certainly, in a court of law, a knowledgeable attorney familiar with the tools used will know that our clinical overinterpretations are not warranted. As an example, an individual with whom one of the authors worked in prior years used the Bender Visual Motor Gestalt Test, a drawing/copying test used to assess visual motor problems in a child client. The individual overinterpreted the test, noting to the parents the child's neurological problems based on the test. Unfortunately for the assessor reporting the results, the child's father happened to be a neurologist, and needless to say was quite interested in how such problems could be diagnosed in his son from a simple drawing test.

Each assessment tool used should follow this pattern, building on one tool to the next in order to develop a clear picture of the client's strengths and weaknesses and to detect common themes and patterns. Using all of the data collected allows you to make generalizations, develop interpretations, and create hypotheses about the reasons for the behaviors. Looking for consistency across results allows the reader to "know" the client.

## Ubiquitous Assessment

Within Ubiquitous Assessment the clinician would, most likely, not have used traditional norm-referenced tools; therefore, the examiner would provide a description of what was learned about the client/student from interactions, observations, and interviews. The following is an example of such a report section of a child experiencing academic problems and social withdrawal at school.

> Jose was described by his mother, classroom teacher, and mental health worker (who were all interviewed for this assessment) as a happy, playful child at home, and in the community. His classroom teacher stated that on the playground at school he tended to be a loner and did not approach other children to play. The interviewees reported that Jose has great potential and appears quite bright when he is interacting with adults. Jose is helpful to adults and his mother stated that he helps her with his younger sibling and tasks around the house. His classroom teacher said that Jose also helps other children in the classroom when others are distressed or unhappy. He puts his arm around them and attempts to help in any way he can although he does this in a quiet, unassuming manner.
>
> Jose was observed on the school playground and at the community park in his neighborhood. He showed good skills at making friends and played well with other children. He was never alone during these times and played at a level commensurate with his age.
>
> Mrs. Morena, Jose's classroom teacher, reported, as a part of the problem-solving consultation process, that Jose had difficulty reading and completing addition and subtraction problems at school. However, while conducting a home observation, Jose's mother gave Jose the grocery list

> and ask Jose to read the list to her to make certain she had not forgotten anything on the list. He was able to do so with ease. When the family went to the grocery store, Jose was in charge of the list and was able to read off to his mother the items, in addition to locating the correct aisle for different food stuffs by reading the signs on each aisle. Jose was also able to do addition and subtraction of goods in the grocery store when asked how much three cans of soup would cost, he was correct; and when asked how much a box of cereal that sold for $3.50 would cost with a 75-cent coupon, he also was able to respond correctly. Thus, Jose has the ability in the real world to do academics that his teacher says he is unable to do in the classroom and he plays well with others in the community. Jose would benefit from interventions that carry over his skills from the community to the classroom. He appears to function very well in the community setting and those skills need to be integrated into the everyday life of the classroom.

Ubiquitous Assessment has as its focus the individual both in assessment and in writing reports addressing the reason for referral. The report should delineate the reason for referral and provide treatment/intervention alternatives. By doing so, the interpretations and findings described in the report increase the treatment validity of the assessment techniques used, and the report is designed specifically for the person who made the original referral (Batsche, 1983; Surber, 1995).

## Report Summary

The report should conclude with a summary, either directly before the recommendations section or following the recommendations section. The summary should be one to two paragraphs, providing a synopsis of the results. New information should not be included in this section. Unfortunately, many readers turn first to the summary section, so make certain that the most relevant information is included here. The important thing to remember is to keep the summary brief.

## Recommendations

Recommendations should be developed in such a way that they will require continuing ongoing consultation with those who will work with the client. Thus, the first statement in this section should include the need for further consultation with the parent and/or teacher. Demonstrating your continued interest to be involved with the client can help those who must work directly with the client day-in and day-out.

So often assessors, once they have completed the report, move on to the next client on their list and never follow up with the first client to determine if any information gathered during their assessment was actually used. Following up with parents, teachers, and other significant individuals in the client's life ensures that the client is not simply doing the same things she/he did before, but actually is benefiting in some way from the information gathered during the assessment process.

Many report readers simply ignore the list of recommendations provided in the report. Writing vague, "pie-in-the-sky" recommendations that cannot be carried out in the home or school setting will be ignored and devalued even if they may appear to be well conceived. Certainly providing positive reinforcement to a client every five seconds could improve the client's behavior, but is this a realistic procedure for a busy parent? By coming to really know the client through the assessment, the writer should be able to develop positive interventions that can be implemented in the home and/or school setting with the assistance of the parent or teacher. Providing areas for improvement and some straightforward concrete methods for working with the client can be helpful to others. Most importantly, the intervention/treatment should be directly related to the initial question or reason for referral, as your job was to determine how best to help the client.

## Last Steps

All reports should be proofread upon final completion. Unfortunately, tools such as spell and grammar checkers, available on all computers today, do not correct all errors. *You* must proofread. This takes time. Make time for it. A report free of misspellings and punctuational/grammatical errors can enhance your professional reputation.

At the very end of your report, your name, professional title, and your degree(s) should appear, with space for your signature. You should only place your signature on the report once you have proofread your report and made all final corrections. Getting in the habit of only putting your name on the report once you have proofread it and made the corrections will ensure that all of your I's are dotted and T's crossed.

## Summary

Reports are difficult to write. Thinking in terms of what would be most helpful to the client/student is where we must begin. As Tallent (1988) stated, "the report writer recognizes (1) the need to be selective of the information to be conveyed and (2) the need to organize this information meaningfully (p.

123). Integrating the information is a necessity if we want to write a report to address the referral question and ensure the client/student receives the services she/he needs to function successfully in the world. Our overarching goal at all times, during assessment and report writing, should be on the individual and how the information we gather allows those in need of our services to make the most out of the information we collect and report. Only by doing so can we truly say we are providing our clients/students with best practices.

# Chapter Nine

## Ethical Considerations

As we define Ubiquitous Assessment to include a continuous process of interactions between the client and the counselor or therapist, ethical considerations remain at the forefront of the practice. Proper ethical conduct both implies and states that the counselor-educator or psychologist-therapist must perform her/his duties in accordance with proper and accepted standards of behavior. Acting in accordance within an ethically correct professional position will, in almost all cases, place the counselor or therapist beyond reproach. As we shall explore, ethical issues are generally presented as problems of confidentiality, scope of practice, scope of competence, and functioning in the best interest of the client. However, there are other, larger areas in which counselors and therapists should consider ethical questions and the role of assessment within our communities. For example, the questions of ethical use of assessment, particularly misuse of standardized tests for high-stakes decision making, raise issues of social justice and fairness (Orfield & Wald, 2000). From the most simple, seemingly innocuous mistake to the most egregious violations of law, ethical issues are critical to the successful implementation of best practices for the school counselor, school psychologist, MFT, and LCSW.

In our discussions with graduate students, we have begun conversations concerning ethical problems with the definition of ethics. The *Random House Unabridged Dictionary* (Flexner, 1993) defines ethics as "the rules of conduct recognized in respect to a particular class of human actions or a particular group, culture, etc." (p. 665). The implication of the rules of conduct is to develop a working definition of right and wrong within an organization or profession. For our purposes, we will examine right and wrong as they relate to issues of assessment and what constitutes the use of best practice. Ethical questions can range from the most simple to the more subtle and complex. Tjeltveit (1999) suggests that ethics have a mysteriousness and require critical thinking. "To think about the ethical character of psychotherapy we need, I think, to be like…sleuths. Although the mystery of therapy has to do with positive human change, not murder, complexities abound, and the skills of the detective can help us to understand and make good decisions about ethics and values in psychotherapy" (p. ix). To maintain ethical correctness requires constant vigilance on the part of the counselor, MFT, and LCSW.

All of the principal professional organizations have scripted sets of ethical guidelines to govern the practice of assessment: American Educational Research Association, American Psychological Association, National Council on Measurement in Education, 1999; American Counseling Association, 1995; and the National Association of School Psychologists, 1992. Each of these professional groups takes a strong stand to maintain ethical obligations, including "professional competency, integrity, honesty, confidentiality, objectivity, public safety, and fairness, all of which are intended to preserve and safeguard public confidence" (Schmeiser, 1995, p. 1). In Schmeiser's Eric Digest report, it is further stated, "Those who are involved in assessment are unfortunately not immune to unethical practices. Abuses in preparing students to take tests as well as in the use and interpretation of test results have been widely publicized. Misuses of test data in high-stakes decisions, such as scholarship awards, retention/promotion decisions, and accountability decisions, have been reported all too frequently. Even claims made in advertisements about the success rates of coaching courses have raised questions about truth in advertising" (p. 1). Sorting out our ethical responsibilities as counselors, psychologists, and therapists requires an examination of the salient issues of confidentiality, client's best interest, scope of practice, scope of competency, and larger questions of social justice and fairness (American Educational Research Association et al., 1999).

Unethical practices can, at the least, impugn the professionalism of the therapist or counselor and at the most egregious level result in firing, arrest, and possibly conviction. To give examples of this continuum of ethical transgressions, we have created three levels corresponding to low, medium, and high levels of ethical impropriety. The lowest levels simply impugn the therapist's credibility, whereas the high levels portend disaster. A simple example of a level one error is to not return a phone call. Taking the message and losing the note under a pile of other documents is easy to do; however, the communicative message to the caller is that their appeal to you was, at the least, of little value to you and at the worst, ignored. The consequence can be a loss of credibility, a chastising call to the supervisor, impugning the work ethic of the therapist, or a discrediting of the agency or school's concern for the client. Simply, the small mistakes can carry significant consequences.

A level two ethical error can create more deleterious results for the clinician. Failure to identify clear boundaries of professional behavior from activities appropriate for nonwork settings can jeopardize one's ability to function with impunity. For example, use of inappropriate jokes, personal conversations, and untoward or improper comments made by coworkers are not considered correct or productive use of time within the office setting. Inappropriate jokes or conversations could be cause for dismissal if practiced at work. Anachronistic cultures of sexism, racism, or other antihumanistic activities should have no place within our society, let alone our schools or mental health settings. Misuse of e-mail or other computer-generated humor can impugn the work ethic and credibility of the counselor or therapist within the office environment. Examples of this type of unethical practice can include personal or business-related phone use during work time, use of the Internet for shopping or "surfing" to relieve the boredom created by a client cancellation, or other misuse of professional time on task. All of these activities can create suspicion of a poor work ethic or lead to serious consequences for the counselor or clinician. Venting and release of professional frustration needs to be done within parameters consistent with good ethical judgment and with the intent of fostering the betterment of the organization's culture. If the therapist needs emotional release or a reprieve from boredom, it is healthy and ethically correct to recognize this and attend to one's own needs appropriately.

The third level of ethical impropriety includes all activities for which the counselor or therapist will be terminated and, most likely, face license revocation. These activities can include but are not limited to, sexual contact with clients, failure to report child abuse or neglect, disrespect of confidentiality laws and procedures, sexual harassment of clients or coworkers, and/or egregiously failing to maintain best practice in one's professional relationship with clients and coworkers. Although these improprieties may seem obvious, counselors, MFTs, psychologists, and LCSWs are not immune from mental health issues of their own. To protect ourselves and our profession, it is important that we help those responsible for supervision to be aware of ethical problems as they arise.

The overarching concept of ethical standards is that we are responsible for the social and educational consequences of our behavior. As we conduct ourselves within our particular work setting, we are responsible for the maintenance of proper and professional conduct. As we work to improve the quality of life for our clients, we must remember that we are also assessed by our clients based upon our behavior and the manifestation of our professional identity. Ubiquitous Assessment implies that as we assess our clients; they, too, are assessing us as therapists or counselors. The distinction between the client's assessment of us and our role is that the overall outcome of each client contact is our responsibility as professionals. Furthermore, beyond our concern for the consequences or outcomes of our work with the individual and family, we need to be aware of the impact we make upon our school or agency and the larger community we serve. Ethical considerations circumscribe all of the counselor or therapist's behavior.

**Ethics as Related to Scope of Practice and Competence**

Performing professional duties within the scope of one's practice is a basic ethical responsibility. Although the notion of practicing within the scope of one's professional training has some obvious features, what is not so clear is the delineation of what the parameters are concerning which assessments fall within each counselor, psychologist, or therapist's scope of competence. To assist the clinician in making ethically correct determinations of test use, most publishers, in accordance with American Psychological Association (APA) recommendations of assessment tools, use a three-tiered system. From the APA Ethical Standards for Psychologists (1953), there is definition of the three-level system.

- Level A: These instruments are straightforward paper and pencil measures that can be administered, scored, and interpreted with minimal training. With the aid of a manual, these tests can be used by responsible non-psychologists such as business executives or educational administrators. This category includes vocational proficiency and group educational achievement tests.
- Level B: These tests require knowledge of test construction and training in statistics and psychology. These products are available to persons who have completed an advanced level course in testing from an accredited college or university, or equivalent training under the supervision of a qualified psychologist. This category includes aptitude tests and personality inventories applicable to normal populations.
- Level C: These tests require substantial understanding of testing and supporting topics. Supervised experience is essential for the proper administration, scoring, and interpretation of these instruments. Typically, Level C tests are available only to persons with a minimum of a master's degree in psychology or an allied field. These instruments include individual tests of intelligence, projective personality tests, and neuropsychological test batteries. (APA, 1953)

It is possible to create further distinctions for duties performed by the professional when we consider the responsibility and ethical questions posed by the issue of scope of competence. Whereas scope of practice implies a set of standards that applies to the entire profession, scope of competence implies that the clinician or counselor is truly able to perform the task at hand. The counselors' and psychologists' scope of practice are defined by the state education codes and the mandates of their school district (National Association of School Psychologists, 1992). MFTs and LCSWs regulations concerning the scope of practice and the scope of competence are set forth by the Business and Professions Code (Riemersma, 2003). Mary Riemersma (2003), the executive director of the California Association of Marriage and Family Therapists, defined the "scope of practice" and "scope of competence" and clarifies the distinctions between the two entities:

> How does a "scope of competence" differ from a "scope of practice"? Scope of competence limits what the individual within the profession may do and is determined by one's education, training, and experience. These two scopes tend to overlap, and in some cases, go hand in hand. One, when practicing marriage and family therapy, has a duty to work within one's scope of practice, but is also limited by scope of competence. Scope of practice is defined for the profession as a whole; scope of competence is individually defined/determined for each marriage and family therapist. (p. 112)

Concerning the use of tests, Riemersma further stated, "One issue that regularly arises in the course of discussing the MFT scope of practice is, may the MFT lawfully administer and evaluate psychological tests. The answer to this question is, of course, like any other work, limited to one's scope of competence. Further, according to the 1984 Attorney General's Opinion, MFTs have the statutory authority to construct, administer, and interpret psychological tests as long as such testing is done within the course of one's practice—i.e., must be done with patients one is also treating" (p. 1).

As further examples of the differences between scope of practice and scope of competence, even though it may be in the scope of practice for psychologists, counselors, MFTs, or LCSWs to provide therapy to individuals with personality disorders, if the particular psychologist, MFT, or LCSW does not have competence, or sufficient competence, to provide therapy to an individual with a specific personality disorder—for example, schizotypal personality disorder—then provision of therapy for that individual may be construed to be outside the therapist's scope of competence. Conversely, if the therapist is a competent massage therapist, it is outside the scope of practice for that psychologist, MFT, or LCSW to perform massage services for their mental health patients.

Recognizing the boundaries of one's professional training and competence is fundamental to the provision and maintenance of best practice in assessment (Salvia & Ysseldyke, 2004). Although it is also a responsibility of test publishers to distribute and advertise materials in an ethical manner, the ultimate determination of appropriate use resides with the clinician. Each of us needs to self-assess our ability and training to decide if a particular test or assessment is within the scope of our competence, knowledge, and practice (Gregory, 2004; Riemersma, 2003).

Ethical conduct is defined for each profession: psychology, counseling, MFT, and LCSW, through the professional organizations and within appropriate business codes. For example, the American Counseling Association's Code of Ethics and Standards of Practice (1995) contributes: "Limits of Competence. Counselors recognize the limits of their competence and perform only those testing and assessment services for which they have been trained. They are familiar with reliability, validity, related standardization, error of measurement, and being used prior to using this type of computer application. Counselors take reasonable measures to ensure the proper use of psychological assessment techniques by persons under their supervision" (p. 36).

**Confidentiality and the Limitations of Client Privilege**

Confidentiality is a concept borrowed from jurisprudence and is related to the notion of privileged information or confidential communications (Flexner, 1993). Originating within English law, confidential communication gave clients the privilege of sharing information with their counsel and restricting its access to the court. Within medicine and psychology, confidentiality works to protect the client from unethical dispersal of information gathered from any counseling, therapy, or consultation (APA, 1992, Principle 5). Ethical release of privileged information, including even the fact that the client is known to a therapist or a mental health organization, is only allowed with the expressed and written consent of the client or when withholding information is a violation of law.

Laws related to the reporting of client information come into effect when the client is posing a danger to herself/himself or others. In addition, individuals who have committed an act of child or elderly physical or sexual abuse must be reported to the appropriate law enforcement agency (Gregory, 2004). "A general ethical principle held by most professional organizations is that confidentiality may be broken only when there is clear and imminent danger to an individual or society" (Salvia & Ysseldyke, 1998, p. 67). In schools and mental health agencies, this responsibility is defined as a part of the work of the mandated reporter.

The mandated reporter is also required to report any threats made by clients toward potential victims. Stemming from a 1967 California law decision that followed the death of college student Tanya Tarasoff, the Tarasoff rule demands that therapists inform potential victims of their client's expressed intent to cause harm to another individual (Wrightsman, Nietzel, Fortune, & Greene, 2002). Also referred to as the duty to warn, Tarasoff is designed to force therapists to recognize their responsibility to protect both the client and the potential victim from causing harm to one another (Gregory, 2004). Many states have followed California's example by requiring therapists to provide reasonable care for both their clients and potential victims of their clients (Gregory, 2004). In the explanation of confidentiality to clients, it is essential that both the protections and the limitations of protections are carefully explained. As cited earlier within the school counselor's chapter, failure to properly orient the client to the limitations of confidentiality can create a major breach of counseling's basic tenet: trust. Best practice dictates the provision confidentiality within its legal limitations.

## Informed Consent and Client Protections of Privacy

Before formal assessment can begin, clients (or in the case of minors, their legal guardians) must be given the opportunity to accept or reject any proposed evaluation. For any individually administered test, this right is defined as having a reasonable understanding of the tests to be administered, their purpose, and potential outcomes of the assessment process. For example, students being referred for assessment for special education need to have the consent of their parents prior to testing. This consent needs to include the parent's comprehension of potential outcomes of the assessment, including the confidentiality of the results. In situations where the client is non-English speaking (their primary language is not English), opportunity for translation into their native language should be provided.

In Ubiquitous Assessment, where the use of informal evaluation methods is the rule, it is even more critical that the process of assessment is explained to the clients and that they give their informed consent to the process. Statements such as, "You will be seen by me for evaluation and assessment for the creation of a plan of care or therapy. Although we may use some formal assessment instruments, the majority of this clinical evaluation will be made by informal techniques such as interviewing, observation, and evaluating any of your past history of psychological interventions." This explanation can help to clarify the assessment process for clients. As with traditional, formal assessments, Ubiquitous Assessments should include a written consent form. This document can support the therapist's claim that this consent was obtained by giving the client sufficient information and that they volunteered to participate in the assessment. The third requirement for informed consent, that the client was competent to understand the process, is the responsibility of the therapist. Through the process of explaining the assessment, it will be clear whether or not the client comprehends the therapist (Gregory, 2004).

A final caveat of assessment is to protect the inviolacy of the client (Groth-Marnat, 2003). For example, in our assessment classes, students are required to participate in an assessment of a classmate. This process includes clinical interviewing, informal observations, and the use of some formal assessments such as the Measures of Psychosocial Development. The assessment is presented to the "client" in the form of a written report and is shared with the client and the professor. To protect the student's inviolacy, we instruct both the examiner and the examinee to remember that this is a part of a class, and that one should disclose only information that is within the bounds of a classroom exercise and not intended to break secrets or invade the privacy of the student. As this rule relates to assessment within mental health settings or schools, clinicians and counselors need to consider how a sense of inviolacy may differ within specific cultures or by individual. For example, if assessment protocols ask if pleasure in sex has been diminished, this may not be appropriate for use with particular religious groups.

## Communicating Assessment Results

In accordance with principles of best practice and the provision of services designed to be in the interest of the client, the communication of assessment results can have positive therapeutic outcomes. This is especially true when the assessment results are communicated in the client's primary language and at a cognitive level appropriate for the individual to comprehend. The key principle is that the client fully understands the conclusions of the assessment (Groth-Marnat, 2003). In Ubiquitous Assessment, the dissemination of assessment results should be therapeutic. As the individual receives the information gleaned from assessment, the therapist and client are engaged in a dialogue and the process acts as a method of validating the results. Valid results that are communicated with sensitivity to confidentiality and client interpretation can be therapeutic or assist the therapeutic process.

Unfortunately, disclosure of the results of the psychological examination is not always met with positive therapeutic outcomes. One of the potentially dangerous and contentious areas of client-therapist relationship can be provoked by the psychological evaluation (Sattler, 1988). Disagreement over diagnostic conclusions of the evaluation can lead to litigation claiming professional malpractice (Wright, 1981). "Complaints include allegations of wrongful use or misuse of tests, wrongful use of derived data, misinterpretation of tests or interviews, invasion of privacy, and violation of confidence" (Sattler, 1988, p. 764). To protect the counselor or psychologist against professional liability, reports should be clear, accurate, and reflect best practice. Here, too, if issues of inviolacy are involved, those potentially damaging of hurtful discoveries need to be eliminated from the report. If the therapist is able to maintain appropriate respect for the client in the psychological evaluation, the trust and integrity of the relationship will be a continuation of the therapy.

By reporting results to the client, the therapist is continuing the conversation and building upon the rapport that has been established. This implies that the results will be communicated positively and that the therapist will purposely direct the evaluative comments to further the client's self-understanding and sense of self-worth. Assessment conducted with this aim eschews labeling and prefers positive conceptualizing of the individual's experience. For example, a depressed client's self-esteem can be enhanced by acknowledging her/his desire for self-improvement and personal growth for participating in therapy. Hope can be reinforced by the therapist's recognition of resiliency factors discovered through the assessment process. Resiliency factors could include client education level, psychosocial supports in the environment, and previously identified personal accomplishments. Connecting on a soul level with the client, the therapist can communicate powerful images keyed to the health of the client (Webb, 2004).

## Ethical Questions of Assessment with Underrepresented Groups

As we stated in our first chapter, Ubiquitous Assessment uses informal and ideographic or individualistic techniques based upon promoting respect for the person through recognition of multicultural and diverse client populations. Ubiquitous Assessment supports the belief that all persons are uniquely representative of a culture, gender identification, spirituality, language, age, ethnicity, and other factors of individuation. This position is consistent with critical multicultural perspectives (Goodman & Carey, 2004). This philosophy relates directly to the American Psychological Association's (APA, 1992) Principle D: Respect for People's Rights and Dignity: "Psychologists are aware of cultural, individual, and role differences, including those due to age, gender, race, ethnicity, national origin, religion, sexual orientation, disability, language, and socio-economic status. Psychologists try to eliminate the effect on their work of biases based on those factors, and they do not knowingly participate in or condone unfair discriminatory practices" (p. 37).

These principles relate to support of culturally and linguistically diverse individuals. As these issues have bearing upon and affect the assessment process, counselors, MFTs, and LCSWs need to actively work to reduce bias. Bias in Ubiquitous Assessment refers to the combination of effects from the lack of knowledge of culturally relevant information for the provision of therapy and the errors inherent in the misuse of psychometric techniques on culturally different individuals or groups (Gopaul-McNicol & Thomas-Presswood, 1998; Jones, 1988; Sandoval et al., 1999). Because of the complexity of cultural and linguistic differences, counselors and therapists need to continually reassess their own competencies and renew their training to enhance skills and develop expertise in the area of multicultural assessment and counseling (Gopaul-McNicol & Thomas-Presswood, 1998).

As culture continuously evolves, it is critical that counselors and therapists remain vigilant and aware of the role of identity and related psychosocial issues. Each community contributes to the subjective reality of the individuals living within its borders. Individuals living in poverty and those repressed by racism, sexism, and other racist identity politics require an openness to understanding this potential conflict within the client's reality. "Race, class, and gender dynamics combine to create a larger playing field with more options for some and a smaller, more limited field for others" (Kincheloe & Steinberg, 1997, p. 107). As counselors and therapists practice Ubiquitous Assessment, they are sensitive to the ethical issues of fairness and its opposite, unequal psychosocial and economic environments, and the tremendous impact these factors have upon the client. Cornel West (1999) sees this issue as an ethical problem for all concerned citizens: "Democracy always raises the fundamental question: What is the role of the most disadvantaged in relation to the public interest? It is similar to the biblical question: What are you to do with the least of these?" (p. 9). These are the ethical questions of the largest scale. Individuals with mental illness are among the most discriminated against in the entire American culture. How we accept these individuals and work to advocate for them reflects our true ethical value system.

Although advances have been made in the creation of assessments designed to achieve fairness in multicultural evaluation, significant issues of reliability and validity of the instruments continues to posit legal and ethical dilemmas for the counselor or therapist (Groth-Marnat, 2003). To ameliorate the assessment process and minimize the effect of bias, sensitivity to the cultural and linguistic qualities of different populations is key to the success of the counselor or therapist. By maintaining openness to diversity and respect for all individuals, the counselor or therapist achieves the greatest possible positive contribution toward the growth of their clients.

As we described in *Critical Multicultural Conversations* (2004), issues of multiculturalism are multifarious and complex. Although many would wish to simplify the problem and erase the differences between individuals with a form of cultural encapsulation (Wrenn, 1985), allowing the thinking that dominant cultural beliefs are reflective of correctness perpetuating the hegemony of white cultural capital (Bourdieu, 1993). Sue, Arredondo, and McDavis (1992) offer:

> There are those who would like to define culture broadly to include race, ethnicity, class, affectional orientation, religion, sex, age, and so forth. As such, multicultural counseling would include not only racial and ethnic minorities, but also women, gays and lesbians, and other special populations. There are those who prefer to limit the discussion of multicultural counseling to what has been referred to as "Visible Racial Ethnic Minority Groups"—African Americans, American Indians, Asian Americans, and Hispanics and Latinos. Those who hold this point of view acknowledge that to some extent all counseling is cross-cultural, but the term can be defined so broadly that it dilutes the focus on racial and ethnic concerns (a primary one being racism) and allows counseling professionals to avoid and omit dealing with the four major groups in our society. (pp. 477–78)

Ethical issues concerning multicultural assessment require a constant vigilance on the part of the counselor or psychologist to maintain not only the minimum standards acceptable but to transcend best practice to achieve a virtuous position (Jordan & Meara, 1990). This means that the counselor moves beyond recognition of cultural difference to a position of valuing the individual and acting in a way that intends to enhance the culture or character of the diverse individual (Cottone & Tarvydas, 2003). Ethical correctness in Ubiquitous Assessment is an honoring of individual differences and a full inclusion of all diverse groups in the provision of best practices of evaluation and therapy in counseling and psychology.

## Ethical Considerations Regarding Referral and Interagency Cooperation

Best practice requires clinicians to refer their clients to other agencies or individuals when the client's needs can be better served or accommodated. An example may include the need for neuropsychological assessment or other assessments outside the scope of the counselor's, MFT's, or LCSW's practice or competence. Using referral, the clinician is in a position to further the trust and respect of the client for the entire mental health field by releasing their "proprietary interest" in the patient or counselee (Bernstein & Hartsell, 2000). The more clinicians clearly articulate their role and scope of practice to their clients, the greater the chances will be that the clients can comprehend the process of therapy.

As therapists work to clarify their professional roles and responsibility, clients can be relieved of their uncertainty and doubt concerning their treatment (Bernstein & Hartsell, 2000). It is of ethical importance that clinicians define themselves for their clients and that other related agencies and practitioners are supported. "A large segment of society already views the mental health profession and its practitioners with skepticism, cynicism, and uncertainty. Public expressions of mutual respect and support among the disciplines will increase public confidence in the profession and induce more people to seek services" (Bernstein & Hartsell, 2000, p. 210). This is especially true within certain cultural groups that perceive therapy as related to weakness or related to rehabilitation for criminal behaviors.

## Ethics in the Use of High-Stakes Assessments

The issue of the ethical propriety of using single measures or tests for the determination of high-stakes decisions continues to provoke ethical debate. For example, deciding to identify a student for special education based upon a handicapping condition of mentally retarded requires the use of multiple measures of intelligence (Sattler, 1988). With regard to the high-stakes issues of promotion and high school graduation, the use of single measures of assessment appears to defy best practice and is unethical (Orfield & Wald, 2000). In an era when our nation is besieged by ethical improprieties in almost every aspect of the public domain from business to government, schools and mental health institutions should take some leadership in exposing ethical inequalities and act to eliminate the misuse of standardized testing. Although the particular issue of assessment is more of an issue confronting the schools, mental health workers and clinicians both serve children of the community and have children of their own attending public schools. Deleterious affects of the use of high-stakes assessments must be seen as a community and social problem, not just a school issue (Kohn, 2000).

Large-group, standardized testing was never designed to provide valid individual assessment or placement decisions (Kohn, 2000). Large-scale assessments have been justified as measures effective for the evaluation of classrooms, schools, and communities. Group tests were never intended to be used to make high-stakes decisions for individual students. In fact, none of the major problems involved in the determination of an individual's test scores or results can be assessed when giving a group assessment. According to Salvia and Ysseldyke (1998), "Five factors impede getting an accurate picture of a student's abilities and skills: the student's ability to understand assessment stimuli, the student's ability to respond to assessment stimuli, the nature of the norm group, the appropriateness of the level of the items (sufficient basal and ceiling), and the students' lack of exposure to the curriculum being tested" (p. 181). All of these issues beg the larger question: Is it ethical to administer high-stakes tests to individual students using group techniques? In fact, misuse of tests with students who are unable to comprehend the assessment stimuli may transcend ethical impropriety: it may be invalid and illegal (Salvia & Ysseldyke, 2004).

Another problem with the possible misuse of tests involves misinterpretation of test results from failure to obtain sufficient information. Meyer et al. (2001) provide an excellent example:

> In psychological testing, the nomothetic meaning associated with a scaled score of 10 on the Arithmetic subtest from the Wechsler Adult Intelligence Scale-Third Edition (Wechsler, 1997) is that a person possesses average skills in mental calculations. In an idiographic assessment, the same score may have very different meanings. After considering all relevant information, this score may mean a patient with a recent head injury has had a precipitous decline in auditory attention span and the capacity to mentally manipulate information. In a patient undergoing cognitive remediation for attentional problems secondary to a head injury, the same score may mean there has been a substantial recovery of cognitive functioning. In a third, otherwise very intelligent patient, a score of 10 may mean pronounced symptoms of anxiety and depression are impairing skills in active concentration. Thus, consistent with Shea's (1985) observation that no clinical question can be answered solely by a test score, many different conditions can lead to an identical score on a particular test. (pp. 143–44)

Basic to the ethics of assessment is the question: Is this test or evaluation in the best interest of the client or examinee? The caveat is to avoid doing harm or causing undue hardship to anyone (American Educational Research Association et al., 1999). According to Gregory (2004), "The functional implication of this guideline is that assessment should serve a constructive purpose for the individual examinee. If it does not, the practitioner is probably violating one or more specific ethical principles" (p. 582). Regarding high-stakes tests, what is the ethical implication when 70 percent of New York's seniors taking a high school exit math test fail and are denied graduation? Even though New York's Education Commissioner, Dr. R. Mills, tabled the 2003 math test results because of the political embarrassment, it is clear that the process was unethical (Winerip, 2003, June 25).

As if high failure rates are not bad enough, one additional question of ethics in the use of high-stakes testing remains: teaching to the test. In authentic assessment, teaching material and assessment of the student's understanding of the subject matter are appropriately connected. In norm-referenced, standardized assessments, teaching to the test was considered to be cheating (Sacks, 2000). Whereas testing companies like Kaplan formerly prepared middle- and upper-class families' children to learn test-taking strategies to improve SAT scores, now schools are almost exclusively focused on teaching both strategies and facts to students in order to increase school's scores. This change in ethics appears questionable and warrants further examination. While it is clear that assessment should reflect and measure specific criterion demonstrating knowledge and comprehension of curriculum, should the opposite also be true? Should curriculum follow the test's content? This does appear to be the case in California as well as in other states across America. At the Agassiz School, a public school in Boston, Mass., one of the fifth-grade teachers, Ms. Rorie, stated, "Everything at the Agassiz is teaching to the state tests. It's deadening for teachers and kids. They follow the state testing curriculum block by block" (Winerip, 2003, June 11). What's worse? Vigorously teaching to standards, and not having the state's test be constructed to assess those standards. This is the case in California. The latest assessment tool chosen for California's annual evaluation, the aptly named, nationally normed California Achievement Test (CAT), does not match the California standards for curriculum and instruction.

What is the message embedded within these two scenarios? Teach to the standards and your school loses; teach to the test and the teachers and children are "deadened" (Delpit, 2003). This is inconsistent with the ethical mandate to avoid negative consequences (American Educational Research Association et al., 1999; Gregory, 2004). All citizens need to be cognizant of this issue. We all want high standards for our students. Evaluation of this type does not improve instruction or student outcomes (Miner, 2000). For assessments to truly improve instruction, there needs to be broad community participation in the process of test development (National Forum on Assessment, 1993). In this manner, inclusionary and democratic principles can return to act for the betterment of our educational communities.

Acting on our client's and children's behalf is in accordance with tenets of best practice and ethical decision making. Maintaining confidentiality, protecting client inviolacy, gaining informed consent, using valid and reliable assessments, practicing within the scope of one's professional practice and competency, and all of the other parameters of good ethical practice are critical to the successful work of the counselor, MFT, and LCSW. Our continuous vigilance is critical to the work of Ubiquitous Assessment. Being ever watchful in an ethical sense, we will be giving our clients the best mental health and educational opportunities for learning and personal growth.

# Chapter Ten

## Ubiquitous Assessment

The field of assessment continues to evolve and benefit from challenges to its hegemony within educational and mental health settings (Orfield & Wald, 2000). A specific example of these challenges includes the 2003 Supreme Court decision supporting affirmative action, *Grutter v. Bollinger.* This position of support for affirmative action was strengthened by the conclusion of the majority of justices supporting the use of qualitative assessments in college admissions (Schmidt, 2003). By supporting a "highly individualized, holistic review of each applicant's file, giving serious consideration to all the ways an applicant might contribute to a diverse learning environment" (O'Connor, 2003, p. S14), the justices were specifically disassociating the admission process from strictly quantitative measurement. In particular, this historic decision was an admonishment for colleges using a quota formula of adding points to the SAT, the Graduate Record Examination (GRE), or other standardized assessments in their administrative efforts to improve diversity. By favoring qualitative measures, the Court encouraged the development of well-reasoned and balanced admissions policies that reflected the diversity of the community. According to Justice O'Connor (2003) in expressing the majority opinion in the *Grutter v. Bollinger* case, "The Law School has determined, based on its experience and expertise, that a 'critical mass' of underrepresented minorities is necessary to further its compelling interest in securing educational benefits of a diverse student body" (p. S13).

An even more recent example of the challenge to formalized testing's dominance or hegemony in high-stakes decision making involves the federal legislative reauthorization of the Individuals with Disabilities Education Act (IDEA) (Lloyd-Jones, 2003). One of the most significant changes that has been recommended includes the development of alternatives to IQ testing as a major component of the qualifying criterion for special education placement (Forrest, 2003). The new emphasis is upon assessing the student's needs within a systems approach featuring the Student Study Team (SST) process (Berninger, 2002). The goal is for psychologists and counselors to immediately deliver interventions and provide appropriate remedial opportunities (Pianta, 2003). The design's purpose is to expedite delivery of instruction and to give prompt intervention to students in need. This really should be no surprise. Since the authorization of IDEA, the mandate was intended to be to educate children in the "least-restrictive educational placement" (*Federal Register*, 1977). In 1986 Lawrence Lieberman wrote, "For those who are failing in regular education classrooms, special education must be the last resort, not the first option" (p. 5).

To promote change in the process, the use of Ubiquitous Assessment can facilitate immediate intervention within the regular education classroom. However, creating a mandate to serve all students needing services to receive support from the school psychologist is a very different role from providing assistance to one or even two hundred students a year. Working within the system, making structural changes, and supporting the teachers to make those accommodations for individual students significantly shifts the role of the school psychologist (Lloyd-Jones, 2003; Pianta, 2003). Consistent with the proposed new regulations from Congress, these authors believe it is time to fulfill the intended mandate of P.L. 94-142 (*Federal Register*, 1977) and to save special education for the most needy and to only serve those students truly handicapped.

As opposed to continuing the cumbersome processes that have been used in the past—for example, the fifty-day timeline for individual psychological evaluation completion—current pressures of time, funding, and societal values are calling for large-scale, rapid, and efficient assessment of mental status or student outcomes. The difference today is that we know that simply testing and sticking the result of a standardized assessment in the cover of a student's cumulative folder is time and money wasted. What is required today is a change in the structure of the classroom and within the walls of the mental health clinic to increase the efficiency and the outcomes for students and clients. What is being demanded is a reduction in the failure rates of these institutions in the delivery of mental health services to students in need of positive interventions (Ringeisen, Henderson, & Hoagwood, 2003).

Because of the proposed changes in IDEA, school counselors and school psychologists will be required to work more efficiently with the entire school community (Lloyd-Jones, 2003). From assisting teachers in the classroom to helping students within the breadth and totality of their school experience, attention to the overall social and mental health needs of the community is the focus of the new mandates (Pianta, 2003; Ringeisen, Henderson, & Hoagwood, 2003). Ubiquitous Assessment supports the development of school interventions that are inclusive of all aspects of the student's development, including prosocial behaviors, classroom behaviors, and all other related school-based phenomena affecting learning (National Research Council, 2000). These conceptualizations of the work of school counselors and school psychologists demand a belief in the goal of process not in the unidimensional pursuit of a specific program seeking a predetermined destination such as special education placement or the empty test score resulting in not qualifying for extra help (Elias, Zins, Graczyk, & Weissberg, 2003).

This same stultifying thinking applies to the overall mental health needs of the individuals and students we serve. As a part of the entire revolution in conceptualizations about systems and outcomes, mental health is turning away from a sickness/medical model to a health/wellness model. According to Short (2003), "the Surgeon General's report calls for a new conceptualization of children's mental health services and a moving away from a traditional, clinical orientation to one that includes a focus upon normal social and emotional development and prevention/early intervention. Essentially, the report promotes a move from a clinical service delivery perspective to a more population-based perspective" (p. 182). This is a call for counselors, school psychologists, MFTs, and LCSWs to change their orientation from a problem-focused approach to an orientation that is less clinical and more empowering for the individual (Short, 2003).

As an ironic result of the new accountability requirements such as NCLB, the quality of the educational experience has been in a diminished role. This is exemplified by the large numbers of dropouts and pushouts within large metropolitan school districts (Schemo & Fessenden, 2003). The same phenomenon occurs within mental health agencies. For example, individuals with mental health issues are often seen briefly by an attending psychiatrist in an emergency, prescribed medication (therapy), and sent home or to the street. Aligned with a recent surgeon general's report to reconceptualize children's mental health services from a strictly clinical orientation to a process that considers a comprehensive consideration of normal developmental and social needs, mental health service providers need to "make real" the treatment and after-care programs these professionals deliver to all members of the community (Short, 2003). The public should no longer be willing to support programs that provide insufficient and inadequate services to its constituents.

Within our schools, a recurring theme has been to focus upon standards-based instruction. The emphasis is upon student outcomes such as passing high school exit exams or achieving scores of average or above (Bushman & Goodman, 2003). This will always make sense for the "average" person or those above average; however, 50 percent of all students are below average. This is what average means. In our mental health centers and schools, the focus has been on outcomes: test results and diagnosis. The acts of teaching and the delivery of therapy have been of secondary importance. Within Ubiquitous Assessment, the emphasis is on instruction and therapy/intervention, and the evaluation of student or client benefit is ongoing. Joining the two processes does not eliminate the need for state tests or diagnostic decisions for MediCal or other insurance billing. Testing and diagnostics appease political and economic constituencies, and unfortunately, this pressure will continue to be part of the reality educators must confront. However, large-scale assessments are only a small piece of the overall function and process of school experience. Ubiquitous Assessment is concerned with the overall, day-to-day process of learning and its facilitation.

Learning and therapy are fundamental to student and client rights. Consistent with recent Supreme Court decisions supporting affirmative action, changes in the SAT to use more qualitative assessment techniques (Schmidt, 2003), and revisions in the evaluation requirements related to the Individuals with Disabilities Education Act (Forrest, 2003), Ubiquitous Assessment provides effective and appropriate techniques for educators and psychologists to meet the assessment needs of students and clients. As we have described for each of the professions (MFT, LCSW, school counselors, and school psychologists), Ubiquitous Assessment provides a valid and reliable methodology linking psychological evaluation with therapeutic interventions or changes in instruction. By minimizing the separation between the two formerly distinct entities, clinicians can more efficiently and effectively provide clients with the services they seek or require. The paradigm shift is to give service, instruction, or therapy/intervention, and to use assessment to enhance the process, not as the primary outcome or, in some cases, the final product (Elias, Zins, Graczyk, & Weissberg, 2003; Pianta, 2003).

## Contributions of Physics and Feminism

Ubiquitous Assessment is the result of reflection upon the practice and teaching of psychological evaluation. As we have struggled with the split between theories and foundations of assessment and the pragmatic practices of the counselor or psychologist, the calling for a unifying theory was apparent. The reductive thinking that created the division between teaching and assessment or the distinction in mental health separating therapy and evaluation of mental status is a result of the either/or, black-and-white thinking that has been endemic within Western thought since modernism's origins (Kincheloe & Steinberg, 1997; Willinsky, 1998). Kincheloe and Steinberg (1997) eloquently describe modernism's effect:

> Sir Isaac Newton extended Descartes' theories with his description of space and time as absolute regardless of context. Clarifying the concept of cause and effect, Newton established modernism's tenet that the future of

> any aspect of a system could be predicted with absolute certainty if its condition was understood in precise detail and the appropriate tools of measurement were employed. Thus, the Cartesian-Newtonian concept of scientific modernism was established, with its centralization, concentration, accumulation, efficiency, and fragmentation. Bigger became better as the dualistic way of seeing reinforced a rationalistic patriarchal expansionist social and political order welded to the desire for power and conquest. Such a way of seeing served to despiritualize and dehumanize, as it focused attention on concerns other than the sanctity of humanity (Fosnot, 1988). (p. 36)

As modernist thinking helped support scientific and political division within the world, psychology grew into a profession that has embraced the separation between assessment and therapy. What has become clear to us, as practitioners, is that this separation between these two entities—assessment and teaching or therapy—is contraindicated. In other words, the purpose of schools and mental health providers is to achieve academic and/or interpersonal learning (Ringeisen, Henderson, & Hoagwood, 2003). These purposes are best achieved by unifying the processes of assessment with teaching and therapy to provide immediate assistance to those needing our expertise (Short, 2003).

Good examples of the paradigm shift that we are suggesting come from the ever-changing world of physics (Greene, 2000; Hawking, 1988; Kaku, 1987) and the feminist movement (Miller, 2003). As postmodernism has grown from modernist refutations, so physics has evolved from Newton's basic observations to complex conceptualizations of the universe. The world of third-millennium physics has been defined through two major theoretical positions: Einstein's theory of relativity (the big bang) and its polar opposite, subatomic quantum physics. "The two theories underlying the tremendous progress of physics during the last hundred years—progress that has explained the expansion of the heavens and the fundamental structure of matter—are mutually incompatible" (Greene, 2000, p. 3). Until recently, these two positions defined the polemic of physics: how do we explain the phenomenon of the universe? String theory provides a method of unifying two extremely divergent theories of our universe's origin (Greene, 2000). "String theory has the potential to show that all of the wondrous happenings in the universe—from the frantic dance of subatomic quarks to the stately waltz of orbiting stars, from the primordial fireball of the big bang to the majestic swirl of heavenly galaxies—are reflections of one grand physical principle, one master equation" (Greene, 2000, p. 5). As string theory attempts to link subatomic quantum physics and its opposite, Einstein's theory of relativity or the big bang theory, Ubiquitous Assessment seeks to connect evaluation processes with instruction or therapy.

Using a combination of formal and informal evaluation techniques, Ubiquitous Assessment provides an effective model for the delivery of therapeutic and educational best practices. Ubiquitous Assessment is a unifying theory; its techniques link not only evaluation and teaching or therapy but it connects with each person as a unique individual within a diverse, multicultural community. The focus is upon the individual and her/his unique, specific situation and the particular experiences that frame her/his life.

In addition to seeing a parallel to physic's string theory, Ubiquitous Assessment draws theoretical support from feminist theory. Consistent with critical pedagogical theory, feminist theory offers unifying concepts to create strength and empowerment. One of the most recent examples of this thinking comes from Jean Miller's (2003) writing with the Wellesley Women's Center. Miller has conceptualized a method of collaboration to promote synergy's strength within human interrelationships. Calling this phenomenon "mutual empowerment," Miller (2003) elaborates on its effectiveness:

> Mutual empowerment is a two-way, dynamic process in which all people in a relationship move toward more effectiveness and power, rather than one moving up while the other moves down. Mutual empowerment is a possibility in all relationships, even when one person clearly has more power than the other, such as parent-child, teacher-student, therapist-patient. The people in these relationships are not equal along such dimensions as age, experience, knowledge of a certain field, and so on. Yet the goal in these types of unequal relationships is similar: for the more powerful person to foster the growth of the other person. The move is toward change, toward equality and mutuality (Miller, 1976). Mutuality means joining together in a kind of relationship in which all participants are engaged, empathic, and growing (Jordan, 1986). Mutual empowerment involves finding new ways to make interactions growth-fostering for everyone in the relationship. (p. 5)

By having everyone benefit, growth becomes the unifying element, and egalitarianism is enhanced. The concept of mutual empowerment is consistent with Ubiquitous Assessment's value upon the individual and the promotion of positive self-worth.

## The Contribution of Conceptual Validity

As Carlos Santana sings in *Smooth*, "Give me your heart, make it real, or else forget about it." "Making it real" or providing truth or veracity is an essential element in human relationships. Two of the most sacred examples of interpersonal connectedness include the loving relationships Santana sings about and the connection between therapists and clients, and in best-case schools, psychologists, counselors, teachers, and their students. That these relationships are valid or real will require an authentic assessment of the achievement of the therapy or school's stated goals. The validity of Ubiquitous Assessment is best evaluated through this type of qualitative assessment. Examining the elements of the immediacy of service delivery, the psychologist's effectiveness in establishing rapport with students or clients, the degree of student or client connectedness, and other important components of successful student or client participation generate data concerning the validity of the educational and therapeutic experience.

Validity in all of its forms (content, construct, criterion, and conceptual), "making it real," is an essential component of Ubiquitous Assessment. As we reviewed earlier within this text, there are three major and traditional types of validity: construct, criterion, and content. There has been a fourth type of validity offered that appears to fit best with Ubiquitous Assessment: conceptual validity (Maloney & Ward, 1976). Conceptual validity posits that the truth or proof of the veracity of one's experience is dependent upon the individual perspective or reality (Maloney & Ward, 1976). Ubiquitous Assessment seeks to make the experience of learning or therapy conceptually valid for the student or client as well as the counselor or therapist.

The perspective offered by conceptual validity is closely aligned with the humanistic view of our world contributed by Carl Rogers (1961). Rogers's belief was that no one else could have our set of personal identity, experience, and abilities. Because each of us is unique, the psychologist or counselor is compelled to assess each person as an individual. How each person compares to the psychologist's conceptualizations of normal is certainly relevant; however, this consideration is secondary to the desire to comprehend the individual and her/his uniqueness. Conceptualizing the client as an individual makes room for many possible explanations of her/his unique adaptation and adjustment to the life circumstances that she/he has encountered. As we continue to examine the uniqueness of each of our students and clients, conceptual validity gains greater recognition and value as a tool in the process of understanding and accepting the student or client's point of view or reality.

In our multicultural world, standardized conceptualizations of normal and the use of techniques that primarily reinforce competitive sorting are not viable, humanistic, or conceptually valid (Bigelow, 2000; Giroux & McLaren, 1994; Kincheloe & Steinberg, 1997; Kohn, 2000; Perry, 2000). As we identify the inadequacies of old paradigms, such as the use of the discrepancy model to select students for special education placement, newer conceptualizations offering assistance to students and clients are becoming available (Stuebing et al., 2002). As we reviewed in the chapter on school psychology, assessment needs to be immediate and the interventions must be effective. To match and honor the diversity that typifies our classrooms and communities, we need to promote Ubiquitous Assessment and attend to the instructional and therapeutic needs of our clients in the here and now. We cannot waste instructional or therapeutic opportunities by limiting our conception of best practice by effectively separating assessment from teaching or treatment. That the student is in our class or that the client is in therapy is sufficient basis for professionals to provide for the individual's needs through positive engagement. Ubiquitous Assessment calls for this style of immediate, gestalt connection between the student or client and their experience of learning or therapy.

## The Value of Rapport

The connection with the student or the client is best defined as rapport. Rapport is a harmonious connection (Flexner, 1993) between two or more individuals. Sympathy is included in the Random House definition, but psychologists prefer the use of the word empathy: relating to the condition of the student or client. The strength of this relationship or rapport is key to the success of all learning and personal growth. Herb Kohl (1994) identifies this concept in his beautiful book, *"I won't learn from you" and Other Thoughts on Creative Maladjustment* and cautions against its absence: the teacher's (or therapist's) inability to develop rapport can be viewed as a mismatch and positive outcomes will be thwarted. This mismatch could be based upon misunderstanding about culture, gender, sexual preference, or any implied "ism" separating the client from the therapist or the student from the teacher. Breaking down the cultural disconnections between those of us who are different requires connection with the conceptualization that we are, in fact, all different, distinct individuals. The work of the therapist is to understand the individual and to accept her/his uniqueness.

Carl Rogers (1961) was modern psychology's original master of unconditional positive regard. He reflects, "I come now to a central learning which has had a great deal of significance for me. I can state this learning as follows: I have found it of enormous value when I can permit myself to understand another person" (p. 18). To further clarify this statement, he adds, "understanding is risky. If I let myself really understand another person, I might be changed by that understanding. And we all fear change. So as I say, it is not an easy thing to permit one's self to understand an individual, to enter thoroughly and completely and empathically into his frame of reference. It is also a rare thing" (p. 18). This condition of unification with the client, understanding and feeling her or his experience, is the heart of rapport. By accepting the client's subjective reality, we create conceptual validity and give the experience meaning. As Herb Kohl (1994) stated, "To agree to learn from a stranger who does not respect your integrity causes a major loss of self. The only alternative is to not learn and reject the stranger's world" (p. 6). Rapport opens us to the other and validates the experience.

Throughout this text, we have emphasized the use of the term *assessment* over the term *test* or other measurement terminology. This is because assessment is a global term and is related most frequently with the psychologist's fundamental tool: the clinical interview. This conversation between the client and the therapist, counselor, or psychologist performs a multiplicity of functions. Not only is the assessment ubiquitously imbedded within the conversation, but the additional functions of therapy, rapport building, relationship sustaining, process affirming, and other important tasks are occurring as well. In this multifaceted dynamic, simply giving a test would be monodimensional, the polar opposite of assessment's complexity. Calling this process Ubiquitous Assessment draws attention to the fact that these processes are occurring throughout the entire encounter between the psychologist or counselor and the client or student.

## Work as Joy and Soul Food

One of the most important ingredients missing within the Western view of education and mental health is the balancing force of soul and an emphasis on those activities that bring us joy (Schultz, 1967; Webb, 2004). To mitigate the dearth of spirituality within schooling and to emphasize the role that soul and joy play in our lives, we often begin our classes on assessment by asking the students: How have you made it this far in life? How have you survived? Implied in this question is the assumption that the road has been filled with challenges, but the individual has weathered these adversities and has survived to tell about them. The answers that we hear represent the hopes and joy our students possess: my God, my children, my faith, my raison d'être. It is this bliss that keeps us buoyed when the weight of life's dark side tries to bring us down.

As therapists, counselors, and psychologists, we confront the same human-condition issues as our students and clients. Integrating life's challenges with a healthy perspective requires that we examine and expand our awareness to include joy, humor, and spirituality within our experience. Balancing the light and the dark sides of life is the challenge of the counselor and psychologist. Lisa Delpit (2003) likens the need to integrate all of our self in the educational process to the experience of African American schooling. She describes the integration as follows: "The aim of African education for the mind could not be separated from education for the body. The body was seen as the divine temple, housing a spirit. As a result, the education for the mind and body was also linked to education for the spirit. Therefore, in the African tradition, it is the role of the teacher to appeal to the intellect, the humanity, and the spirituality in their students" (p. 16). For counselors, psychologists, and therapists, this interconnecting equates to our seeing all the parts of the person before us: her/his color, gender, identity, and spirit.

For many who come to us as students or clients, there have been tremendous and disproportionate challenges in their way. Not all have had "equal opportunity" or access to achieving success. Michelle Cooper (2003) contributes,

> Since the founding of the nation, democratic ideals—the beliefs that all human beings have equal value, deserve equal respect, and have equal opportunity to exercise their freedom to participate in all aspects of society—have been recognized as the national creed. However, the historic reality of the United States suggests that the realization of these democratic ideals has yet to be achieved. Within this society, there have always been people, traditionally racial minorities and women, who bear scars of having lived as marginalized and stigmatized persons. For these Americans, in particular, democracy's promises of recognition, opportunity, equality, and justice remain largely unfulfilled. (p. 75)

Cooper's comments could also include gay, lesbian, or transgendered individuals, people with disabilities, and all other underrepresented groups. For these students and clients, we need to recognize the circumstances surrounding her/his personal and social-political struggle in order to understand the enormity of her/his path to success (Gray, 1999; McLaren & Carlson, 1996).

Connecting with students and clients requires a soulfulness and spiritual presence in addition to clinical skills and expertise (Webb, 2004). As E. M. Forester sensitively requested in his literary challenge to those who formerly supported colonialism's divisions, "Only connect." The connections between our self and the significant others that we serve—our students, parents, and clients—are the manifestation of our commitment to providing best practice within a spirit of mutual empowerment (Miller, 2003). When this connection is working best, the greatest learning and personal growth potential is released and a sense of equanimity is achieved. Sylvia Boorstein (2002), in her recent work on Buddhism's contribution to mental health, reflects upon equanimity's value as an essential outcome of paying attention. As we pay attention to our students and clients, we develop better insights into their struggles, and we are better able to connect to the significance these conflicts possess.

Seeing the struggles our clients carry from their perspectives, the challenges of comprehending the reality that these individuals experience, can pose not only professional issues but personal problems for us within our work. Many of the clients and students whom we see present us with significantly stressful dilemmas. Empathizing with our client or student and simultaneously upholding sufficient clinical distance is the finest point of best practice. Because this balance is so difficult to maintain, we sometimes fail to achieve it. Irving Yalom (1996) describes the issues of countertransference within the therapist, Ernest, as he struggles over his erotic feelings for his client, Carolyn:

> Ernest knew he needed help. First, he turned again to the professional literature on erotic transference and found more there than he had expected. For one thing, he was comforted by the knowledge that, for generations, other therapists had struggled with his dilemma. Many had pointed out, as Ernest had concluded on his own, that the therapist must not avoid the erotic material in therapy or respond in a disapproving or condemning fashion lest the material be driven underground and the patient feel that her wishes are dangerous and damaging. Freud had insisted that there was much to be learned from the patient's transference. In one of his exquisite metaphors, he said that to fail to explore erotic transference would be analogous to summoning a spirit from the spirit world and then sending it away without asking it a single question. (p. 271)

As we experience our humanness and as Yalom suggests from his side of the couch, it is not unusual for us to need to participate in therapy to relieve some of the pressure and conflict that the opposing forces of transference (the client's subconscious projection of repressed feelings toward the therapist) and countertransference (the arousal of repressed feelings within the therapist by the client as expressed by Ernest) create (Hunt, 1994). In the view of many clinicians, our need for participation in a therapeutic process could be considered essential (Kopp, 1971).

While working as a school counselor at the Oyster River Middle School in Durham, N.H., one of our fellow staff members committed suicide. When I received the call, there was an overwhelming feeling of sadness coupled with a tremendous sense of inadequacy and insecurity. Why didn't I see this coming? Why didn't this colleague share her feelings with me? What was missing in me that Debbie (a fictional name) couldn't share her feelings with me? Inadequacy was beginning to turn to guilt about my professional shortcomings. During a gestalt exercise at a New England regional American Counseling Association conference, I broke down while experiencing a chairs "dialogue" with Debbie.* Through the experience of talking to Debbie and as I continued to explore my feelings, therapy was calling me to see what was behind my guilt.

For a two-year period, I participated in individual and group therapy. The therapy was called psychomotor therapy and its guru, Al Pezo, was a New Hampshire resident. Although Al was not my therapist, his spirit was there in the bodies of co-therapists Sue Mautz and Craig Cleeves. The therapy included a combination of structures designed by the therapists to accentuate the point of the psychomotor intervention. For me, the problem was that I was trying to hold everything up, and I couldn't possibly be responsible for everything, especially my colleague's completed suicide. Could I?

The metaphoric structure for my therapy included creating a physical resistance by covering my chest with large pillows. The therapists and other group members began the structure by gently pushing down on the pillows while I tried to "hold it up." Gradually, as the pressure increased, I soon realized that I could not succeed: I couldn't hold them up. The result and learning for me was in the letting go. I broke down. My determined resistance was gone, and the tears were the release of the pain of what I had perceived as my biggest professional failure. The pain was literally gut wrenching, and through the agony, I released the hurt I had hidden. This therapy was hard physical and psychological work, but the benefit was equally significant. Not only was I able to forgive myself; I was able to let go of the absurd notion that I could be available for everyone and responsible for everything. I realized that no matter what the issue, I cannot always hold up or cope or create the happy ending. I am human, and I have limits.

Another learning of therapy was to look for the irony. The strong must allow weakness in order for the person to grow and maintain strength. Conversely, the weak must look inside to see their inner strengths and courage. Yin and yang continue to play their parts, and as we expand our awareness, we learn more of our duality. For a mindful educator or psychologist, there is learning to be gained in each encounter.

In our journey to grow and improve our ability and skills, we need to continue to examine ourselves and hone our awareness of the joys and soulful

---

* The chair dialogue is a Gestalt Therapy technique. In this technique, the client is directed by the therapist to talk to an imaginary individual seated in a chair across from the client. Generally, this imaginary individual is a significant person and the conversation concerns an unresolved issue. The term "unfinished business" has also been associated with this technique. The dialogue with the empty chair gives the client an opportunity to have the conversation they wished they could have to get out unresolved feelings.

energy that has brought us to our current position with work, home, and self. Paying attention and being mindful is the highest compliment we can bestow upon ourselves and those with whom we are present (Conze, 1959). As we grow to experience the richness of life and all of its components, we will increase our ability to help others find their joy and fulfillment (Watts, 1972). This is a mission worthy of our full attention. Within each of us is the power to make the world a better place. As psychologists and counselors, we contribute caring, respect, and deep understanding of the value and worth of each individual. In this way we heal ourselves (May, 1990).

## The Affirmation of Assessment

Many of the arguments within this text may lead the reader to assume that the process of assessment is somewhat diminished in its role because of these authors' work to enmesh evaluation techniques within educational and therapeutic process. In fact, the opposite is in effect. We believe that assessment has the preeminent role in the process of therapy and instruction because individuals need specific and individualized treatments and teaching. No one receives best-practice teaching or therapy when she or he is treated generically. Each individual requires a unique educational experience or therapeutic intervention based upon a deep understanding of the diversity she/he represents (Nieto, 1996; Sleeter, Gutierrez, New, & Takata, 1996). In no way can this be conducted without individual assessment.

The point of Ubiquitous Assessment is to gently and subtly imbed the evaluation within the therapeutic process in such a way that the student or the client can experience the connection as educational or therapeutic. One of our favorite images of the evaluation process involves the initial assessment of Randle P. McMurphy (Jack Nicholson) in the film *One Flew Over the Cuckoo's Nest* (1975). The plot of the film centers on McMurphy having been sent to a state psychiatric hospital for evaluation to determine his mental status. During the initial evaluation, the psychiatrist deftly interviews McMurphy and creates an exceptionally strong rapport. As McMurphy smokes his cigarette, he admits to fighting and having had sexual relations with a fifteen-year-old, but he discounts his behaviors by adding that "Rocky Marcianno had forty fights, and he's a millionaire." McMurphy's antisocial personality is not lost on the psychiatrist, but the clinical interview is so subtle that it could easily be mistaken for casual conversation. As the topics switch from the psychiatrist's photograph of a recently captured salmon to matters of McMurphy's incarceration, the transitions are smooth. McMurphy sums up the interview by saying, "I'm gonna cooperate with you 100 percent, Doc." As the film proceeds, it becomes abundantly clear that the opposite of McMurphy's testimony more closely resembles the truth. Such is the reality of relationships with individuals with antisocial personality disorder.

For educators, psychologists, and counselors, assessment is not only a prerequisite for teaching and therapy but it must continue throughout the relationship. As we continue to reevaluate our progress, we see the outcomes of our teaching and interventions and we create a reinforcing loop (Senge, 1990). Therefore, the learning and growth is mutual for the teacher/therapist and the student/client. We both grow from our experience.

### The Need for Research within Ubiquitous Assessment

As we have articulated throughout this text, the processes of assessment and therapy or instruction have been identified as closely connected within a clinician's or educator's daily practice. Although these authors have alluded to the seamless quality of Ubiquitous Assessment's processes, little research is available to validate these conclusions. We would encourage and welcome quantitative and qualitative study of the theories and practices of Ubiquitous Assessment. Regardless of the name of the process of linking assessment and instruction or therapy, we believe that the more these activities are combined, the more effective and efficient will be the outcomes of instruction and therapy.

William James (Coles, 1977) cautioned, "Originality cannot be expected in a field like this, where all the attitudes and tempers that are possible have been exhibited in literature long ago, and where any new writer can immediately be classed under a familiar head" (p. 542). In many ways it may appear to some that we have traveled back to psychology's roots and abandoned the "scientific" work of most of the last century. More correctly, we believe that the new scientific contributions, such as the example of string theory's unifying possibility, are recognizing that in the nonlinear business of education and psychology, simple modernist solutions such as group achievement testing are failing our students (Swope & Miner, 2000). The same oversimplification of mental health processes is causing failures for psychological service delivery as well (DuPaul, 2003). Turning schizophrenics back into their bushy lairs or onto cold streets with a therapy consisting of a handful of medication is not best practice either. Mental health practitioners need to be the advocacy force pushing politicians to create healthy alternatives to street life and criminal survival activities such as stealing food from locked cars.

Ubiquitous Assessment is calling for reexamination of the fundamental and essential qualities of the therapist/counselor connection or rapport. This includes a refutation of the norm-referenced, standardized testing and the continued diminishing of the interpersonal relationship so critical to learner and client growth. The importance of the progress of the last century cannot be overlooked; however, to get lost in the economic realities of mass-produced mental health services and No Child Left Behind (NCLB) accounting of Annual Yearly Progress (AYP) is to succumb to centuries-old puritanical, work-ethic driven, commodification of what should be the root humanistic and egalitarian purposes of education and psychology. Although NCLB's intent to promote scientifically based, research-proven intervention is laudable, much more research supports qualitative and authentic assessment for student interventions, hence the recent *Grutter v. Bollinger* decision (Schmidt, 2003). Ubiquitous Assessment affirms belief in the individual practitioner, and we trust the clinical judgment of the counselor or psychologist to perform in accordance with accepted standards for best practice. Within this method, there is ample room for individuality and diversity on both sides of the couch.

Questions for future research within Ubiquitous Assessment include the use of formal evaluation within the practice of clinicians. How much emphasis is placed upon the results of formal assessment? In which situations is the use of formal assessment mandated? Which formal assessments are the most commonly used? In what way does the clinician perceive there to be a balance between the use of formal and informal techniques? Is Ubiquitous Assessment an activity of most clinicians: Are clinicians assessing continuously throughout the therapeutic experience? And for school psychologists and counselors: Are educational psychologists continuously assessing student strengths and concerns? How is this input used to create effective interventions for students within the classroom? Is the connection between the therapist or psychologist enhanced through Ubiquitous Assessment?

Science has, in some ways, betrayed us. In our attempts to objectively evaluate (standardization) students and clients, we have subtly removed ourselves from connecting on a personal level and placed a clinical detachment between us. As Alan Watts (1961) explains, "We have been seeing all along that although Western science started out by trying to gain the greatest objectivity, the greatest lack of involvement between the observer and the observed, the more diligently this isolation is pressed, the more impossible it is found to be" (p. 106). Ubiquitous Assessment works to fully connect the clinician and the client and to drop the authoritative guru stance of the all-knowing healer. The pedagogical difference is that we join the student or the client as an ally in their quest for learning and self-improvement. We are together with the student or the client, not boundaryless but connected with a joint purpose. As we drop our authoritative discourse (McLaren, 1997), we assume a position of relative equality with the student or client. We do not relinquish our leadership in the process, but our position is egalitarian not authoritarian. This position is aligned with Shelly Kopp's (1988) admonishment, *If You Meet the Buddha on the Road, Kill Him*. We have no one other than ourselves to create and maintain our path through life. As therapists and educators, we must always try to remember that our clients and students are responsible for their choices and actions, too. Our role is to help and to guide, but we do not change others: we change ourselves.

Last, we change ourselves and help our students and clients develop healthy paths within the context of the family and culture where we both live. Although we are ultimately and existentially alone, we actually live with and as a part of something larger than ourselves: our family, our culture, and our community. Within these contexts, it is essential that we consider our role as educators and therapists and our contribution to and support from the larger psychosocial world where we work and live. In an earlier book, we discussed the interconnections that we share (Goodman & Carey, 2004). Habermas (1984) called this phenomenon of interconnectedness universality: all people share a right to "self-development and self-realization" (Warren, 1995, p. 167). For us, as psychologists, counselors, and therapists, we gain from and simultaneously contribute to a community that supports individuals and groups representing diversity and democratic manifestations of equal treatment of one another. As we perceive Ubiquitous Assessment to be the seamless interrelationship between assessment and therapy, we, too, see an interconnectedness between the counselor/therapist and the community within which she/he works and lives. Sustaining ourselves and our community are also parallel processes. Concomitantly, the same degree to which we are maintained and supported, there will be a direct influence upon the work that we provide for our students and clients. Ubiquitous Assessment unites the circle and seeks to bring together all of the entities working to provide social justice within the community into one force for change. In this democratic and critical method, we can learn to connect our professional responsibilities with the personally satisfying experience of being a part of creating a larger, more psychologically supported community based upon principles of social justice and meaningful connections between the participants.

# APPENDIX

**SOPHOMORE COUNSELING FORM**

Student's Name: ______________________ Date: ______________

I. Items listed below that are checked are those that were covered with your student on the above date.

A. ___ Credits earned to date __________ Credits still needed for graduation _______

B. ___ Classes needed for makeup* ______________________
*See four year plan

**CALIFORNIA HIGH SCHOOL EXIT EAXM:** English __________ Math __________

C. ___ College Plans: UC Campus (ACT of SAT and SAT II) ______________

CSU Campus (ACT or SAT). JC Campus Private University ____________

D. ___ College Testing: 9th ______________
10th ______________
11th ______________
12th ______________

E. ___ Grade Point Average: High School ________ CSU ________ UC ________

F. ___ NCAA Eligibility: Sport(s) ______________________

G.

| Junior Year | Senior Year |
|---|---|
| English | English |
| U.S. History | Government/Economics |
| P.E. | P.E. |
| Math | Math |
| | |
| | |
| | |
| | |

H. 10th grade Summer School __________ 11th grade Summer School __________

II. Co-Curricular Activity ______________________ (CSF) _____

COMMENTS: ______________________________________

______________________________________

______________________ ______________________
Parent's Signature Parent's Signature

______________________ ______________________
Student's Signature Counselor's Signature

Junior Conference – Class of 2005

**Name**: ______________________________ **Date**: ______________

**Total Credits to Graduate**: _____ **Total Earned Credits to Date**: _____ **Credits Deficient**: _____

| CALIFORNIA HIGH SCHOOL EXIT EXAM | TESTS | NCAA |
|---|---|---|
| Verbal _____ Math _____ | SAT _____ SAT II _____ ACT _____ | _____ |

**Graduation Course Requirements**

| | School Year 03 – 04 | School Year 04-05 |
|---|---|---|
| English | _____ | _____ |
| Math | _____ | _____ |
| Science (Life) | _____ | _____ |
| Science (Physical) | _____ | _____ |
| Health/Geog | _____ | _____ |
| World History | _____ | _____ |
| US History | _____ | _____ |
| Gov/Econ | _____ | _____ |
| Foreign Lang/Art | _____ | _____ |
| Physical Education | _____ | _____ |

**Course work (credits) to complete during summer**: ______________________________

**Senior Schedule**: ___________, ___________, ___________, ___________,

___________, ___________, ___________, ___________.

**Post High School Options**: ______________________________ Other: ______________

**Notes**: ______________________________________________________

______________________________________________________________

______________________________________________________________

______________________________
**Student Signature**

______________________________
**Counselor Signature**

Senior Conference – Class of 2004

**Name**: ______________________________ **Date**: ______________

**Total Credits to Graduate**: _____ **Total Earned Credits to Date**: _____ **Credits Deficient**: _____

| **CALIFORNIA HIGH SCHOOL EXIT EXAM** | **TESTS** | **NCAA** |
|---|---|---|
| **Verbal** _____ **Math** _____ | **SAT** _____ **SAT II** _____ **ACT** _____ | _____ |

**Graduation Course Requirements: (semesters remaining)**

**Senior Schedule**

| | **Fall Semester 03-04** | **Spring Semester 03-04** |
|---|---|---|
| English | _____ | _____ |
| Math | _____ | _____ |
| Science (Life) | _____ | _____ |
| Science (Physical) | _____ | _____ |
| Health/Geog | _____ | _____ |
| World History | _____ | _____ |
| US History | _____ | _____ |
| Gov/Econ | _____ | _____ |
| Foreign Lang/Art | _____ | _____ |
| Physical Education | _____ | _____ |

**Additional course work needed**: __________, __________, __________, __________,

__________, __________, __________, __________.

**Post High School Options**: ________________________________________

**Notes**: ________________________________________

________________________________________

________________________________________

______________________________
**Student Signature**

______________________________
**Counselor Signature**

**PERSONAL DATA FORM — ADOLESCENT**

(To be completed with parent or guardian)

**Identifying Information**

Student's Name:________________________________ Sex (M/F):____ Date of Birth:__________

Address:______________________________________ Phone:____________________

School Attending:_________________________________ District/City:____________________

School Principal:_________________________________ Counselor:____________________

Mother's Name:________________________ Age:________ Occupation:________________

Father's Name:________________________ Age:________ Occupation:________________

Address and phone (if different from above):_______________________________________

________________________________________________________________________________

Name of employer(s):_______________________________ Work phone:____________________

| Siblings Name | Sex | Age | School and Grade |
|---|---|---|---|
| | | | |
| | | | |
| | | | |
| | | | |
| | | | |
| | | | |

Family Pediatrician:_______________________________ Phone:____________________

Address:________________________________________________________________________

Counseling status: None__________ Currently receiving______________ Past________________

Psychiatrist/Psychologist:___________________________ Phone:____________________

Address:________________________________________________________________________

Patient(s) in family:______________________________________________________________

________________________________________________________________________________

Feelings about counseling:________________________________________________________

________________________________________________________________________________

________________________________________________________________________________

**Relationships**

Please make a brief statement under each of the following headings indicating how the student gets along with each of the people listed below, including reaction to conflicts and ability to resolve or handle them.

With father:____________________________________________________________________

________________________________________________________________________________

________________________________________________________________________________

________________________________________________________________________________

With mother:___________________________________________________________________

________________________________________________________________________________

________________________________________________________________________________

________________________________________________________________________________

With siblings:___________________________________________________________________

________________________________________________________________________________

________________________________________________________________________________

________________________________________________________________________________

**PERSONAL DATA FORM — ADOLESCENT (continued)**

With neighborhood friends:

With schoolmates and close friends:

**Areas of Communication**

Are there any areas that the student feels unable to discuss freely with you, such as matters pertaining to sex? Please explain:

**Health Status**

Student's present state of health: Excellent________ Satisfactory________ Poor________

If poor, explain:

Physical disabilities:

Nervous habits (bedwetting, soiling, thumb sucking, fingernail biting, etc.):

Personality traits (circle any that apply):

| | | |
|---|---|---|
| Easily excited | Daydreams constantly | Feels inadequate |
| Cries easily | Seems preoccupied | Perfectionist |
| Inhibited Withdr | awn | Easily frustrated |
| Holds feelings in | Craves attention | Overly aggressive |
| Moody Disagreeable | | Fights authority |
| Nothing bothers them | Likes to show off | Easily angered |
| Depressed Overly | competitive Shows | temper |
| Hyperactive Ove | rconfident | Submissive |
| Passive, unresponsive | Hates to be alone | Easily controlled |
| Lethargic | Overly sensitive to criticism | Fearful |
| Slow moving | Hates to be wrong | Shy |
| Happy-go-lucky Won' | t accept blame | Uncommunicative |
| Prefers solitude | Self-deprecating | Overly talkative |
| Short attention span | Self-conscious | Easily embarrassed |

Please explain any items circled above:

*Page 3*

**PERSONAL DATA FORM — ADOLESCENT (continued)**

**Health History**

Date of last physical examination:________________ Examined by:________________________

Nature of any adverse findings:________________________________________________

________________________________________________________________________

List any diseases of a serious nature that student has had, including approximate date of occurrence and length of illness:________________________________________________

________________________________________________________________________

________________________________________________________________________

List any accidents of a serious nature that have occurred, including approximate dates and periods of disablement. Also state whether temporary or permanent disabilities resulted:________________

________________________________________________________________________

________________________________________________________________________

**Developmental History**

Approximate age when student first: Walked________________ Began to talk:________________

Was weaned:____________ Was toilet trained:______________

Make a statement describing your recollection of student's preschool experiences, including any significant events, tragedies, or conflicts that you feel may have contributed to present problems or difficulties:

________________________________________________________________________

________________________________________________________________________

________________________________________________________________________

Describe student's social, emotional, and physical development up to the present time. Has development in these areas been in tune with peers' development, or otherwise? Have there been any special problems in these areas?________________________________________________

________________________________________________________________________

________________________________________________________________________

Has student attained puberty yet? If so, at what age? Make a statement with regard to any problems during this transition period.________________________________________________

________________________________________________________________________

________________________________________________________________________

Have there been any unusual events, situations, tragedies, or influences during student's past history (not already mentioned under preschool experiences), which may have contributed to present difficulties or problems?________________________________________________

________________________________________________________________________

________________________________________________________________________

________________________________________________________________________

________________________________________________________________________

**School History**

Describe progress through school to the present, including any academic difficulties encountered, teacher-pupil conflicts, peer conflicts, etc.:________________________________________________

________________________________________________________________________

________________________________________________________________________

________________________________________________________________________

________________________________________________________________________

________________________________________________________________________

________________________________________________________________________

________________________________________________________________________

Estimate of student's academic ability (superior, above average, average, below average, slow learner):

________________________________________________________________________

# References

Achenbach, T. M. (1991). *Manual for the Child Behavior Checklist/4–18.* Burlington: University of Vermont, Department of Psychiatry.

Alessi, G. J., & J. H. Kaye. (1983). *Behavioral assessment for school psychologists.* Washington, DC: National Association of School Psychologists.

Alexander, D., & S. Clark. (1998). Keeping "the family" in focus during patient care. In *Essentials of family medicine,* edited by P. D. Sloane, L. M. Slatt, P. Curtis, and M. H. Ebell. Baltimore, MD: Williams and Wilkins.

Allen, I. (2001). *Preventing suicide: Individual acts create a public health crisis.* Washington, DC: Center for the Advancement of Health.

Alper, S., P. J. Schloss, & C. N. Schloss. (1995). Families of children with disabilities in elementary and middle school: Advocacy models and strategies. *Exceptional Children* 62(3), 261–70.

American Counseling Association. (1995). *Code of ethics and standards of practice.* Alexandria, VA: Author.

American Educational Research Association, American Psychological Association, & National Council on Measurement in Education. (1999). *Standards for educational and psychological testing.* 2nd ed. Washington, DC: American Psychological Association.

American Guidance Service. (1999). *Behavior assessment system for children.* Circle Pines, MN: American Guidance Service.

American Psychiatric Association. (2000). *Diagnostic and statistical manual of mental disorders.* 4th ed., text revision. Washington, DC: American Psychiatric Association.

———. (1987). *Diagnostic and statistical manual of mental disorders.* 3rd ed., revised. Washington, DC: American Psychiatric Association.

American Psychological Association. (1993). Guidelines for providers of psychological services to ethnically, linguistically, and culturally diverse populations. *American Psychologist* 48, 45–48.

———. (1992). Ethical principles of psychologists and code of conduct. *American Psychologist* 47, 1597–611.

———. (1953). *Ethical standards of psychologists.* Washington, DC: Author.

Anastasi, A. (1988). Psychological testing (5th edition). New York: Macmillan.

Apple, M. W. (1996). Dominance and dependency: Situating *The Bell Curve* within the conservative restoration. In *Measured lies: The bell curve examined,* edited by J. Kincheloe, S. Steinberg, and A. Gresson, 51–69. New York: St. Martin's Griffin.

Asimov, N. (2003). Standards tougher on diverse schools. *San Francisco Chronicle*, 23 December, 19 & 23.

Associated Press. (2003). School chief failed literacy test. *The Boston Globe*, August 4, B2.

Barnett, D. W. (2002). Best practices in early intervention. In *Best practices in school psychology-IV*. Vol. 2, edited by A. Thomas and J. Grimes, 1247–62. Washington, DC: National Association of School Psychologists.

Barnett, D. W., S. Bell, & K. T. Carey. (1999). *Designing preschool interventions: A practitioner's guide*. New York: Guilford.

Barnett, D. W., & K. T. Carey. (1992). *Designing interventions for preschool learning and behavior problems*. San Francisco: Jossey-Bass.

Barnett, D. W., R. Collins, C. Coulter, M. J. Curtis, K. Ehrhardt, A. Glaser, C. Reyes, S. Stollar, & M. Winston. (1995). Ethnic validity and school psychology: Concepts and practices associated with cross-cultural professional competence. *Journal of School Psychology* 33(3), 219–34.

Bateson, G. (1958). *Naven*. Palo Alto, CA: Stanford University Press.

Batsche, G. M. (1983). The referral oriented consultative assessment report writing model. In *Communicating psychological information in writing*, edited by J. Grimes, 27–43. Des Moines: Iowa Department of Public Instruction.

Beck, A. T., A. J. Rush, B. F. Shaw, & G. Emery. (1979). *Cognitive therapy of depression*. New York: Guilford Press.

Begala, P. (2000). *Is our children learning? The case against George W. Bush*. New York: Simon & Schuster.

Bell, T. (2002). State adopts new school tests. *San Francisco Chronicle*, 26 April, A1.

Berninger, V. (2002). Best practices in reading, writing, and math assessment-intervention links: A systems approach for schools, classrooms, and individuals. In *Best practices in school psychology-IV*. Vol. 1, edited by A. Thomas and J. Grimes, 851–65. Bethesda, MD: National Association of School Psychologists.

Bernstein, B. E., & T. L. Hartsell. (2000). *The portable ethicist for mental health professionals: An A–Z guide to responsible practice*. New York: John Wiley & Sons.

Bernstein, R. (1988). Metaphysics, critique, and utopia. *Review of Metaphysics* 42, 267.

Berry, W. (1986). *Home economics*. San Francisco: North Point Press.

Bettelheim, B. (1983). *Freud & man's soul*. New York: Alfred A. Knopf.

Bigelow, B. (2000). Standards and multiculturalism. In *Failing our kids: Why the testing craze won't fix our schools*. Milwaukee, WI: Rethinking Schools.

Bijou, S. W., R. F. Peterson, & M. H. Ault. (1968). A method to integrate descriptive and experimental field studies at the level of data and empirical concepts. *Journal of Applied Behavior Analysis* 1, 175–91.

Bijou, S. W., R. F. Peterson, F. R. Harris, K. E. Allen, & M. S. Johnson. (1969). Methodology for experimental studies of young children in natural settings. *Psychological Record* 19, 177–210.

Boehner, J. (2003). The improving education results for children with disabilities act. *Bill summary, House Education & the Workforce Committee.* Washington, DC.

Boorstein, S. (2002). *Pay attention, for goodness' sake.* New York: Ballantine Books.

Boughner, S. R., S. F. Hayes, D. L. Bubenzer, & J. D. West. (1994). Use of standardized assessment instruments by marital and family therapists: A survey. *Journal of Marital and Family Therapy* 20, 69–75.

Bourdieu, P. (1993). *The field of cultural reproduction.* New York: Columbia University Press.

Bowers, K. S., & D. Meichenbaum (Eds.). (1984). *The unconscious reconsidered.* New York: Wiley.

Braginsky, B. M., D. D. Braginsky, & K. Ring. (1969). *Methods of madness: The mental hospital as a last resort.* New York: Holt, Rinehart, and Winston.

Braus, J. A., D. Wood, & L. E. LeFranc. (1993). *Environmental education in the schools: Creating a program that works.* Washington, DC: Peace Corps, ICE Publications. Also available at www.peacecorps.gov/library/pdf/M0044_enveduc.pdf

Brown, L., & D. Hammill. (1990). *Behavior Rating Profile.* 2nd ed. Austin, TX: Pro-Ed.

Burke, S. K., & P. Farber. (1997). A genogrid for couples. *Journal of Gay and Lesbian Social Services* 7(1), 13–22.

Bushman, J., & G. S. Goodman. (2003). What teaching the standards really means. *Leadership* 33(2, November/December).

Buurma, D. (1999). *The family play genogram: A guidebook.* Summit, NJ: Author. Available from 67 Valley View Avenue, Summit, NJ 07901.

Carey, K. T. (2004). Ethnic validity. In G. Goodman & Karen Carey (Eds.) *Critical Multicultural instruction.* Cresskill, NJ: Hampton Press.

———. (1989). *The treatment utility potential of two methods of assessing stressful relationships in families: A study of practitioner utility.* Unpublished PhD diss., University of Cincinnati.

Carver, C. S., & M. F. Scheier. (1999). Optimism. In C.R. Snyder (Ed.) *Coping: The psychology of what works*, 182–204. New York: Oxford University Press.

Cattell, R. B. (1940). A culture free intelligence test, Part 1. *Journal of Educational Psychology* 31, 161–79.

Centers for Disease Control. (1992). *Youth suicide prevention programs: A resource guide.* Atlanta: U.S. Department of Health & Human Services.

Central Valley Educational Research Consortium (CVERC). (2004). *Specific Strategies for Successful Schools.* Fresno: California State University, Fresno.

———. (2002). *What works: Characteristics of high-performing schools in the Central Valley.* Fresno: California State University.

———. (2000). *Looking for success.* Fresno: California State University.

Charles, C. M. (1995). *Introduction to educational research.* 2nd ed. White Plains, NY: Longman.

Chomsky, N. (1999). *Profit over people.* New York: Seven Stories Press.

Clark, C. (1975). The Shockley-Jensen thesis: A contextual appraisal. *Black Scholar* 6(10), 2–11.

Coles, R. (1977). William James: Selected writing. New York: Book-of-the-Month Club.

Communication Companies International. (1989). *True Colors.* Corona, CA: Author.

Congress, E. P. (1994). The use of culturegrams to assess and empower culturally diverse families. *Families in Society* (November).

Conze, E. (1959). *Buddhism: Its essence and development.* New York: Harper Torchbooks.

Cook, A. (2003). High-stakes testing. *New York Times*, 14 July, 16.

Cooper, J. O., T. E. Heron, & W. L. Heward. (1987). *Applied behavior analysis.* Columbus, OH: Merrill.

Cooper, M. A. (2003). Academic freedom and the challenges of September 11. In *Thought and Action: The NEA Higher Education Journal* 19(1), 75–85.

Corey, G. (1977). *Theory and practice of counseling and psychotherapy.* Belmont, CA: Wadsworth Publishing.

Cottone, R. R., & V. M. Tarvydas. (2003). *Ethical and professional issues in counseling.* 2nd ed. Upper Saddle River, NJ: Merrill/Prentice Hall.

Creswell, J. W. (2002). *Educational research: Planning, conducting and evaluating quantitative and qualitative research.* Upper Saddle River, NJ: Merrill Prentice Hall.

CTB/McGraw-Hill. (2002). *Terra Nova.* 2nd ed. Monterey, CA: Author.

Delpit, L. (2003). Educators as "Seed People" growing a new future. *Educational Researcher* 7(32), 14–21.

Dowrick, S (1991). *Intimacy and solitude: Balancing closeness and independence.* New York: Norton.

Dunlap, G., & L. Kern. (1996). Modifying instruction activities to promote desirable behavior: A conceptual and practical framework. *School Psychology Quarterly* 11, 297–312.

DuPaul, G. J. (2003). Commentary: Bridging the gap between research and practice. In *School Psychology Review* 32(2), 178–80.

Elias, M. J., J. E. Zins, P. A. Graczyk, & R. P. Weissberg. (2003). Implementation, sustainability, and scaling up of social-emotional and academic innovations in public schools. *School Psychology Review* 32, 303–19.

Elliott, C. D. (1990a). *DAS introductory and technical handbook*. San Antonio, TX: Psychological Corporation.

———. (1990b). *Differential abilities scales: Administration and scoring manual.* San Antonio, TX: Psychological Corporation.

Ellis, A., & R. A. Harper. (1975). *A new guide to rational living.* North Hollywood, CA: Wilshire Book.

Endicott, J., & R. L. Spitzer. (1978). A diagnostic interview: The schedule for affective disorders and schizophrenia. *Archives of General Psychiatry* 35, 837–44.

Fagan, T. K., & P. S. Wise. (2000). *School psychology: Past, present, future.* Washington, DC: National Association of School Psychologists.

*Federal Register.* (1977). Volume 42, number 163 (August 23), p. 42496–42497, 121a.530.

First, M. B., R. L. Spitzer, M. Gibbon, & J. B. W. Williams. (1996). *Structured clinical interview for axis one DSM-IV: Disorders research version-Patient edition* (SCID-I/P, Version 2.0). New York: New York State Psychiatric Institute.

Flexner, S. B. (1993). *Random House unabridged dictionary.* 2nd ed. New York: Random House.

Flores, L. Y., & E. M. Obasi. (2003). Positive psychological assessment in an increasingly diverse world. In *Positive psychological assessment*, edited by S. J. Lopez and C. R. Snyder. Washington, DC: American Psychological Association.

Ford, J. (1996). What is chaos, that we should be mindful of it? In *The new physics*, edited by Paul Davies. Cambridge: Cambridge University Press.

Forrest, T. (2003). New changes in IDEA: An interview with Allan Lloyd-Jones, Special education consultant to the California Department of Education. *CASPToday* (Summer).

Forsyth, R. L., T. Ansley, L. Feldt, & S. Alnot. (2001). *Iowa Tests of Educational Achievement.* Chicago: Riverside Publishing.

Foucault, M. (1965). *Madness and civilization: A history of insanity in the age of reason.* New York: Vintage Press.

———. (1970). *The order of things: An archeology of the human sciences.* New York: Vintage Press.

Fraser, J. W. (1997). Love and history in the work of Paulo Freire. In *Mentoring the mentor: A critical dialogue with Paulo Freire,* edited by P. Freire. New York: Peter Lang Publishing.

Freire, P. (1998). *Pedagogy of hope: Reliving Pedagogy of the Oppressed.* New York: Continuum.

———. (1970). *Pedagogy of the Oppressed.* New York: Continuum.

Frierson, R. L., M. Melikian, & P. Wadman. (2002). Principles of suicide risk assessment: How to interview depressed patients and tailor treatment. In *Postgraduate medicine online.* www.postgradmed.com/issues/2002/09_02/frierson4.htm.

Gerson, R., & S. Shellenberger. (1999). *The genogram-maker plus for Windows and Macintosh.* Macon, GA: Humanware. Computer software.

Gill, E., & B. Sobol. (2000). Engaging families in therapeutic play. In *Children in therapy: Using the family as a resource,* edited by C. E. Bailey. New York: Norton.

Giroux, H. A. (1997). *Pedagogy and the politics of hope: Theory, culture and schooling.* Boulder, CO: Westview Press.

———. (1992). *Border crossings: Cultural workers and the politics of education.* New York: Routledge.

Giroux, H. A., & P. McLaren. (1994). *Between borders: Pedagogy and the politics of cultural studies.* New York: Routledge.

Goodman, G. S. (2002). *Reducing hate crimes and violence among American youth: Creating transformational agency through critical praxis.* New York: Peter Lang Publishing.

———. (1999). *Alternatives in education: Critical pedagogy for disaffected youth.* New York: Peter Lang Publishing.

Goodman, G. S., & K. T. Carey, Eds. (2004). *Critical multicultural conversations.* Cresskill, NJ: Hampton Press.

Goodman, R. (2003). Letter to the editor. *Boston Globe,* 7 December, B12.

Gopaul-McNicol, S., & T. Thomas-Presswood. (1998). *Working with linguistically and culturally different children.* Needham Heights, MA: Allyn & Bacon.

Gough, H. G. (1987). *California Psychological Inventory manual.* Palo Alto, CA: Consulting Psychologists Press.

Gould, S. J. (1981). *The mismeasure of man.* New York: W. W. Norton.

Gramsci, A. (1971). *Selections from the Prison Notebooks.* New York: International Publishers.

Gray, M. L. (1999). *In your face: Stories from the lives of queer youth.* New York: Harrington Park Press.

Greene, B. (2000). *The elegant universe: Superstrings, hidden dimensions, and the quest for the ultimate theory.* New York: Vintage Press.

Greenwood, C. R., J. J. Carta, D. Kamps, & J. Delquadri. (1995). *Ecobehavioral assessment system software.* Kansas City, KS: Juniper Gardens Children's Center.

Gregory, R. J. (2004). *Psychological testing.* Boston: Allyn and Bacon.

Griffin, G. A. (1991). Interactive staff development: Using what we know. In *Staff development for education in the 90s*, edited by A. Lieberman and L. Miller, 243–58. New York: Teachers College Press.

Groth-Marnat, G. (2003). *Handbook of psychological assessment.* 4th ed. Hoboken, NJ: John Wiley and Sons.

Gutkin, T. B., & M. J. Curtis. (1990). School-based consultation: Theory and techniques. In *Handbook of school psychology*, edited by C. R. Reynolds and T. B. Gutkin, 796–828. New York: Wiley.

Habermas, J. (1994). *The past as future.* Trans. Max Pensky. Lincoln: University of Nebraska Press.

———. (1984). *The theory of communicative action.* Vol. 1. Boston, MA: Beacon Press.

Hall, E. T. (1989). *Beyond culture.* New York: Doubleday.

Harcourt Brace Educational Measurement. (1996). *Stanford Achievement Test.* 9th ed. San Antonio, TX: Psychological Corporation.

Harcourt Educational Measurement. (2002). *Metropolitan Achievement Test.* 8th ed. San Antonio, TX: Author.

Hardy, K. V., & T. A. Laszloffy. (1995). The cultural genogram: Key to training culturally competent family therapists. *Journal of Marital and Family Therapy* 21(3), 227–37.

Hartmann, D. P. (1984). Assessment strategies. In *Single case experimental designs: Strategies for studying behavior change.* 2nd ed., edited by D. H. Barlow and M. Hersen, 107–39. New York: Pergamon.

Hathaway, S. R., & J. C. McKinley. (1940). A multiphasic personality schedule (Minnesota) I.: Construction of the schedule. *Journal of Psychology* 10, 249–54.

Hawking, S. (1988). *A brief history of time.* New York: Bantam Books.

Hayes, S. C., & R. O. Nelson. (1986). Assessing the effects of therapeutic interventions. In *Conceptual foundations of behavioral assessment*, edited by R. O. Nelson and S. C. Hayes, 461–503. New York: Guilford.

Haywood, C. H. (1988). Dynamic assessment: The learning potential assessment device. In *Psychoeducational assessment of minority children: A casebook*, edited by R. L. Jones. Berkeley, CA: Cobb & Henry.

Hebdige, D. (1979). Subculture: The meaning of style. New York: Routledge.

Heller, K. A., W. H. Holtzman, & S. Messick. (1982). *National research council (U.S.) panel on selection and placement of students in programs for the mentally retarded.* Washington, DC: National Academy Press.

Helzer, J. E., L. N. Robins, J. L. Croughan, & A. Welner. (1981). Renard Diagnostic Interview: Its reliability and procedural validity with physicians and lay interviewers. *Archives of General Psychiatry* 38, 393–98.

Hendrickson, R. M. (1996). The bell curve, affirmative action, and the quest for equity. In *Measured lies: The bell curve examined*, edited by J. Kincheloe, S. Steinberg, and A. Gresson, 351–65. New York: St. Martin's Griffin.

Herrnstein, R. J., & C. Murray. (1994). *The bell curve.* New York: Free Press.

Hightower, A. D., D. Johnson, & W. G. Haffey. (1995). Best practices in adopting a prevention program. In *Best practices in school psychology-III*, edited by A. Thomas and J. Grimes. Washington, DC: National Association of School Psychologists.

Hinds, M. (2000). *Violent kids: Can we change the trend.* Dubuque, IA: Edward J. Arnone Publisher.

Hirsh, E. D., J. F. Kett, & J. Trefil. (1991). *The dictionary of cultural literacy: What every American needs to know.* Boston: Houghton Mifflin.

Hobbs, N. (1966). Helping disturbed children: Psychological and ecological strategies. *American Psychologist* 21, 1105–15.

Hoff, L., & E. Berman. (1986). The sexual genogram. *Journal of Marital and Family Therapy* 12(1), 39–47.

Holder, J. (1999). *Adventurelore: Adventure-based counseling for individuals and groups.* Holmes Beach, FL: Learning Publications.

Holmes, S. A., & G. Winter. (2003). Fixing the race gap in 25 years or less. *New York Times*, 29 June, section 4, 1 and 14.

Hooks, B. (2001). *All about love: New visions.* New York: Perennial Books.

Hoopes, M. H., & J. M. Harper. (1987). *Birth order roles & sibling patterns in individual and family therapy.* Rockville, MD: Aspen Publishers.

Hoover, H. D., S. B. Dunbar, & D. A. Frisbie. (2001). *Iowa Tests of Basic Skills.* Chicago: Riverside Publishing.

Hopkins, B. L., & J. A. Hermann. (1976). Evaluating interobserver reliability of interval data. *Journal of Applied Behavior Analysis* 10, 121–26.

House, J. (2004). Accommodating under section 504 of the rehabilitation act: A fair break for every student. In *Critical multicultural conversations*, edited by G. S. Goodman and K. T. Carey, 299–324. Cresskill, NJ: Hampton Press.

Hunt, M. (1994). *The story of psychology*. New York: Anchor Books.

Ingersoll, S., & D. LeBoeuf. (1997). Reaching out to youth out of the educational mainstream. *Juvenile Justice Bulletin* (February), 1–11.

Jardine, D. W. (2000). *"Under the tough old stars": Ecopedagogical essays*. Brandon, VT: Foundation for Educational Renewal.

Jensen, A. R. (1969). How much can we boost IQ and scholastic achievement? *Harvard Educational Review* 33: 1–123.

Jesse, R. C. (1989). *Children in recovery: Healing the parent-child relationship in alcohol/ addictive families*. New York: W. W. Norton.

Jimerson, S. R., E. Campos, & J. Greif. (2003). Toward an understanding of definitions and measures of school engagement and related terms. *California School Psychologist* 8, 7–27.

Johnson, M. (2001). *Attention deficit disorder*. Discovery Health.com, at Health.discovery.com/diseasesandcond/encyclopedia/2799.html.

Jones, R. L. (1988). *Psychoeducational assessment of minority group children: A casebook*. Berkeley, CA: Cobb & Henry.

Jordan, A., & N. Meara. (1990). Ethics and the professional practice of psychologists: The role of virtue and principles. *Professional Psychology: Research and Practice* 21(2), 107–14.

Kaku, M. (1987). *Beyond Einstein*. New York: Anchor Books.

Kanfer, F. H., & L. Gaelick. (1986). Self-management methods. In *Helping people change: A textbook of methods*. 3rd ed., edited by F. H. Kanfer and A. P. Goldstein, 283–345. New York: Pergamon.

Kanpol, B. (1997). *Issues and trends in critical pedagogy*. Cresskill, NJ: Hampton Press.

Karp, S. (2001). Bush plan fails schools. *Rethinking Schools Online* (Spring). www.rethinkingschools.org

Kastner, L. (2003). Failed students, plenty of blame. *New York Times*, 2 August, 14.

Kaufman, A., & N. Kaufman. (1998). *Kaufman Tests of Educational Achievement-Normative Update-Comprehensive form manual*. Circle Pines, MN: American Guidance Service.

Kelves, D. J. (1968). Testing the army's intelligence: Psychologists and the military in World War I. *Journal of American History* 55, 565–81.

Kerr, M. C., & Bowen, M. (1988). *Family Evaluation.* New York: Norton.

Kesey, K. (1970). Sometimes a great notion. New York: Bantam.

Keyes, C. L. M., & J. L. Magyar-Moe. (2003). The measurement and utility of adult subjective well-being. In *Positive psychological assessment*, edited by S. J. Lopez and C. R. Snyder. Washington, DC: American Psychological Association.

Kincheloe, J. L., & S. Steinberg. (1997). *Changing multiculturalism.* Buckingham, U.K.: Open University Press.

———. (1996). Who said it can't happen here? In *Measured lies: The bell curve examined*, edited by J. Kincheloe, S. Steinberg, and A. Gresson, 351–65. New York: St. Martin's Griffin.

Kincheloe, J. L., S. Steinberg, & A. Gresson (Eds.). (1996). *Measured lies: The bell curve examined.* New York: St. Martin's Griffin.

King, J. (1996). Language of hoodoo social science. In *Measured lies: The bell curve examined*, edited by J. Kincheloe, S. Steinberg, and A. Gresson, 177–92. New York: St. Martin's Griffin.

Kohl, H. (1994). *"I won't learn from you" and other thoughts on creative maladjustment.* New York: W. W. Norton.

Kohn, A. (2000). *The case against standardized testing.* Portsmouth, NH: Heinemann Press.

———. (1999). *The schools our children deserve: Moving beyond traditional classrooms and "tougher standards."* Boston, MA: Houghton Mifflin.

———. (1998). *What to look for in a classroom…and other essays.* San Francisco: Jossey-Bass.

Kopp, S. (1988). *If you meet the Buddha on the road, kill him: The pilgrimage of psychotherapy patients.* New York: Bantam Books.

———. (1971). *Guru: Metaphors from a psychotherapist.* New York: Science and Behavior Books.

Kozol, J. (1991). *Savage inequalities: Children in America's schools.* New York: HarperCollins.

Kratochwill, T. R., S. N. Elliott, & P. Carrington Rotto. (1995). School-based behavioral consultation. In *Best practices in school psychology-III*, edited by A. Thomas and J. Grimes. Washington, DC: National Association of School Psychologists.

Kubler-Ross, E. (1981). How I became interested in death and dying. In *What helped me when my loved one died*, edited by E. A. Grollman. Boston, MA: Beacon Press.

Lemann, N. (2003). A decision the universities can relate to. *New York Times*, 29 June, section 4, 14.

Lewin, T., & J. Medina. (2003). To cut failure rate, schools shed students. *New York Times*, 31 July, A1 and A21.

Lieberman, L. L. (1986). Special educator's guide to regular education. Newtonville, MA: GloWorm Publications.

Lincoln, Y. S., & E. G. Guba. (1986). But is it rigorous? Trustworthiness and authenticity in naturalistic evaluation. In *Naturalistic evaluation*, edited by D. D. Williams, 73–84. San Francisco: Jossey-Bass.

Linn, R. L., & N. E. Gronlund. (2000). *Measurement and assessment in teaching*. 8th ed. Upper Saddle River, NJ: Merrill.

Lloyd-Jones, A. (2003). New Changes in IDEA: An interview with Allan Lloyd-Jones, special education consultant to the California Department of Education. *CASP Today* (Summer), 8–9.

Lopez, S. J., C. R. Snyder, & H. Rasmussen. (2003). Striking a vital balance: Developing a complementary focus on human weakness and strength through positive psychological assessment. In *Positive psychological assessment*, edited by S. J. Lopez and C. R. Snyder. Washington, DC: American Psychological Association.

Lourde, A. (1984). *Sister outsider*. Freedom, CA: Crossing Press.

Lukas, S. (1993). *Where to start and what to ask: An assessment handbook*. New York: W. W. Norton.

Macewan, A. (2000). Why business likes more testing. In *Failing our kids: Why the testing craze won't fix our schools*. Milwaukee, WI: Rethinking Schools.

MacLeod, J. (1995). *Ain't no makin' it*. Boulder, CO: Westview Press.

Maloney, M. P., & M. P. Ward. (1976). *Psychological assessment: A conceptual approach*. New York: Oxford University Press.

Markwardt, F. (1998). *Peabody Individual Achievement Test-Revised-Normative Update*. Circle Pines, MN: American Guidance Service.

Marshall, C., & G. B. Rossman. (1995). *Designing qualitative research*. 2nd ed. Thousand Oaks, CA: Sage.

Maslow, A. H. (1968). *Toward a psychology of being*. New York: Van Nostrand Reinhold.

May, R. (1990). *The wounder healer*. Speech to the American Counseling Association annual meeting, Houston, TX.

McGoldrick, M., R. Gerson, & S. Shellenberger. (1999). *Genograms: Assessment and intervention*. New York: Norton.

McLaren, P. (1999). *Schooling as a ritual performance: Toward a political economy of educational symbols and gestures*. Lanham, MD: Rowman & Littlefield.

———. (1997). *Revolutionary multiculturalism: Pedagogies of dissent for the new millennium*. Boulder, CO: Westview Press.

———. (1996). White supremacy and the politics of fear and loathing. In *Measured lies: The bell curve examined*, edited by J. Kincheloe, S. Steinberg, and A. Gresson, 343–50. New York: St. Martin's Griffin.

McLaren, P., & D. Carlson. (1996). Education as a political issue: What's missing in the public conversation about education? In *Thirteen questions: Reframing education's conversation*. 2nd ed., edited by J. L. Kincheloe and S. R. Steinberg. New York: Peter Lang Publishers.

McNeil, L. (2000). The educational costs of standardization. In *Failing our kids: Why the testing craze won't fix our schools*. Milwaukee, WI: Rethinking Schools.

Merrell, K. W. (1994). *Assessment of behavioral, social, and emotional problems*. New York: Longman.

Messick, S. (1989). Validity. In *Educational measurement*. 3rd ed., edited by R. L. Linn, 13–103. New York: Macmillan.

Meyer, G. L., S. E. Finn, L. D. Eyde, et al. (2001). Psychological testing and psychological assessment. *American Psychologist* 56, 128–65.

Miller, G. A. (1969). Psychology as a means of promoting human welfare. *American Psychologist* 24, 1063–75.

Miller, J. B. (2003). Telling the truth about power. In *Research and Action Report* 25(1, Fall/Winter). Wellesley, MA: Wellesley College for Women.

———. (1976). *Toward a new psychology of women*. Boston: Beacon Press.

Millon, T. (1983). *Millon Clinical Multiaxial Inventory manual*. 2nd ed. Minneapolis, MN: National Computer Systems.

Miner, B. (2000). Origins of the latest testing craze. In *Failing our kids: Why the testing craze won't fix our schools*. Milwaukee, WI: Rethinking Schools.

Minuchin, S. (1974). *Families and family therapy*. Cambridge, MA: Harvard University Press.

Missouri Department of Mental Health. (2003). *Alcohol pharmacology*. Jefferson City, MO: Division of Alcohol and Drug Abuse.

Morawetz, A., & G. Walker. (1984). *Brief therapy with single-parent families*. New York: Brunner/Mazel Publishers.

Morrison, T. (1994). *The Nobel lecture in literature, 1993*. New York: Alfred A. Knopf.

National Association of School Psychologists. (2003). *Position statement on school psychologists' involvement in the role of assessment*. Washington, DC: National Association of School Psychologists.

———. (1992). *Principles for professional ethics*. Silver Springs, MD: Author.

———. (n.d.). What is a school psychologist? Washington, DC: National Association of School Psychologists.

National Commission on Excellence in Education. (1983). *A nation at risk: The imperative for educational reform*. Washington, DC: U.S. Government Printing Office.

National Forum on Assessment. (1993). *Principles and indicators for student assessment systems*. Cambridge, MA: Author.

National Research Council. (2000). *From neurons to neighborhoods: The science of early childhood development*. Washington, DC: National Academy Press.

Nelson, R. O., & S. C. Hayes. (1986). The nature of behavioral assessment. In *Conceptual foundations of behavior assessment*, edited by R. O. Nelson and S. C. Hayes, 1–40. New York: Guilford.

Nieto, S. (1996). *Affirming diversity: The sociopolitical context of multicultural education*. White Plains, NY: Longman.

*No Child Left Behind Act*. (2002). Public Law 107-110, 1st session (January 8).

Nordquist, V. M., & S. Twardosz. (1990). Preventing behavior problems in early childhood special education classroom through environmental organization. *Education and Treatment of Children* 13, 274–87.

O'Connor, S. (2003). *Grutter v. Bollinger,* 02–241. Washington, DC: U.S. Supreme Court.

Ogbu, J. U. (1995). Literacy and black Americans: Comparative perspectives. In *Literacy among African-American youth*, edited by V. L. Gladsden and D. A. Wagner. Cresskill, NJ: Hampton Press.

Olson, D. H., J. Portner, & Y. Lavee. (1985). *FACES III: Family adaptability and cohesion evaluation scales*. St. Paul, MN: Family Social Service.

Orfield, G., & J. Wald. (2000). Testing's unequal impact. In *Failing our kids: Why the testing craze won't fix our schools*. Milwaukee, WI: Rethinking Schools.

Orpinas, P., A. M. Horne, & D. Staniszewski. (2003). School bullying: Changing the problem by changing the school. *School Psychology Review* 32(3), 431–44.

Page, T. J., & B. A. Iwata. (1986). Interobserver agreement: History, theory, and current methods. In *Research methods in applied behavior analysis*, edited by A. Poling and R. W. Fuqua, 99–126. New York: Plenum.

Papp, P., O. Silverstein, & E. A. Carter. (1973). Family sculpting in preventive work with well families. *Family Process* 12(25), 197–212.

Parenti, M. (1996). *Dirty truths*. San Francisco, CA: City Lights Books.

Perls, F. (1969). *In and out of the garbage pail*. Lafayette, CA: Real People Press.

Perry, M. (2000). *Walking the color line: The art and practice of anti-racist teaching*. New York: Teachers College Press.

Peterson, D. R. (1968). *The clinical study of social behavior*. New York: Appleton-Century-Crofts.

Pianta, R. C. (2003). Commentary: Implementation, sustainability, and scaling up in school contexts: Can school psychology make the shift? *School Psychology Review* 32(3), 331–35.

Pianta, R. C., & D. J. Walsh. (1996). *High-risk children in schools.* New York: Routledge.

Power, M. J. (2003). Quality of life. In *Positive psychological assessment*, edited by S. J. Lopez and C. R. Snyder. Washington, DC: American Psychological Association.

Psychological Corporation. (2001). *Wechsler Individual Achievement Test.* 2nd ed. San Antonio, TX: Author.

Rasmussen, H. N., J. E. Neufeld, J. C. Bouwkamp, L. M. Edwards, A. Ito, J. L. Magyar-Moe, J. A. Ryder, & S. J. Lopez. (2003). Environmental assessment: Examining influences on optimal human functioning. In *Positive psychological assessment*, edited by S. J. Lopez and C. R. Snyder. Washington, DC: American Psychological Association.

Rebellon, C., J. Brown, & C. L. M. Keyes. (2000). Mental illness and suicide. In *The encyclopedia of criminology and deviant behavior, Volume 4: Self destructive behavior and disvalued identity*, edited by C. E. Faupel and P. M. Roman, 426–29. London: Taylor & Francis.

Reich, R. B. (2003). The real supply side. *American Prospect* (October), 40.

Remen, R. N. (2000). *My grandfather's blessings: Stories of strength, refuge, and belonging.* New York: Riverhead Books.

Reynolds, C. R., & R. W. Kamphaus. (1992). *Behavior Assessment System for Children.* Circle Pines, MN: American Guidance Service.

Riemersma, M. (2003). *Scope of practice: Do you know the difference between scope of practice and scope of competence?* www.camft.org/staticcontent/articles/scopeofpractice.htm.

Ringeisen, H., K. Henderson, & K. Hoagwood. (2003). Context matters: Schools and the "Research to Practice Gap" in children's mental health. *School Psychology Review* 32(2), 153–68.

Robins, L. N., J. E. Helzer, J. L. Croughan, & K. S. Ratcliff. (1981). National Institute of Mental Health Diagnostic Interview Schedule. *Archives of General Psychiatry* 38, 381–89.

Rodenhauser, P., & R. E. Fornal. (1991). How important is the mental status examination? *Psychiatric Hospital* 22, 256–62.

Rogers, C. (1961). *On becoming a person: A therapist's view of psychotherapy.* Boston, MA: Houghton Mifflin.

Roid, G., & L. Miller. (1997). *Leiter-*R *manual.* Wood Dale, IL: Stoelting.

Rosenfield, S., & T. A. Gravois. (1999). Working with teams in the school. In C. R. Reynolds & T. B. Gulkin (Eds.), *Handbook of school psychology* (3rd Ed.), 1025–40. New York: Wiley.

Sackett, G. P. (1978). Measurement in observational research. In *Observing behavior: Vol. 2. Data collection and analysis methods*, edited by G. P. Sackett, 25–43. Baltimore: University Park Press.

Sacks, P. (2000). Changing ethics. In *Failing our kids: Why the testing craze won't fix our schools*. Milwaukee, WI: Rethinking Schools.

Salvia, J., & J. Ysseldyke. (1998). *Assessment*. 6th ed. Boston: Houghton Mifflin.

Salvia, J., & J. Ysseldyke. (2004). *Assessment*. 9th ed. Boston: Houghton Mifflin.

———. (2004). *Assessment in special and inclusive education*. 9th ed. Boston: Houghton Mifflin.

Sandoval, J., C. L. Frisby, K. F. Geisinger, J. Ramos-Grenier, & J. D. Scheuneman. (1999). *Test interpretation and diversity: Achieving equity in assessment*. Washington, DC: American Psychological Association.

Satir, V. (1972). *Peoplemaking*. Palo Alto, CA: Science and Behavior Books.

Sattler, J. M. (2001). *Assessment of children: Cognitive applications*. 4th ed. San Diego: Jerome Sattler, Publisher.

———. (1988). *Assessment of children*. 3d ed. San Diego, CA: Jerome Sattler, Publisher.

Savage, J. E., & A. V. Adair. (1980). Testing minorities: Developing more culturally relevant assessment systems. In *Black psychology*. 2nd ed., edited by R. L. Jones. New York: HarperCollins.

Scannell, D. P. (1996). *Tests of achievement and proficiency*. Chicago: Riverside Publishing.

Schemo, D. J. (2003). For Houston schools, college claims exceed reality. *New York Times*, 28 August, 14.

Schemo, D., & F. Fessenden. (2003). Gains in Houston's schools: How real are they? *New York Times*, 3 December, 18.

Schmeiser, C. B. (1995). *Ethics in assessment*. 30 January. www.ericfacility.net/ericdigests/ed391111.html. ED 391111.

Schmidt, P. (2003). Affirmative action survives, and so does the debate. *Chronicle of Higher Education* (July 4), S1–4.

Schultz, W. C. (1967). *Joy: Expanding human awareness*. New York: Grove Press.

Senge, P. (1990). *The fifth discipline: The art and practice of the learning organization*. New York: Doubleday.

Shaker, P., & E. E. Heilman. (2002). Advocacy versus authority—Silencing the education professoriate. In *Policy perspectives: Examining public policy issues in teacher education.* Vol. 3, no. 1. Washington, DC: American Association of Colleges for Teacher Education.

Shinn, M. R. (1989). *Curriculum-based measurement: Assessing special children.* New York: Guilford.

Shohat, E., & R. Stam. (1994). *Unthinking Eurocentrism: Multiculturalism and the media.* New York: Routledge.

Short, R. J. (2003). Commentary: School psychology, context, and population-based practice. *School Psychology Review* 32(2), 181–84.

Slattery, P. (1996). A quantum analysis of *The bell curve.* In *Measured lies: The bell curve examined*, edited by J. Kincheloe, S. Steinberg, and A. Gresson, 291–301. New York: St. Martin's Griffin.

Sleeter, C. E., W. Gutierrez, C. A. New, & S. R. Takata. (1996). Race and education: In what ways does race affect the educational process? In *Thirteen questions: Reframing education's conversation.* 2nd ed., edited by J. L. Kincheloe and S. R. Steinberg. New York: Peter Lang Publishers.

Soto, G. (1999). Werewolf friends. In *A Natural Man.* San Francisco, CA: Chronicle Books.

Spring, J. H. (1972). Psychologists and the war: The meaning of intelligence in the Alpha and Beta tests. *History of Education Quarterly* 12, 3–15.

Stiggins, R. J. (2001). *Student-involved classroom assessment.* 3rd ed. Upper Saddle River, NJ: Merrill Prentice Hall.

Street, P. L. (2003). The kids aren't all right. *In These Times*, 1 September, 23–25.

Strosahl, K. D., & M. M. Linehan. (1986). Basic issues in behavioral assessment. In *Handbook of behavioral assessment.* 2nd ed., edited by A. R. Ciminero, K. S. Calhoun, and H. E. Adams, 12–46. New York: Wiley.

Stuebing, K. K., J. M. Fletcher, J. M. LeDoux, G. Reid Lyon, S. E. Shaywitz, & B. A. Shaywitz. (2002). Validity of IQ-discrepency classifications of reading disabilities: A meta-analysis. In *American Educational Research Journal* 39(2), 469–518.

Sue, D. W., & D. Sue. (1999). *Counseling the culturally different: Theory and practice.* 3rd ed. New York: John Wiley & Sons.

Sue, D. W., P. Arredondo, & R. J. McDavis. (1992). Multicultural counseling competencies and standards: A call to the profession. *Journal of Counseling & Development* 70, 477–86.

Suen, H. K., & D. Ary. (1989). *Analyzing quantitative behavioral observation data.* Hillsdale, NJ: Wiley.

Surber, J. M. (1995). Best practices in a problem-solving approach to psychological report writing. In *Best practices in school psychology-III*, edited by A. Thomas and J. Grimes. Washington, DC: National Association of School Psychologists.

Swope, K., & B. Miner. (2000). *Failing our kids: Why the testing craze won't fix our schools*. Milwaukee, WI: Rethinking Schools.

Tallent, N. (1988). *Psychological report writing*. 3rd ed. Englewood Cliffs, NJ: Prentice Hall.

Taylor, L. S., & C. R. Whittaker. (2003). *Bridging multiple worlds: Caes studies of diverse educational communities*. Boston: Allyn and Bacon.

Tharinger, D., & M. Stafford. (1995). Best practices in individual counseling of elementary-age students. In *Best practices in school psychology-III*, edited by A. Thomas and J. Grimes. Washington, DC: National Association of School Psychologists.

Thorndike, R. M. (1997). Measurement and evaluation in psychology and education. 6th ed. New York: Macmillan.

Tindall, G. A., & D. B. Marston. (1990). *Classroom-based assessment: Evaluating instructional outcomes*. Columbus, OH: Merrill.

Tjeltveit, A. C. (1999). Ethics and values in psychotherapy. New York: Routledge.

Tombari, M., & G. Borich. (1999). *Authentic assessment in the classroom: Applications and practice*. Englewood Cliffs, NJ: Merrill Prentice Hall.

Tyler, F. B., D. R. Brome, & J. E. Williams. (1991). *Ethnic validity, ecology, and psychotherapy: A psychosocial competence model*. New York: Plenum.

U.S. Department of Health & Human Services. (1998). *Suicide: A report of the Surgeon General*. Rockville, MD: Author.

U.S. Public Health Service. (1999). *The surgeon general's call to action to prevent suicide*. Washington, DC: Department of Health & Human Services.

van Wagtendonk, R. (2000). Bush admits drunk driving. *Radio Netherlands* www.rnw.nl/hotspots/html, 3 November.

Vangay, J. (2004). Unique problems and opportunities within the Southeast Asian family. In *Critical multicultural conversations*, edited by G. S. Goodman and K. T. Carey. New York: Peter Lang Publishing.

Vedder-Dubocq, S. (1990). *An investigation of the utility of the Parenting Stress Index for intervention decisions*. Unpublished PhD dissertation, University of Cincinnati.

Vorst, J. (1986). *Necessary losses: The loves, illusions, dependencies, and impossible expectations that all of us have to give up in order to grow*. New York: Ballantine Books.

Walker, D. K. (1983). *Socioemotional measures for preschool and kindergarten children*. San Francisco: Jossey-Bass.

Warren, M. E. (1995). The self in a discursive democracy. In *The Cambridge companion to Habermas*, edited by S. K. White. Cambridge, England: Cambridge University Press.

Watts, A. (1972). *The book: On the taboo against knowing who you are.* New York: Vintage Books.

———. (1961). *Psychotherapy east and west.* New York: Ballantine Books.

Webb, W. D. (In Press). *The soul of counseling.* Atascadero, CA: Impact Publishers.

Wechsler, D. (2003). *Wechsler Intelligence Scale for Children.* 4th ed. San Antonio, TX: Psychological Corporation.

———. (1991). *Wechsler Intelligence Scale for Children.* 3rd ed. San Antonio, TX: Psychological Corporation.

———. (1974). *Manual for the Wechsler Intelligence Scale for Children-Revised.* Cleveland, OH: Psychological Corporation.

Wellstone, P. (2000). A harsh agenda: High-stakes testing is being abused in the name of accountability—and almost always to the detriment of our children. In *Failing our kids: Why the testing craze won't fix our schools.* Milwaukee, WI: Rethinking Schools.

West, C. (1999). The moral obligations of living in a democratic society. In D. Batstone & E. Mendieta (Eds.), *The good citizen.* New York: Routledge.

Whetstone, B. (2000). *How to get togetherness: Improving AD/HD and ODD relationships in families and classrooms.* Laconia, NH: Bert Whetstone, Publisher.

Whiston, S. (2000). *Principles and applications of assessment in counseling.* Belmont, CA: Brooks/Cole.

White, M. B., & K. J. Tyson-Rawson. (1995). Assessing the dynamics of gender in couples and families: The gendergram. *Family Relations* 44, 253–60.

Williams, R. (1974). Scientific racism and I.Q.: The silent mugging of the black community. *Psychology Today* 7, 32–41.

Willinsky, J. (1998). *Learning to divide the world: Education at empire's end.* Minneapolis: University of Minnesota Press.

Wilson, F. E., & I. M. Evans. (1983). The reliability of target behavior selection in behavioral assessment. *Behavioral Assessment* 5, 15–33.

Winerip, M. (2003). Holding back a pupil: A bad idea despite intent. *New York Times*, 21 May, A1.

———. (2003). Where prepping for state tests is the road not taken. *New York Times*, 11 June, A25.

———. (2003). 70% failure rate? Try testing the testers. *New York Times*, 25 June, A24.

Winter, G. (2003). California report tallies cost of "exit exam." *New York Times*, 2 May, A30.

———. (2003). California will wait until 2006 to require high school graduates to pass exam. *New York Times*, 10 July, A29.

Witt, J. C., & G. M. Gresham. (1986). Review of the Wechsler intelligence scale for children-revised. In J. J. Kramer & J. C. Conoley (Eds.), *The Ninth Mental Measurement Yearbook*, 1351–56. Lincoln, NE: The University of Nebraska Press.

Wolery, M. (1989). Using direct observation in assessment. In *Assessing infants and preschoolers with handicaps*, edited by D. B. Bailey Jr. and M. Wolery, 64–96. Columbus, OH: Merrill.

Woodcock, R. W., K. S. McGrew, & N. Mather. (2001). *WJ-III tests of cognitive abilities and tests of achievement.* Itasca, IL: Riverside Publishing.

Wrenn, C. G. (1985). Afterward: The culturally encapsulated counselor revisited. In P. Pederson (Ed.), *Handbook of cross-cultural counseling and therapy.* (323–29). Westport, CT: Greenwood Press.

Wright, H. F. (1967). *Recording and analyzing child behavior.* New York: Harper & Row.

Wright, R. H. (1981). Psychologists and professional liability (malpractice) insurance: A retrospective review. *American Psychologist* 36, 1485–93.

Wrightsman, L., M. Nietzel, W. Fortune, & E. Greene. (2002). *Psychology and the legal system.* 5th ed. Pacific Grove, CA: Brooks/Cole Publishing.

Yalom, I. D. (1996). *Lying on the couch.* New York: Harper Perennial.

———. (1989). *Love's executioner & other tales of psychotherapy for anyone who's ever been on either side of the couch.* New York: Harper Collins.

Yeaton, W. H., & L. Sechrist. (1981). Critical dimensions in the choice and maintenance of successful treatment. Strength, integrity, and effectiveness. *Journal of Consulting and Clinical Psychology* 49, 156–67.

Ysseldyke, J. E., & S. L. Christenson. (2002). *Functional assessment of academic behavior: Creating effective learning environments.* Longmont, CO: Sopris West.

Ysseldyke, J. E., & M. L. Thurlow. (1993). *Self-study guide to the development of educational outcomes and indicators.* Minneapolis: National Center on Educational Outcomes, University of Minnesota.

Zarb, J. M. (1992). *Cognitive-behavioral assessment and therapy with adolescents.* New York: Bruner/Mazel.

Zimmerman, M. (1994). *Interview guide for evaluating DSM-IV psychiatric disorders and the mental status examination.* East Greenwich, RI: Psych Products Press.

Zins, J. E., & W. P. Erchul. (1995). Best practices in school consultation. In *Best practices in school psychology-III*, edited by A. Thomas and J. Grimes. Washington, DC: National Association of School Psychologists.

Zins, J. E., & S. G. Forman (Eds.). (1988). Mini-series on primary prevention: From theory to practice. *School Psychology Review* 17(4).

Ziskin, J. (1981). *Coping with psychiatric and psychological testimony*. 3rd ed., 2 vols. Venice, CA: Law and Psychology Press.

# Author Index

# Subject Index

## J



## K

# Studies in the Postmodern Theory of Education

*General Editors*
*Joe L. Kincheloe & Shirley R. Steinberg*

Counterpoints publishes the most compelling and imaginative books being written in education today. Grounded on the theoretical advances in criticalism, feminism, and postmodernism in the last two decades of the twentieth century, Counterpoints engages the meaning of these innovations in various forms of educational expression. Committed to the proposition that theoretical literature should be accessible to a variety of audiences, the series insists that its authors avoid esoteric and jargonistic languages that transform educational scholarship into an elite discourse for the initiated. Scholarly work matters only to the degree it affects consciousness and practice at multiple sites. Counterpoints' editorial policy is based on these principles and the ability of scholars to break new ground, to open new conversations, to go where educators have never gone before.

For additional information about this series or for the submission of manuscripts, please contact:

Joe L. Kincheloe & Shirley R. Steinberg
c/o Peter Lang Publishing, Inc.
275 Seventh Avenue, 28th floor
New York, New York 10001

To order other books in this series, please contact our Customer Service Department:

(800) 770-LANG (within the U.S.)
(212) 647-7706 (outside the U.S.)
(212) 647-7707 FAX

Or browse online by series:

www.peterlangusa.com